Governing Tsarist Russia

PETER WALDRON

First published 2007 by
PALGRAVE MACMILLAN
Houndmills, Basingstoke, Hampshire RG21 6XS and
175 Fifth Avenue, New York, N.Y. 10010
Companies and representatives throughout the world

PALGRAVE MACMILLAN is the global academic imprint of the Palgrave
Macmillan division of St. Martin's Press, LLC and of Palgrave Macmillan Ltd.
Macmillan® is a registered trademark in the United States, United Kingdom
and other countries. Palgrave is a registered trademark in the European
Union and other countries.

ISBN-13: 978–0–333–71717–2 hardback
ISBN-10: 0–333–71717–1 hardback
ISBN-13: 978–0–333–71718–9 paperback
ISBN-10: 0–333–71718–X paperback

This book is printed on paper suitable for recycling and made from fully
managed and sustained forest sources. Logging, pulping and manufacturing
processes are expected to conform to the environmental regulations of the
country of origin.

A catalogue record for this book is available from the British Library.

A catalog record for this book is available from the Library of Congress.

10   9   8   7   6   5   4   3   2   1
16   15   14   13   12   11   10   09   08   07

Printed and bound in China

182779338

European History in Perspective
General Editor: Jeremy Black

Benjamin Arnold   *Medieval Germany*
Ronald Asch   *The Thirty Years' War*
Nigel Aston   *The French Revolution, 1789–1804*
Nicholas Atkin   *The Fifth French Republic*
Christopher Bartlett   *Peace, War and the European Powers, 1814–1914*
Robert Bireley   *The Refashioning of Catholicism, 1450–1700*
Donna Bohanan   *Crown and Nobility in Early Modern France*
Arden Bucholz   *Moltke and the German Wars, 1864–1871*
Patricia Clavin   *The Great Depression, 1929–1939*
Paula Sutter Fichtner   *The Habsburg Monarchy, 1490–1848*
Mark Galeotti   *Gorbachev and his Revolution*
David Gates   *Warfare in the Nineteenth Century*
Alexander Grab   *Napoleon and the Transformation of Europe*
Martin P. Johnson   *The Dreyfus Affair*
Tim Kirk   *Nazi Germany*
Ronald Kowalski   *European Communism*
Paul Douglas Lockhart   *Sweden in the Seventeenth Century*
Kevin McDermott   *Stalin*
Graeme Murdock   *Beyond Calvin*
Peter Musgrave   *The Early Modern European Economy*
J. L. Price   *The Dutch Republic in the Seventeenth Century*
A. W. Purdue   *The Second World War*
Christopher Read   *The Making and Breaking of the Soviet System*
Francisco J. Romero-Salvado   *Twentieth-Century Spain*
Matthew S. Seligmann and Roderick R. McLean
Germany from Reich to Republic, 1871–1918
David A. Shafer   *The Paris Commune*
Brendan Simms   *The Struggle for Mastery in Germany, 1779–1850*
David Sturdy   *Louis XIV*
David J. Sturdy   *Richelieu and Mazarin*
Hunt Tooley   *The Western Front*
Peter Waldron   *The End of Imperial Russia, 1855–1917*
Peter Waldron   *Governing Tsarist Russia*
Peter G. Wallace   *The Long European Reformation*
James D. White   *Lenin*
Patrick Williams   *Philip II*
Peter H. Wilson   *From Reich to Revolution*

European History in Perspective
Series Standing Order
ISBN 0–333–71694–9 hardcover
ISBN 0–333–69336–1 paperback
(outside North America only)

You can receive future titles in this series as they are published by placing a standing order.
Please contact your bookseller or, in the case of difficulty, write to us at the address below
with your name and address, the title of the series and the ISBN quoted above.

Customer Services Department, Palgrave Ltd
Houndmills, Basingstoke, Hampshire RG21 6XS, England

Governing Tsarist Russia

Contents

List of Figures; Chronology

List of Figures

Chronology

Romanov monarchs, 1689–1917

Peter I (the Great)	1689–1725
Catherine I	1725–1727
Peter II	1727–1730
Anna	1730–1740
Ivan VI	1740–1741
Elizabeth	1741–1761
Peter III	1761–1762
Catherine II (the Great)	1762–1796
Paul I	1796–1801
Alexander I	1801–1825
Nicholas I	1825–1855
Alexander II	1855–1881
Alexander III	1881–1894
Nicholas II	1894–1917

Preface

This book owes much to discussion with many colleagues and friends, both at conferences and seminars and in less formal settings across lunch and dinner tables. I am especially grateful to Gill Cookson, Clare Crowley, Simon Dixon, Peter Durrans, John Flanagan, Janet Hartley, Dominic Lieven, David Moon, Jon Pemberton, David Saunders, Richard Stites and Peter Wilson, all of whom have provided sage advice and counsel.

I have been fortunate to be able to work in a variety of libraries and archives with rich holdings of materials relating to Tsarist Russia. The incomparable Slavonic Collection of the National Library of Finland has been an essential resource over many years; its staff and working conditions provide the most fruitful environment imaginable for an historian of Russia, and my work could not have been accomplished without being able to utilise this extraordinary library in Helsinki. It has been paralleled by the Russian State Historical Archive in St Petersburg; it has been an inspiration to work in this archive, located in the Senate and Synod Palaces on the banks of the Neva, an environment which witnessed the actual making of the history I have studied. The great equestrian statue of Peter the Great – the *Bronze Horseman* of Pushkin's poem – that stands outside the archive's buildings has been an ever-present reminder of the weight of history that envelopes St Petersburg. The very air of Petersburg is heavy with the knowledge that events of great vibrancy and gravity have gripped the city right through the three centuries of its existence: there are few cities on the globe where the echoes of the past are so rich and pervasive. It is a great sadness that this archive has now been moved away from the historic centre of St Petersburg and that the daily journey to the archive is no longer one that involves wending my way past the ornamented, deep green Winter Palace and the lustrous golden-spired Admiralty. I have also been fortunate to work in two other great libraries in St Petersburg, the Library of the Academy of Sciences, *BAN*, and the Russian National Library, the *Publichka*. St Petersburg is one of the greatest cradles of culture in the world: it has given birth to some of the most outstanding art, music and literature ever created. The custodians of its cultural heritage have laboured under very great tribulations to preserve intact these great libraries and archives and I, and every other historian of imperial Russia, owe them a deep debt of gratitude.

PETER WALDRON

Introduction: Building the Russian State

Tsarist Russia from Peter the Great to Nicholas II

The Romanov dynasty first came to power in Russia in 1613 at the end of a long period of political instability. The seventeenth century was a time of mixed fortunes for Russia, and the accession to the throne in 1682 of the 10-year-old Peter appeared to presage a further period of uncertainty. But by the time Peter reached the age of 18, he had taken power for himself, and his more than 30 years on the throne transformed Russia. Peter the Great began the process of modernising both state and society, setting them on a path that was to persist until the end of the Tsarist regime in 1917. Peter's armies defeated the Swedes and established Russia as the dominant state in Baltic Europe, thrusting Russia into the ranks of the Great Powers. At home, Peter drew on western technology and expertise to begin the process of modernising the Russian economy, and his insistence on developing Russia's military strength meant that the state's economy came under continual pressure to increase its output. The apparatus of the Russian state was reshaped by Peter as he drew on western models to create new structures for both central and local governments, while ensuring that his own autocratic power remained intact. Peter's priorities set the pattern for Russia's development over the next two centuries, as its rulers sought to maintain and enhance Russian international influence and to retain their own power at home.

Warfare was an ever-present preoccupation of the eighteenth-century Tsarist state. Russia went to war frequently to protect its newly acquired status as a Great Power and to acquire new territory.

Conflict in northern Europe and with the Ottoman Empire was especially frequent. By 1783 Russia had taken control of the Crimea on the northern shores of the Black Sea and in the 1790s it helped in the dismemberment of Poland, taking possession of a large proportion of the Polish lands. Russia's ties with Europe grew closer, especially with the accession to the throne of the German-born Catherine II in 1762. The new empress was determined to demonstrate her credentials as a member of the European enlightenment, and she presented to the outside world the image of a monarch in the mainstream of European culture and thought. Catherine was not, however, prepared to do anything that would weaken her own position domestically and she rejected calls to liberalise the Russian state and Russia's social structures. Catherine's long reign consolidated Russia's power: her regime was able to defeat Pugachev's rebel peasant army in the 1770s, and was also able to expand its empire. By the time Catherine died in 1796, Russia was firmly established as a stable and powerful state. Russia's international standing was shown even more obviously during the Napoleonic Wars, when Bonaparte's invasion of Russia in 1812 ended in ignominious retreat and Russian troops marched into Paris in 1814 with Tsar Alexander I at their head.

Russia's greater engagement with Europe brought about wide discussion of the nature of the relationship between the Romanov state and its western neighbours. The accession to the throne in 1801 of Alexander I sparked hopes that the new Emperor would take the steps that his grandmother, Catherine, had baulked at and would espouse reform. Alexander's first years as Tsar gave some hope that he would soften the grip of autocracy on Russia, but within a decade it became clear that the new monarch had no intention of making any real reform. On Alexander's death in 1825, there was an attempt to place his brother Constantine on the throne, in the hope that he would introduce reform. But the Decembrist revolt lacked any public support, and the plotters proved unable to secure sufficient military support to stage a palace rebellion. Tsar Nicholas I was able to put the rebellion down with ease, but the fear of further revolt dominated his 30 years on the throne. Nicholas imposed a deeply repressive regime on Russia, strengthening both censorship and the secret police, but he was not wholly averse to contemplating reform. The issue of serfdom played a critical role in Russian thinking during the first half of the nineteenth century, and calls for the emancipation of Russia's serfs were amplified as the contrast between Russia's serf economy and the economies of Europe became sharper. In the 1840s Nicholas agreed to reforms that affected the state peasants, but he drew back from contemplating rural reform more widely across the empire. Russia's military might was severely tested by the Crimean War of 1854–56, when Russian forces were defeated by Britain and France on Russia's own soil.

The death of Nicholas I in the middle of the war appeared to offer an opportunity for Russia to embark on a fresh course and the new emperor, Alexander II, instituted a major series of reforms during the 1860s. The emancipation of the serfs in 1861 was their centrepiece, but they also encompassed the legal system, local government, education and the army. The implementation of reform, however, stimulated the appetite of much of educated Russian society for further change: Alexander II was assailed by calls for the autocracy itself to give up some of its power. The emperor vacillated over this, and in 1881 he was assassinated shortly before he was due to approve the introduction of a very limited element of popular representation in the work of the Russian government.

The final two Russian emperors presided over a society that was changing dramatically. During the 1890s, Russia's industrial development accelerated sharply as Sergei Witte, the shrewd Finance Minister, developed a set of economic policies that created a stable framework for investment in the Russian economy. The rural economy began to change as both peasants and nobles took advantage of the emancipation of 1861 to create new patterns of life in the countryside, while Russia's small middle class became more vocal and prominent. At the same time, Russia became more closely drawn into the network of European politics, making a formal alliance with France in 1894 and concluding an agreement with Britain over areas of common imperial interest in 1907. Both Alexander III and his successor Nicholas II were deeply conservative men who set their face against making any reform to Russia's political structures. Even when revolution and defeat in war with Japan threatened to topple the Tsarist regime in 1905, Nicholas II had to be pushed into agreeing to the establishment of an elected parliament, the Duma.

After 1905, an uneasy domestic peace held sway in Russia. Rebellion had been quelled, but popular discontent was still widespread and the iron hand of the state was very evident in maintaining order. A reforming Prime Minister, Stolypin, found his plans frustrated as conservatism regained the initiative after the tumult of 1905. The

First World War created a deep crisis for Russia, as its much-vaunted army suffered catastrophic defeats and Russia's economy was very slow to adapt to the demands of wartime. The political establishment was unable to unify Russian society behind the war effort and by the end of 1916 food shortages were becoming evident in Russia's cities. When demonstrations and strikes broke out in the capital in February 1917, the Tsarist regime was powerless to resist.

On 2 March 1917, Tsar Nicholas II abdicated the Russian throne 'for the salvation of Russia and the preservation of the army at the front' as he explained in his diary.[1] The following day, his brother Grand Duke Mikhail Alexandrovich refused to take the throne, bringing the Romanov dynasty's three centuries of rule in Russia to an end. The collapse of Romanov rule was very rapid. Demonstrations began on the streets of Petrograd – the wartime name for St Petersburg – on 23 February when workers took to the streets protesting at the shortages of food that were affecting the city. A general strike broke out in the capital two days later as more than 200,000 workers abandoned their jobs. By 27 February it was clear that the troops garrisoned in the capital could not be relied upon to put down the revolt that was seizing hold of Petrograd. As soon as it became clear that the loyalty of the army was disintegrating, it was evident to both civilian and military authorities that the Tsarist regime was doomed. The chief official responsible for the city, General A. P. Balk, noted that at headquarters 'the atmosphere was depressing. The agony of the government had begun. Sobbing started. A captain . . . wept hysterically . . . [his] detachment had just refused to carry out his orders.'[2] It took only a little more than a week from the initial outbreak of trouble in Petrograd to bring about the complete downfall of the Tsarist state.

Nicholas II put up little resistance to the idea of abdication. He accepted the views put to him by both his senior generals and political leaders that there was no alternative but for him to give up the throne, and made only a very limited attempt to challenge the need for him to abdicate. His brother was equally determined not to become Tsar, knowing that the throne was a poisoned chalice that would destroy him too. Grand Duke Mikhail questioned Russia's political leaders about his own personal safety if he became emperor: he was told in no uncertain terms that they 'could not vouch for his life'.[3] The Romanovs thus gave up their power with barely a whimper. Three centuries of their rule came to an end with immense speed and with their traditional supporters showing themselves unwilling to stand up to support their rulers. The power that the Romanov monarchs had demonstrated both at home and abroad proved to be a chimera. The mighty Russian army had been humiliated by the Germans during the First World War, losing control of great swathes of the western territories of the empire during the spring and summer of 1915. And in February 1917 the authority of the Tsarist regime crumbled away in its own capital, with the people of Petrograd refusing to be cowed by the symbols of imperial power that defined the physical environment of the city. Almost overnight, Russia appeared to have been transformed from being the most powerful of European states into the weakest.

This easy collapse of the Russian monarchy has informed the way in which the history of the Tsarist state has been approached. When Lenin took power in Russia in October 1917, the Bolsheviks believed that they were acting out a process that was ordained by impersonal and objective historical forces. Informed by Marx's over-arching theory of historical materialism, they traced the roots of their success back through the nineteenth century, identifying the features of Russian historical development that were pointers towards the success of their revolution. The history of Tsarist Russia that was written in the Soviet Union was teleological. Working backwards from the 'Great October Socialist Revolution' of 1917, Soviet histor-ians emphasised the tradition of Russian popular revolt during the eighteenth and nineteenth centuries, explaining rebellion in both countryside and city as part of the sweep of historical development that was to lead to the inevitable triumph of the Bolshevik party. One of the standard works on the last decades of Tsarism, written in the 1980s, regarded the imperial regime as inevitably doomed to destruction and saw the 'crisis of autocracy reflected in all aspects of the economic, social and political life of the country'.[4] Soviet history also devoted immense attention to the intellectual history of revolu-tion in Russia, magnifying the significance of minor thinkers and creating a coherent 'Russian revolutionary tradition' that provided the theoretical background for popular rebellion. At the same time, this teleology was imposed on the history of the Tsarist regime. Soviet history began from the premise that the wreck of Tsarism was inev-itable and that its history must be analysed through the prism of its certain and inevitable failure. The Soviet approach to the eighteenth- and nineteenth-century Russian state was, with few exceptions, to concentrate on the features of its history that exemplified the weakness of the state and that presaged its eventual ruin. The twin tracks of Soviet history mirrored each other: a state that was inherently weak and doomed to destruction was paralleled by a society that was intrinsically revolutionary. Soviet historians saw the seeds of Romanov collapse and of Bolshevik triumph at every turn.

Unsurprisingly, this approach coloured accounts of the history of Russia written outside the confines of the Soviet Union. Even though Soviet historians condemned the 'bourgeois falsifiers of history' who had the temerity to write the history of Russia from a standpoint that was not determined by the hegemony of Marxist–Leninist thinking, significant elements of western histories of Tsarist Russia were conditioned by the Soviet approach. Western historians too laid immense stress on the development of a working class in Romanov Russia, tracing the roots of the emergence of a revolutionary consciousness among the Russian urban population. As well, the eventual failure of Tsarism conditioned much of western historical writing about the nature of the Russian state and the society over which it ruled. Western history too picked out the features of Russian history that were to lead to the twin revolutions of 1917, focussing on the fragility of Tsarist power and on the social challenges that were a continual threat to the state's existence long before the eventual victory of revolution. Richard Pipes, for example, wrote that 'the trappings of imperial omnipotence [after 1762] served merely to conceal the monarchy's desperate weakness'.[5] The collapse of the Soviet Union, the failure of the Bolshevik experiment and the disintegration of the historic Russian empire since 1991 have allowed historians – both in Russia and in the wider world – to take a very different view of the history of Tsarism. The inevitability of Bolshevik triumph has been exposed as an illusion, since the 74 years of Soviet rule ended as ignominiously as had the Tsarist empire. The communist period of rule proved to be, not the enduring final stage of the development of human society that Marx predicted, but merely a single episode in Russia's history. The Soviet state was held in place by an apparatus of coercion, seen at its zenith in Stalin's terror of the 1930s, but then subsiding into a regime of banal repression until it finally collapsed, bereft of any social support. Since 1991, it has been argued that Bolshevism itself was an anomaly in Russia's history, and renewed interest has been taken in the final decades of Tsarism, with continuities identified between the Russia of Nicholas II and the post-1991 situation.

The long concentration on explaining the history of eighteenth- and nineteenth-century Russia in terms of the events of 1917 has obscured important issues. The ease with which Tsarism was toppled has led to a concentration on the roots of the Romanov regime's weakness, ignoring the real strength that Tsarism demonstrated over many generations. Such an approach to this period of Russian history fails to acknowledge the features of the Russian autocracy that differentiated it from other European monarchical states and that allowed it to endure for so long. The strength of the Russian state was evident to contemporaries: even during its final decades the empire was recognised as one of the Great Powers, despite its military setbacks in the Crimea in the 1850s and against Japan in 1904-05. Russian imperial expansion was perceived, especially by the British, as posing a severe threat to the stability of the international order. The internal policies of Tsarism were regarded as ferocious by outsiders and the Russian state was feared as the most repressive in Europe.

The Romanov regime had survived unscathed and had been able to resist calls for reform right through the eighteenth and nineteenth centuries. Uniquely among European monarchies, the Tsarist state was successful in staving off demands for some form of liberal constitution until 1905. This was in sharp contrast to the experience of other states: the British monarch had been deposed in the 1640s and the 1688 settlement that legitimised the restored monarchy placed severe limits on the powers of the monarch. Successive extensions to the franchise during the nineteenth century changed the British political landscape beyond recognition. The French Revolution had removed France's monarchy and, even though restored monarchs continued to hold sway in France for much of the nineteenth century, the power of the eighteenth-century kings was never again replicated. The role of the people in the French state steadily grew and the establishment of the Fourth Republic in 1871 finally laid the French monarchy to rest. The Habsburg empire was forced to concede significant autonomy to its Hungarian domains in 1867 and universal male suffrage was established in the remainder of the empire by 1906. Even Bismarck's Prussia and the German empire that came into existence after 1871 had the powers of the monarch limited by an elected assembly. The Russian autocracy, however, proved able to sustain its position even when threatened by internal rebellion, such as the great Pugachev uprising in the 1770s, and was able to put down the

1905 revolution successfully. The coercive forces at the disposal of the Tsarist regime were powerful enough to prevent most major outbreaks of revolt, and were able to deal a firm blow to those outbursts that did occur. Until 1905, the autocrat was able to restrict the expression of political opinion through censorship, the use of emergency powers and the activities of the political police so that it was very difficult for opposition to take hold among the articulate elites of Russian society. The inherent strength of the Romanov regime enabled it to survive a series of shocks that could have proved fatal to the Tsarist state. It was able to deal with widespread popular rebellion in the 1770s and in 1905, and to cope with lost wars in the Crimea in the 1850s and against Japan in 1905. Nicholas II proved powerful enough to claw back some of the constitutional concessions that were forced out of him in 1905, rendering the elected Duma much less powerful than its protagonists had hoped.

The success of the Tsarist state in restoring its authority after the disasters of 1905 appeared to demonstrate that the Romanovs had regained the initiative and that Russia would continue as an autocracy, largely untouched by the pressures of reform that had compelled each of the other European powers to introduce some form of constitutional government and to limit the power of the monarch. The Russian economy had begun to industrialise rapidly in the 1890s, bringing greater prosperity to the empire, while Russian society was starting to break free from its traditional rural structures. A nascent Russian bourgeoisie was emerging as the landed nobility slowly declined in social significance, and business and the professions grew in importance. Society was gaining an existence autonomous of the state, and a civil society was slowly coming into being. In these circumstances, it has been argued that Tsarism was on the way to achieving an equilibrium that was allowing social development, while maintaining the essentials of autocratic politics.[6] This optimistic view of the nature of Tsarist Russia assumed that the Romanov regime was amenable to the development of a state and society that were developing on lines that would bring Russia towards convergence with western European models. But, the later Romanovs were deeply resistant to giving up any of their power, and Russia was becoming more polarised after 1905. The prospects for Russia's development were fatally interrupted by the First World War, which heaped crisis upon crisis for the Tsarist state and destroyed it within the space of three years.

The record of the Romanovs in maintaining their position is the more remarkable, given the pressures which the Russian state faced between 1700 and 1900. For more than 50 of these 200 years, Russia was at war with other European states. Wars took place regularly during the eighteenth and nineteenth centuries, and Russia was only once at peace for more than 30 consecutive years during these two centuries. War placed great strains upon the state in two ways: it required large amounts of both money and men. The Russian state was consistently successful in raising revenue and in conscripting troops to enable it to engage in armed conflict. It was able to engage in frequent conflicts that absorbed significant amounts of both human and financial resources, at the same time as expanding its territorial reach in both Europe and Asia. The Russian state drew new lands into its domains in an almost continuous process for more than 150 years after 1700. It acquired lands with dramatic contrasts in geography and climate, populated by peoples with the greatest variety of languages and religions of any state on the globe. Alongside these demonstrations of its external power, Tsarist Russia maintained a very tight grip on its internal authority so that by 1900 the Tsar was the most powerful monarch in Europe.

This book aims to explain the reasons for the Tsarist state's enduring power. The relationship between Russia and Europe had been defined by Peter the Great at the beginning of the eighteenth century when he drew on the western model of economic development and raided Europe's technological treasure-house to push forward the development of Russia itself. But Peter wanted nothing to do with European political developments and this set the course for the following two centuries. The Romanov regime was exceptional in Europe in being able to retain its absolute power for so long. It was able to develop an intellectual foundation for its rule that did not simply mirror the theories about the divine right of monarchs to rule that were a feature of western states in the medieval and early modern periods. The Russian state recognised the differences that existed between its society and those of its neighbours to the west and did not seek to ape the political theories that legitimised western monarchies. In particular, the Romanovs rejected the developments in political ideas that suggested that monarchies could only continue to exist if they gained the consent – whether explicit or implicit – of the peoples over whom they ruled. The men and women who occupied the Russian throne proved to be doughty defenders of their authority. They were inculcated with the belief that their autocratic power had been bestowed upon them by God and that each monarch must pass on this power intact to their successor. Although a very few Russian sovereigns – in particular Catherine II and Alexander I – dallied with western political and social theories, they always drew back from anything other than intellectual engagement with them. Although Catherine II prided herself on her sympathies with the principles of the European Enlightenment and developed closer ties to western thinkers than any of her fellow sovereigns, she was always insistent that these ideas had little practical relevance for Russia itself.

The Tsarist state's authority grew from deep social roots. Even though the Romanovs rejected any hint that their power rested upon the consent of their people, they nevertheless constructed a social alliance with the Russian nobility that enabled them to keep a tight grip on power. The state and nobility reached an implicit bargain: the nobility would offer their unconditional support to the autocratic state in return for being given their own unlimited authority over the serf population of the empire. The social structures of Russia thus buttressed the state's political organisation, but the power of the Tsars was dependent on being able to maintain control over the entire population, whether they be nobles, peasants or townspeople. The state could not rely entirely upon these social bonds to exert its authority across its domains and it constructed an elaborate system of institutions that enabled it to rule effectively. Russia's central government, operating from the deep-yellow ministerial buildings of official St Petersburg, was largely unrestricted by western concepts of legality.

The ethos of autocracy demanded that law take second place to the interests of the state and that the apparatus of government could operate without being constrained by legal norms. The St Petersburg ministries were able to exert immense power across Russia's domains and their local agencies possessed equally wide powers. It was vital, in the immense Russian state where communications could be very slow, to allow local authorities considerable latitude in the actions they could take to ensure social stability and to maintain order. The Romanovs put institutions in place in the provinces that had sufficient autonomy to act on their own initiative, as well as establishing a system of policing that could impose severe restrictions on the population. The regime's disdain for legal constraints and its intense craving to retain absolute power was shown by its reliance on emergency powers in the final decades of its existence; the state was determined not to concede any of its authority and instead sought to tighten the screw on its subjects. The Tsarist state was remarkably successful at imposing its power over the great multitude of non-Russian nationalities that were ruled from St Petersburg. The clear view of Russian identity that the state articulated explicitly during the 1830s – Official Nationality – provided a vision for the empire's rulers. They wanted to construct a state in which the political, religious and cultural values were those of its Russian rulers, and they were not prepared to allow their subject peoples any real latitude to develop their own identity. The Tsarist regime based its power across the empire on its military strength. It ensured that it could conscript a huge army year after year – a process that in itself provided its subjects with a persistent reminder of the state's power. Alongside this, Russia proved able to maintain its finances securely. The regime recognised that it must be able to collect its revenues successfully if it was to continue to sustain its military and international position. Russia's huge army depended on the regimes ability to pay, feed and equip its soldiers. The heart of Russian power lay in men and money, without a sound financial basis the state's military ambitions would collapse, and without a brutally effective system of conscription the Tsarist regime could not have imposed its power at home and abroad.

Despite the formidable and enduring authority of the Russian autocracy, however, it did crumble away in 1917. The book seeks to identify the sources of its eventual failure, even as the Russian state put on an outward show of might. The regime itself helped to plant the seeds of its own downfall. Autocratic power was founded on total control of every aspect of the Russian state and society. But, in the 1860s the state began to dismantle some of the essential elements of its power. Emancipating the serfs broke the crucial link that existed between the regime and the nobility and undermined the control of the rural population. At the same time, the state for the first time gave a degree of autonomy to sections of society by reforming the judicial system and by establishing elected local councils across European Russia. The Romanovs pursued policies that proved contradictory; despite their efforts to retrieve their authority in the last decades of the nineteenth century, they were unable to turn the clock back. In the end, the Romanovs proved unable to adapt their state to the changed social environment after 1861.

PART I

THE ETHOS OF AUTOCRACY

Chapter 1: The Ideology of Tsarism

The imperial Russian state was an autocracy, ruled over by a succession of emperors and empresses from the accession of Peter the Great to the throne in 1689 until the abdication of Nicholas II and the end of the Romanov dynasty more than two centuries later in 1917. Each of these rulers had their own priorities and the way in which the state was governed changed significantly as monarchs and times changed. But, the principles on which the Romanov monarchs of the eighteenth and nineteenth centuries based their rule over the empire remained constant. The rulers of imperial Russia had a fundamental and consistent view of their own position and of the way in which their empire should be ruled. This provided them with a certainty about their own position that made it easier for them to see off challenges to their authority and that enabled them to deal with opposition in a ruthless and forthright manner.

Autocracy

Russian monarchs believed that they were ordained by God to rule over their empire as autocrats. While the concept of the divine right of kings had been successfully challenged in both practical and theoretical terms in western Europe since the seventeenth century, in Russia it remained supreme. The Russian intellectual climate was to a large extent resistant to accepting ideas that had originated in the West, as Russian elites argued that Russia occupied a special place in Europe. The view that prevailed among Russia's political elites was that Russia was a part of the broader European world, but that it stood separate and was not destined to follow the western model, either in political or in economic terms. From the reign of Peter the Great onwards, Russia sought to exploit western European technology, but these economic ties were kept strictly separate from politics. Russia was characterised as a society that bore fundamental differences from the rest of Europe. Its population was overwhelmingly rural, and even in 1897, when the first empire-wide census was conducted, more than 80 per cent of the population lived in the countryside. More than this, Russia's huge peasant population was argued to be especially volatile, requiring strong and decisive government to prevent it from erupting into spontaneous and inchoate rebellion. This was the root of Russia's 'otherness': its social distinctiveness required a very different polit-ical structure. This sparsely populated, rural society needed, it was believed, strong central control if it was to be able to operate as a coherent political entity. The concept of popular consent to govern-ment that had begun to emerge in the West during the seventeenth century found few echoes in Russia. Although Catherine II corres-ponded with the leading lights of the French Enlightenment and saw herself as being in the mainstream of European thought, she had no intention of seeing these ideas put into practice in the Russian empire. Russian monarchs continued to insist that they gained their authority directly from God, and that the population of the empire was too unsophisticated to play any part in the structures of government. Furthermore, the nature of Russian government had to be entirely different from the character of regimes to Russia's west. The strong central authority that was needed to maintain order in the Russian empire could only be provided by a regime that was all-powerful and could exert absolute authority over the population. Russia's political system was destined to remain an autocracy.

It was clearly convenient for successive Russian monarchs to argue the case for autocracy. None of them wanted to see their own power curtailed, and they were supported by officials whose careers and authority depended on the maintenance of the autocratic system of government. There was, therefore, a powerful systemic inertia that worked against change taking place. However, the reasons for the maintenance of autocracy ran much deeper. The authority of the Russian state rested on what were shaky foundations. It was only in the fifteenth and sixteenth centuries that a single united Russian state had developed from the Muscovite princedom, centred on Moscow itself.

Since then, Russia had expanded at breakneck speed: the inhospitable lands of Siberia to the east were colonised by Russians, and they succeeded in reaching the Pacific Ocean for the first time in 1639. The Russians did not need to venture overseas to acquire their empire: there were vast tracts of land ripe for the picking in Siberia and in Central Asia. The expansion of the state continued almost unbroken for nearly 200 years from the beginning of the eighteenth century. The rich natural resources of Siberia were a powerful incentive for explorers to put up with the harsh climate and difficult terrain and to stamp Russian authority on the land. Scientific and military expeditions ranged widely across the wilderness areas of northern and eastern Siberia to explore the riches that Russia had acquired. During the nineteenth century, Russia acted to colonise regions to the south. The mountainous Caucasus region was only brought under the control of the empire in the early nineteenth century and it continued to be troublesome for St Petersburg. Central Asia was the final area to be added to the empire's domains, with major military campaigns in the middle of the nineteenth century to subdue the indigenous populations and establish Russian rule. The Russian state did not have the settled frontiers of Britain or France, nor had it undergone the long and gradual process of political development that characterised many of its western neighbours. The Russian empire continued to expand until almost the end of the period of Romanov rule, meaning that the state was permanently in a condition of flux and that consolidation was difficult. This process was very different from the imperial expansion that other European states underwent. For most imperial states, colonies were overseas and physically separate from the metropolitan power, and their acquisition came about as a result of the metropolitan state's political and economic strength. Colonial difficulties could produce problems for the imperial power, but these did not often threaten the integrity of the imperial state itself. The Russian experience was entirely different. Russia's acquisition of empire did not involve explorers venturing overseas and this produced advantages for the Russian state in terms of the ease of the empire's growth. But, it also presented the Russian state with severe problems. Imperial difficulties could not be easily isolated from the heartland of the state, and Russia lacked the protective insulation that oceans and great distances provided for the British and the French when they faced problems with their colonial possessions.

Russian rule was not always welcome to the peoples over whom they ruled. Military campaigns were needed to subdue the Caucasus and Central Asia, and these regions required continual garrisoning to ensure that the Russians could continue their dominance. Other parts of the empire provided even greater challenges: Russia acquired a large part of Poland when the Polish state was dismembered in the 1790s. While Prussia and Austria-Hungary also gained parts of the Polish state, it was Russia that seized the largest share. The Poles loathed their new Russian masters and rebelled against them in 1830 and with even greater ferocity in 1863. Finland had been gained from the Swedes in 1808 and presented the Russians with few problems until the end of the nineteenth century and the advent of attempts to Russify the country and to destroy Finnish autonomy. A determined campaign of sullen civil discontent by the Finns then made life very difficult indeed for the Russians. Russia's empire thus presented its rulers with significant problems that shaped their method of government. Much of the state was, in effect, newly conquered and the Russians had no opportunity to consolidate a region into the empire before embarking on new imperial conquests. The government was continually having to cope with the addition of new areas and seeking ways of creating a coherent state. The challenges to Russian power that were presented by this process of imperial expansion had an important impact on the empire's model of government. The threats that were posed by the ever-expanding empire persuaded its rulers that only powerful central authority could successfully guarantee the survival and coherence of the empire.

This belief was reinforced by the state's need to maintain control over the population of its heartland. Russia was the most populous European state and, in addition, its population was spread thinly across a huge area. The sheer vastness of the state's territory made it imperative for the Tsarist regime to be able to maintain tight control of its population and to be capable of quelling rebellion before the state itself could be threatened. There were successive instances of peasant rebellion that made the state all too aware of its fragile grip on power. In 1606–07, 1670–71, 1707–08 and lastly in the 1770s, there were huge yet incoherent peasant uprisings that made monarchs and their advisers fear for their authority. The Pugachev rebellion in the 1770s was especially disturbing, since Catherine II imagined herself to be an 'enlightened' ruler whose rule should encourage the people of the Russian empire to feel grateful for the benefits that she munificently bestowed upon them. The apparent ingratitude of the people who rallied to Pugachev confirmed in Catherine and her successors the view that Russia required ruling with an iron fist. This was the attitude that prevailed until the very end of the Tsarist regime. Peasant rebellion was put down with severity whenever it occurred and the state took particular care to be alert to the possibility of rural unrest and to recognise the most practical ways of dealing with it. One of the motives for the emancipation of the serfs in 1861 was an increase in peasant disturbances during the 1850s: although the absolute number of uprisings was small, the increase in unrest that they represented was sufficient to worry the emperor and his advisers and to persuade them that reform was needed to stave off the threat of more serious rebellion in the future. On this occasion, the regime took the view that the most effective method of maintaining control was to recognise that change had to take place. But this was a rare move. The state's more usual response to rural unrest was demonstrated in 1905 when there were more than 3000 separate instances of peasant rebellion across the empire. The government attempted to quell rebellion by force, only making concessions when it was clear that coercion was not succeeding. But, after the announcement of reforms in the autumn of 1905, the government again went on the offensive in the countryside, despatching troops to put down disturbances with great brutality.[1] The supposed predilection of the Russian people for rebellion was a powerful weapon in the regime's continuing espousal of autocracy.

Autocracy was the cornerstone of the principles that governed the way in which Russian monarchs ruled their empire. It invested the monarch with power that was unparalleled among the rulers of the Great Powers and its implications were immense. The Russian sovereign, free from any of the limitations that a parliament could place upon his authority, was able to make law as he wished. Autocracy meant that the monarch possessed unlimited authority and, in effect, that every decision that he made had the effect of law.[2] The nature of law in the Tsarist empire was very different from its status in western Europe. As limitations were gradually placed upon monarchs' authority in the West, it became accepted that the monarch too was subject to the same laws that governed the behaviour of the population of a state. This fundamental concept of modern western political thinking was never accepted in Russia. Law was something that was imposed by the state on its population, but that the state itself – personified by the sovereign – did not need to abide by. The idea of the rule of law that lay at the heart of western societies from the late eighteenth century did not take root in Russia. The Russian state stood above the law. This was manifested in a number of ways. The monarch's decisions were law and, although imperial Russia possessed a formal system by which law should be made, through the bureaucratic institution of the Senate, in practice the word of the Tsar represented law. This had important implications for the ways in which law was implemented for ordinary Russians. Since the monarch essentially stood above the law, so the ruler's representatives throughout the empire were also able to act with impunity with the same sort of extra-judicial privileges as the sovereign. This was institutionalised through the system of administrative justice that became commonplace in the empire. While western models of justice required that criminal offences be tried by courts, and that punishment could only be imposed in line with formal legislation, these principles never took hold in imperial Russia. Ordinary Russians were subject to the administrative decisions of the state's officials, and local officials could pass judgement on people and impose sentences without reference to any form of judicial authority. Imprisonment and fines were the most common punishments that could be meted out, but Russians could also be sentenced to internal exile and expelled from their home region, if local officials believed that an individual's behaviour warranted it.

It was only in 1864 that the first signs of an independent legal system began to be introduced in the Russian empire, but the Tsarist regime soon realised that these innovations threatened its traditional freedom to act as it wished and it began to find ways to evade the new judicial system. The 1864 reforms introduced jury trials in Russia, and also established an independent judiciary, appointed for life and paid sufficiently well that they had no need to take bribes. These innovations offered a sharp contrast to the underlying traditions of Russian government by establishing an autonomous source of authority in the Russian state, and the regime soon sought to re-establish its control over the legal process. The assassination of Tsar Alexander II by a group of revolutionaries in 1881 provided the impetus for this attempt at reaction: legislation was introduced that allowed the government to introduce a state of emergency in areas of the empire. This effectively allowed the state to bypass the judicial process completely and to revert to its traditional practices of imposing order on its population as it saw fit. This arbitrary treatment of the population was a direct and logical corollary of autocracy: the sovereign believed that the Russian state and its people were for him to deal with as he saw fit, and this meant that he could not be restricted by law or regulation. The concept of autocracy was not just related to the person of the monarch: it had repercussions for each individual Russian, whether they were a government official or a peasant farmer deep in the heart of the countryside. Autocracy conjures up images of an opulent court in which people fawned upon the emperor, seeking to ingratiate themselves with the sovereign, knowing that decisions and favours could flow their way. But, autocracy was also reflected in the popular experience of ordinary Russians who had no proper recourse against the actions of the regime's officials and who were subject to the arbitrary whims of low-level rural officialdom. The ethos of autocracy stretched right through Russian society from the emperor to the lowliest rural policeman or tax collector. It meant that not just the sovereign, but also each government official, was imbued with the idea that they could act with impunity in their dealings as agents of the state. For the sovereign, this could mean the ability to embark on war without any need to take formal advice from any institution of government. For a rural bureaucrat, it could mean confining a peasant to the cells on the basis of flimsy or non-existent evidence. The practice of autocracy thus touched the lives of every inhabitant of the Russian empire.

Attempts to modify this autocratic model of ruling proved consistently unsuccessful. For most of the eighteenth century, Russian monarchs revelled in the power that it brought them. Peter the Great's dynamic reshaping of the institutions of the Russian state and his desire to give Russian society a western-orientated outlook was accomplished largely through the use of his huge personal power and with the threat of sanctions and retribution against those who challenged or disagreed with him. Catherine II, while presenting herself to the outside world as a monarch who was in the mainstream of the ideas of the Enlightenment that were taking hold in western Europe, ruled Russia in a way that was much more traditional. Even though the ideas that Catherine read and discussed with her intellectual correspondents advanced the concept of human liberty, Catherine would not emancipate the Russian peasants from serfdom. She continued to assert that the ideas that were emanating from the West were not appropriate for Russian conditions: this was the argument of Russian exceptionalism that was used by each of Russia's rulers to justify the maintenance of very different political and social systems in their empire. In the first half of the nineteenth century, Nicholas I's Minister of Education, Sergei Uvarov, attempted to provide the Russian autocracy with an intellectual justification for its method of government. His theory of 'Official Nationality' attempted to demonstrate that Russia's rulers were not simply motivated by a desire for unlimited power, but that they also had the interests of their subjects at heart. Uvarov believed that autocracy was the only viable form of government for Russia. 'Autocracy', he wrote, 'constitutes the main condition of the political existence of Russia. The Russian giant stands on it as the cornerstone of his greatness', but Uvarov was insistent in drawing a distinction between autocracy and despotism. He described Russia's autocracy as 'strong, humane and enlightened' and placed Russia in an overall tradition of monarchical development.[3] He believed that monarchs came to recognise that they could only rule successfully if they became 'enlightened' and that, far from weakening their authority, this would lead to what Uvarov described as 'maturity' and more effective government.

Right through the nineteenth century, the ideal of autocracy and the power that it bestowed upon the monarch was upheld by successive sovereigns. The only exception to this pattern was during the early part of the reign of Alexander II, who succeeded to the throne during the Crimean War. For the first decade of his reign, Alexander was convinced that Russia had to reform and needed to emulate western models of development. The 'Great Reforms' of the 1860s brought about fundamental change in Russia, but they did not succeed in altering Russia's political culture. Alexander II grew wary of reform, especially after an assassination attempt on him in 1866, and the growth of revolutionary movements during the 1870s made the regime much more ambivalent about the wisdom of political reform. After Alexander II's assassination in 1881, the new emperor – his son, Alexander III – moved decisively away from reform and reasserted the virtues of autocracy. This ethos was continued by Russia's last emperor, Nicholas II, who resisted attempts to encroach on his autocratic authority with extreme stubbornness. Even after the events of 1905, and the establishment of an elected parliament in Russia, the emperor continued to believe that he retained his full powers as an unlimited monarch.

Orthodoxy

Autocracy and the preservation of monarchical authority rested at the heart of the Tsarist regime's beliefs. Other elements, however, buttressed this central political dogma. Pure politics alone was insufficient to bind the empire together, and the Romanov regime needed to find other ways of ensuring that its subjects accepted the authority of the monarchy, and preventing them from rebelling. Religion played a crucial role in this process. The ties between the Tsarist regime and the Russian Orthodox Church were very strong and gave the regime a means of communicating with the population of the empire that added significantly to its capacity. The theology of Russian Orthodoxy complemented the political ideas of the Russian autocracy. The Russian church had split away from eastern Orthodoxy in the fifteenth century, taking advantage of the weakness of the Byzantine church and establishing itself as what it believed was the true Christian church. The Russian church reflected the political beliefs of the state; Russia possessed a particular spiritual role inside the Christian world. The Roman Catholic Church, according to Orthodox beliefs, had shown itself to have left the true Christian path and the same was true for the Byzantine church. Russia was destined to be the 'third Rome', the real repository of Christian values and beliefs. In religious terms, the Orthodox Church cultivated the same concept of Russian distinctiveness that the state encouraged. For the church, Russia was entirely separate from the Christian traditions of the remainder of Europe, and the Orthodox hierarchy sought to stamp out other Christian religions within the Russian empire. In the case of Roman Catholicism, this was made easier by the Catholic Church's identification with the empire's increasingly rebellious Polish subjects and the state's desire to see every manifestation of Polish nationalism stamped out. Protestant religions were viewed with rather less disfavour, since there was no significant national group that espoused Protestantism and posed a threat to the integrity of the state. The Orthodox Church made strenuous efforts to convert people to Orthodoxy from other religions, believing that it offered the only true route to salvation. There was, however, a wider motivation at work. The identification of the Orthodox Church with the imperial Russian state meant that the attraction of new adherents to Orthodoxy was an important way of integrating new populations into the empire. Converting new Russian subjects to the Orthodox religion served the interests of both church and state; the Orthodox Church was able to claim that it had acquired new adherents to the true religion, while for the state, conversion to Orthodoxy symbolised that new believers had accepted the attributes of Russian nationality and the authority of the Russian state.

The Orthodox Church played an important part in the formation of the state's identity. Peter the Great had recognised the utility of the spiritual authority and had sought to integrate the Church into the apparatus of the state itself. Metropolitan Feofan Prokopovich had reciprocated by providing an intellectual justification for Peter's absolutism. In 1721, Peter established the Holy Synod as a collegial body of bishops to run the Church, but tried to ensure that the Church was closely linked to the state by appointing a lay official as the Synod's Chief Procurator – its chief official.[4] For much of the eighteenth century, the Church was able to continue to run itself and found little interference from the state and the Chief Procurator in its affairs. It was able to impose its own canon law and to regulate its own ecclesiastical affairs, while the Church's bishops possessed significant autonomy. From the beginning of the nineteenth century, however, the state began to take a much closer interest in the Orthodox Church as it appreciated its potential utility as a means of sustaining the government's authority over an increasingly troublesome population. The Church appeared to offer the state a means of exerting influence and control over its subjects through an institution that was not tainted with the overt authority of the state itself. Orthodoxy provided a further advantage to the state, as it derived its power from the spiritual sphere. While Russians might baulk at obeying the commands of the state and its agents, believing that they were acting unjustly and were simply behaving in the oppressive manner to which they had become accustomed, the Orthodox Church's authority derived from God and the messages that its priests preached from the pulpit each week could have a greater impact on the Church's flock.

The Orthodox Church had to be cautious in the extent to which it became directly involved with the policies of the government, lest it simply become seen by Orthodox believers as an arm of the state, but the Church recognised that its own interests were also served by promoting social stability and obedience to authority. The most obvious example of the Church's links to the state centres on the emancipation of the serfs in 1861. The monumental significance of this measure, and the extreme trepidation with which the government approached granting freedom to tens of millions of serfs, meant that it wanted to invest the event with a particular gravity. The emancipation proclamation itself was written by Filaret, the Metropolitan of Moscow, and it was read from Orthodox pulpits across Russia in March 1861.[5] The Church did realise that its interests did not always coincide with those of the government, and during the nineteenth century there was substantial conflict between church and state as the Orthodox Church sought to extend its independence and to reform itself. But, despite these tensions, the Church always recognised that its central interest was at one with the state's own priority: the maintenance of order and the preservation of strong central authority. The Church needed the protection of the state if it was to thrive and it was therefore prepared to support the government at times of crisis. During the first decade of the twentieth century, when revolt threatened the stability of the empire, priests were called upon to read messages from the pulpit to encourage their parishioners to obey the legitimately constituted authorities of the state. The Orthodox Church possessed a further advantage for the state; it had a vast network of priests who were in close and frequent contact with the rural population of the empire. Russia had more Orthodox priests than policemen during the nineteenth century and their position as an integral part of rural society gave them access to the population that was denied to the state's own servants.

Orthodoxy also played a significant part in the legitimation of the imperial regime. The monarchs saw religious ritual as playing a vital part in their lives, even if they did not themselves hold deep religious beliefs. Catherine II ensured that she participated fully in all the Orthodox ceremonies that were demanded of a Russian monarch, even though she had no sincere commitment to Orthodoxy herself. She did, however, recognise the importance of the Church in helping to ensure the stability of the Russian state and took steps to ensure that the Church recognised the primacy of the state. Even though the Orthodox Church had helped in cementing Catherine's seizure of power from her husband, Peter III, in 1762, the new empress wanted to make it plain where real power resided. The Orthodox hierarchy had some hope that Catherine might allow them greater autonomy in the way in which they governed the Church, in recognition of the Church's part in bringing her to power. Instead, however, Catherine secularised the Church's lands and dealt severely with Metropolitan Arsenii of Rostov, who emerged as the chief opponent of secularisation. He was tried for *lèse majesté* and in 1767 imprisoned in conditions of great harshness until he died 5 years later.

Other Romanovs showed a greater personal devotion to the Orthodox faith. Nicholas I displayed a simple religiosity but also demonstrated an abiding interest in the promotion of Orthodoxy across his empire. Conflict with Turkey in the late 1820s helped to intensify Nicholas's religious faith; he began to see Russia as the standard bearer of Christendom in defending the shrines of the Holy Land and to emphasise the links between Russia's present and its past. This was evident in the attention that Nicholas paid to the construction of new churches in Russia: he wanted to see religious buildings that would demonstrate the identification of Orthodoxy with the Russian people. The most substantial example of this was the construction of a new Orthodox cathedral in Moscow. Nicholas wanted to see a cathedral 'in ancient Russian taste' and the building was to be on a monumental scale, combining motifs from Russia's Byzantine past with elements of its more recent heroic present.[6] The building took almost half a century to complete. The two final Russian emperors were the most devout of Russia's monarchs. Both Alexander III and Nicholas II married foreign brides; Romanov tradition required that these women convert to Orthodoxy and take Russian names. Both Empress Maria Fedorovna and especially Nicholas II's wife, Alexandra Fedorovna, embraced Orthodoxy with enthusiasm. Nicholas II and his empress both possessed a genuine and mystical devotion to the Orthodox Church. Nicholas fervently believed that he had been appointed to his task as emperor by God and that it was his duty to ensure that he handed the empire on to his heir in the same condition as he had inherited it from his father. The deep religious springs of Nicholas's convictions help to explain his dogged and stubborn resistance to making reform: the emperor clearly believed that by taking such steps he would be betraying his inheritance and that he would have to answer for this to God.

Russian monarchs continued to believe in the divine nature of their power long after their western European counterparts had abandoned this viewpoint. This reliance on Orthodoxy had important consequences for the development of the Russian state. Successive Tsars believed that their power derived from the Almighty, and they therefore rejected any suggestions that their power could gain any legitimacy from other sources. The commanding place of Orthodoxy in the nature of Russia's statehood, combined with the commitment of the spiritual power to autocracy, made it impossible for sovereigns to contemplate sharing power with any other group or institution. Any recognition of the place of popular opinion in the government of the Russian empire aimed a dagger at the whole ethos of the empire and threatened the fundamental ideas that gave the Romanovs their legitimacy.

Nationality

Uvarov's doctrine of Official Nationality identified the third element of Russian uniqueness as nationality. While it was easier to define the nature of autocracy and of Orthodoxy, nationality remained a much more nebulous concept. It represented both the popular application of Orthodoxy and autocracy, as well as encapsulating the historic mission that Uvarov and like-minded thinkers believed to be Russia's destiny. He defined Russian identity as unique and separate and insisted that Russia should find its own solutions to the issues that confronted it in the mid-nineteenth century. Uvarov believed that the imperial Russian state had both the duty and the right to direct the development of each of its subject peoples. The tradition of romantic nationalism that was prominent across Europe during the 1830s and 1840s helped to support this approach and it found expression in both the state's policies towards its non-Russian national groups and in the ways in which the state projected itself to its people. The visits of Nicholas I to Moscow in 1848 and 1849 showed how closely the emperor wished to identify himself with Russia's history and national identity. Nationalists saw the appearance of Nicholas I in the Kremlin as representing 'the union of Tsar and people' and viewed the monarch as the embodiment of Russia's national character.[7] These manifestations of Russian nationhood were a persistent part of Romanov behaviour and were reflected in the ways in which the monarchs sought to identify themselves with Russia itself and to show that they were a true part of the Russian nation. Even Peter the Great, the most European-orientated of Russia's rulers, wanted to demonstrate that he was a true Russian. His utilisation of western models was designed to allow Russia to develop as rapidly as possible and to be able to challenge the great powers of Europe on their own terms, rather than to see Russia's distinctive identity subsumed into an alien pan-European culture. For most of the eighteenth and nineteenth centuries, Russia's monarchs were consciously determined to preserve and strengthen national identity. The western pattern of development appeared increasingly unpalatable and unsuited to Russia's particular nature. Russia remained a state that was dominated by the rural world in a way that was not true of any other European power. The peasantry continued to form the overwhelming majority of the population, and Russia's economy and society took only very slow and faltering steps towards industrialisation. This was the fundamental element of Russian identity that successive rulers wanted to protect and maintain: the traditional social structures of the empire provided the base to sustain their autocratic regime. Before 1861, the enserfed peasantry were the counterpoint to the autocratic state; the absolute power that the monarch wielded could really only be exercised in a society where the rights of the majority of the population were limited or, as under serfdom, essentially non-existent. It was therefore in the interests of the state to maintain Russia's traditional social structures and to freeze Russia's identity in the pre-emancipation mould.

The nature of Russian nationhood was, however, a question that was continually debated from Peter the Great's era onwards. While the political imperatives that pointed towards the preservation of autocracy remained strong and constant, Russia could not be immune from the wider processes of social and economic change that gathered pace in Europe from the 1750s onwards. The onset of industrial revolution had a crucial impact on Russia itself, even though the Russian economy lagged far behind the other European Great Powers. Peter the Great had thrust Russia firmly onto the European stage with his dramatic military victories over the Swedes at Poltava in 1709 and the formalisation of Russian dominance of northern Europe through the Peace of Nystad in 1721. But continued military success required that Russia's armies be equipped to a level that would allow them to sustain their triumphs. As western Europe became more and more technologically sophisticated, Russia could not be unaffected by the improvements to weaponry and equipment that industrialisation was bringing. Even though, for political reasons, Russia's rulers might hanker after the continuation of the rural-based economy that enabled them to remain in power, their intense desire to retain Russia's international status forced them into a paradoxical position. Once Russia had become one of the Great Powers through Peter's military successes at the beginning of the eighteenth century, no Russian monarch could countenance any weakening in the state's international position. The prestige that came from Russian Great Power status enhanced the status of the empire and also provided great personal prestige to successive monarchs. The zenith of Russian power was reached in 1814, when Alexander I entered Paris at the head of his troops following Napoleon's defeat.[8] It became impossible for any of his successors to contemplate any reduction in Russian military power, and they had to accept that the largest single element of the state's budget would be devoted to the army and navy. Once it had decided to participate fully in the international politics and wars of Europe, Russia was therefore committed to aping the West. Retaining its status as a Great Power meant, inevitably, that Russia had to follow the western pattern of economic development so that it could produce the weapons and equipment that would enable its armies to match the performance of other European military machines. Thus, the adventurings of Peter the Great set the pattern for Russian nationhood over the following two centuries: each of his successors saw Russia as an integral part of the European state system and was loathe to do anything that would weaken its international standing. But, this element of Russian national identity conflicted with the domestic priorities that monarchs set during the eighteenth and nineteenth centuries, determined to preserve their autocratic power and to retain the social structures that enabled them to rule as absolute monarchs; the view of Russian national identity that the state wanted to foster domestically was very different from the image that it projected abroad.

The nature of Russian nationality was thus a complex and contro-versial area. Should Russia identify itself with its traditional heritage and seek to pursue a path of development that would enable it to remain a rural-based society and economy? Or should it seek to embrace the West, with the implications that this had for both its social and political structures? For Uvarov, the architect of the concept of Official Nationality, the answer was clear. He stressed that it was vital to identify Russia's distinctive elements and thus to establish a Russian identity that set the country apart from western Europe. He contrasted the collapse of religious and civic institutions in much of Europe with Russia, which had 'retained a warm faith in the sacred principles without which she cannot prosper, gain in strength, live'. Uvarov believed that Russia could learn from the exper-ience of western Europe but that it must not slavishly follow the path that Europe had taken. In particular, Russia must not follow a path that led towards any weakening of monarchical authority. For Uvarov, the French Revolution had shown very clearly that republicanism was wholly inappropriate for European states, leading only to disaster and the breakdown of authority. Russia therefore had to pursue a balancing act, weighing the necessity of economic and social change against the dangers that this could present to the political fabric of the state.

The positions adopted by Slavophiles – who emphasised Russia's uniqueness – and Westernists – who stressed the need for Russia to follow Europe – during the nineteenth century simply mirrored the paradox that continually confronted Russia's rulers: what were the limits of Russian engagement with Europe? This part of the intellectual foundations of Tsarism was much more complex than its simple reliance on autocracy and the Orthodox religion and it was made more difficult by the nature of the imperial state that Russia became during the eighteenth and nineteenth centuries.

Imperial growth also presented challenges to the definition of Russia's identity. The Tsarist empire drew no distinction between metropolis and colonies. Russian imperial expansion did not involve Russians taking ship for foreign lands, as in the case of the other great European empires, but was a gradual and at times almost imperceptible process of Russians moving further across the Eurasian landmass from their Muscovite heartland. The Russian empire was therefore an integral part of the metropolitan state, without any physical separation between the Russian part of the empire and its non-Russian colonies. The empire was ruled as a single integral state, and the imperial government did not regard its newly acquired possessions as colonies. It governed them in much the same way as it did Russia's European centre and viewed them as simply more troublesome elements of its possessions, requiring more extreme types of coercion to control them. The empire came to include more than a hundred different national groups spread across an expanse of land that stretched from the western border with Austria-Hungary and the German states to the Pacific Ocean, more than 4500 miles distant. The Russian empire was both ethnically and nationally Russian by origin and rule, *russkii*, and owned by Russia, *rossiiskii*. While the terminology of the Russian language provided for a distinction between these two concepts, this was not reflected in other languages, which simply described the empire as Russian, leaving aside the complexities of this unusual and integrated imperial state. The definition of Russian nationality thus presented exceptional difficulties to the rulers of the Russian state and its ideologues.

The principles upon which the Tsarist state rested gave it very significant strengths. Russian monarchs felt confident of their power in a way that few other European monarchs were, and believed fervently that they were ruling in the best interests of their subjects. They believed that their particular brand of autocracy was a natural consequence of Russia's physical and social conditions and they never believed that they presided over a despotic, tyrannical regime. Russian rulers were convinced that their patriarchal regime was uniquely suited to the nature of the lands and peoples over whom they ruled and that their subjects benefited from the autocratic regime. This view was shared by many Russians. The peasant population of the empire traditionally saw the Tsar as 'batiushka', the Little Father who was devoted to his people and had their best interests at heart. Russian peasants could not deny that, at times, they were treated with great harshness by the state's officials, but they believed for the most part that the emperor was unaware of the exactions that his people were suffering and that, if he knew of their troubles, he would intervene to improve their lot. The nineteenth-century Slavophile Iurii Samarin described the peasants' faith in the Tsar:

> The nobility has separated the common people from the tsar. Standing as an obstacle between them, it conceals the common people from the tsar and does not permit the people's complaints and hopes to reach him. It hides from the people the bright image of the tsar, so that the tsar's word does not get to simple people, or does so in distorted form. But the common people love the tsar and yearn for him and the tsar, for his part, looks fondly upon the common people, whom he has long intended to deliver from their woes. And some day, reaching over the heads of the nobles, the tsar and the people will respond to one another.[9]

This espousal of 'naive monarchism' by much of the peasant population of the empire was of great utility to the state in acting as a brake on discontent and in promoting social stability, although it has been suggested that this peasant monarchism was insincere and that the peasantry simply adopted it as a strategy to conceal their fundamental histility to their lords.[10] Successive rulers projected the Russian autocracy to their people as a paternalist regime, distant from the apparatus of coercion that was the usual means of contact between state and people. This vision of the nature of Russian domestic power continued to inform the outlook of monarchs until the very end of the Romanov regime. Related to most of the ruling families of Europe, the later Romanovs were clearly aware of the ways in which other monarchs had seen their powers limited and, in extreme cases such as that of the French monarchy, entirely destroyed. Russia's monarchs retained a fundamental confidence in the security of their own position, even at times of crisis. When opposition was manifested, the most common reaction of Russia's rulers was to see it as representing only a minority of opinion and to portray opponents as un-Russian. Even though the grievances that rebels voiced were often justified, the Tsarist state dealt with it by intensifying its repressive policies, believing that applying its traditional methods of control would restore the situation. Both monarchs and people deluded themselves in their understanding of the nature of political power.

Unlimited autocracy gave the Romanov regime powers that were unmatched by other European monarchs. By the mid-nineteenth century, the Russian Tsar was the most powerful monarch in Europe, able to wield power to an extent that his fellow monarchs had long forgotten. With no formal institutions to act as a check on the power of the emperor, he was able to exert an authority that could not be formally challenged and this allowed him to act in ways that belied the paternalist image that successive Tsars espoused. The assassination of emperor Alexander II in 1881 was followed by the enactment of draconian emergency legislation, allowing the state to dispense with the normal apparatus of justice in areas of the empire that it identified. The Tsarist regime believed that it was essentially omnipotent across its empire and could act without fear of any legal or institutional challenge.

The state's identification of its political character with religion and with Russia's national identity provided the Romanovs with a potent weapon to proclaim their legitimacy and the futility of opposition to their rule. But it also contained dangers that became evident during the second half of the nineteenth century. When Uvarov formulated the trinity of Orthodoxy, Autocracy and Nationality in 1832, he intended that it should act as a means to unite the empire's subjects around the Romanov regime. In the wake of the Decembrist revolt of 1825 that had presented a challenge to the accession of

Nicholas I to the throne, and of the revolution in France at the end of the eighteenth century, Uvarov believed that the Russian state's stability required the explicit identification of ruler and subjects. Official Nationality was to be a potent means to bring together the peoples of the empire. The development of nationalist thinking across Europe in the middle of the nineteenth century brought a significant shift in official views on the nature of the Russian nation. Official Nationality came to be interpreted from the 1870s onwards as radical nationalism, driving Russia towards seeing its national characteristics and identity as superior to those of both its subject peoples and its European neighbours. Russian nationalism formed an important part of the intellectual climate of the final half-century of Tsarism and the St Petersburg regime's tactics helped to ensure that nationality became a divisive, rather than a unifying force across the empire. The unthinking application of Official Nationality proved, in the end, to weaken the Russian state by antagonising non-Russians and by engendering hostility to Russia and Russians from many non-Russian nationalities.

The same processes were at work with both the political and religious elements of Tsarism. Aggressive Russian nationalism was often accompanied by attempts to impose Orthodoxy upon non-Russian peoples, sometimes by offering inducements to the non-Orthodox to convert. At the same time, action was taken to restrict non-Orthodox religions by limiting the numbers of their churches and by making it difficult for them to recruit and retain sufficient priests. In many parts of the empire, Russian Orthodoxy became an intrinsic element of aggressive nationalism and was promoted alongside the Russian language as superior to the beliefs of non-Russian peoples. The nature of autocracy too became much more sharply defined as greater threats assailed the Romanovs. By the final quarter of the nineteenth century, the Russian state believed itself to be in significant danger as it witnessed the development of articulate and radical opposition to its very existence. The state's perception of danger pushed it further along the path towards a ferocious defence of its position. The sobriquet earned by the final Romanov Tsar of 'Nicholas the Bloody' gives some indication of how far the ruling elite had moved away from the paternalism that had been the outward image of Russian rulers. While Russian monarchs had never eschewed the use of force to sustain their position at times of crisis, the level of coercion that was utilised during and after 1905 was significantly greater than anything that the peoples of the empire had previously experienced. The regime's insistence on preserving its autocratic powers intact brought it into open conflict with many of its subjects and, even after the establishment of an elected parliament – the Duma – in 1905, the efforts of the regime to frustrate the Duma's ambitions served to further antagonise many Russians. Nationality, Orthodoxy and Autocracy were double-edged weapons: they could each be utilised as methods to enhance the cohesiveness of the Russian empire, and the Russian state was highly successful in securing the unity of its domains for most of its existence. But the ideology of Tsarism could also be unleashed on the empire in an aggressive fashion that only served to increase the centrifugal forces pulling the empire apart.

Chapter 2:   Monarchs

More than a dozen Romanovs occupied the Russian throne between 1682 and 1917. They ranged from the physically imposing Peter I to the shy and reserved Nicholas II, from the German-born Catherine II to the intensely Russian Alexander III. Children succeeded to the throne: in 1740 Ivan VI became Tsar when he was just two months old, but was deposed only a year later. Gender was no bar to the throne, as for most of the eighteenth century empresses ruled the Russian empire. Russia's sovereigns were men and women with varied and individual characters. Catherine II prided herself on her rationality and intellect and maintained friendships with the leading figures in the European Enlightenment, leaving a body of her own writings that illuminate her approach to ruling. In sharp contrast, her son and successor, Paul I, acted with no sensitivity to the people on whom he depended for his power and paid the price when he was strangled to death in his own bedroom after less than five years as emperor. Some of Russia's rulers were dedicated to the work of government. Even though Nicholas II did not enjoy the business of government and wished that he could concentrate on his dual passions of the army and his family, he conscientiously ploughed his way through the interminable documents that were a feature of the Russian bureaucratic state, annotating them in the margins. His grandfather Alexander II, was one of Russia's most energetic rulers during his first decade on the throne, but in the 1870s he gradually lost interest in much of the work of government, occupying himself with personal distractions and only displaying a reawakened interest in the reality of ruling at the very end of the decade. Some Tsars clearly revelled in the ceremony of monarchy: Paul's brief reign was filled with a concentration on the outward trappings of kingship. His successor Alexander I, however, loathed this aspect of the role of emperor, enjoying only military parades. Even though the position of monarch required a certain uniformity from its occupants, they were each able to adapt the role to fit their own preferences.

The formal title of the Russian monarch indicates the extent of their power. The final Romanov, Nicholas II, was formally described as

> Emperor and Autocrat of all the Russias, of Moscow, Kiev, Vladimir, Novgorod, Tsar of Kazan, Tsar of Astrakhan, Tsar of Poland, Tsar of Siberia, Tsar of Tauric Khersones, Tsar of Georgia, Lord of Pskov, and Grand Duke of Smolensk, Lithuania, Volhynia, Podolia, and Finland, Prince of Estonia, Livonia, Courland and Semigalia, Samogitia, Bielostok, Karelia, Tver, Iugra, Perm, Vyatka, Bulgaria, and other territories; Lord and Grand Duke of Nizhnii Novgorod, Chernigov; Ruler of Riazan, Polotsk, Rostov, Iaroslavl, Belozero, Udoria, Obdoria, Kondia, Vitebsk, Mstislav, and all northern territories; Ruler of Iveria, Kartalinia, and the Kabardinian lands and Armenian territories – hereditary Ruler and Lord of the Cherkess and Mountain Princes and others; Lord of Turkestan, Heir of Norway, Duke of Schleswig-Holstein, Stormarn, Ditmarsch, Oldenburg, and so forth, and so forth, and so forth.

This collection of titles, accumulated since the emergence of the rulers of Moscow as the dominant power in the Russian lands, emphasised the immense authority that the Russian ruler had acquired across the Eurasian landmass. The Tsar's writ ran from Finland to the Pacific Ocean and from the arctic north of Siberia to the mountainous Caucasus and to the arid deserts of Central Asia. The personal power that was invested in the individual who occupied the Russian throne was reflected in the title of Tsar. Derived from the same linguistic root as the Latin Caesar, it encapsulated the absolute authority that the monarch possessed, but even this had not proved sufficient for Peter the Great. He added the title of emperor to his list of appellations, both to stress the European dimensions of Russian authority and also to emphasise the imperial nature of the growing state.

The formal power of the monarch was intensely individual. Russian rulers had to depend upon an expanding bureaucracy to govern their empire and a ministerial system of government was formally instituted in 1802, but until 1905 there was no position of prime minister. The monarch was both head of state and head of government and had to fulfil both the ceremonial tasks associated with the role of representing the Russian state and the day-to-day work of governing the empire. Some monarchs took their responsibilities as head of government very seriously and devoted significant amounts of time to meeting with ministers and considering the documents that the bureaucracy produced. Nicholas I saw himself as the 'commander' of the Russian state and wanted to ensure that he was well informed about the condition of the empire so that he could govern effectively.[1] However, the deficiencies of the Russian bureaucratic machine and the ethos that permeated it during Nicholas I's reign placed obstacles in the way of effective government. Nicholas was mistrustful of much of what was reported to him. He was a hard taskmaster and, unsurprisingly, officials did have a tendency to put a favourable gloss on the reports they made to the monarch.

Nicholas sought to gain a more accurate picture of his domains in a number of ways. He embarked on frequent and extensive personal tours of the empire: in 1830 he visited Moscow, Novgorod, Warsaw and Helsinki to inspect aspects of government provision, but even though the emperor tried to gain an accurate picture of conditions by arriving unannounced, it proved very difficult to keep details of his visits secret, and officials were usually able to ensure that the monarch received a favourable impression of their areas of responsibility. Nicholas also attempted to evade the bureaucratic machine by establishing special committees to examine particular issues: between 1826 and 1847 he created ten separate bodies to examine aspects of the problem of serfdom and to suggest ways in which the condition of the Russian peasantry could be improved.[2] A secret committee was also established by the emperor in 1829 to try to learn lessons from the poor performance of Russia's troops in war with Turkey. These *ad hoc* bodies were only part of the Tsar's attempts to govern more effectively: he added the infamous Third Section to the Imperial Chancellery to function as a secret police and to keep the emperor well informed on the mood and activities of his subjects. The efforts made by the Tsar to ensure that he was properly able to govern his empire had some success; they suffered, however, from the same flaws as the regular bureaucracy of the empire. The absolute dominance of the monarch in the process of government meant that his subordinates were often wary of disagreement with the emperor, fearful of the impact that this could have on their careers. The monarch's work was made more difficult by the absence of any proper secretariat to support the Tsar in his work. Even the final Tsar, Nicholas II, worked without a personal secretary and, alongside the deliberations on policy that occupied his time, he also had to carry out the most basic tasks, such as addressing envelopes for his letters.

Russian rulers could grow bored with the work of government. The absence of proper institutional structures to coordinate the Russian government meant that, when this happened, there was no established prime minister to take responsibility and instead the empire could become dominated by whoever happened to be the monarch's current favourite. Catherine II's work as empress was closely bound up with the succession of men with whom she had close personal relationships. Grigorii Potemkin was the most celebrated of Catherine's lovers – he may well have married her secretly in 1775 – and he carried out a wide variety of commissions for the empress until his death in 1791. He played an especially important role in reforming the Russian army, even after he had been supplanted in Catherine's affections by others, but he occupied his position almost wholly as a result of the empress's favours, rather than through his tenure of government office. While Catherine had the strength of character to dispense with men whose utility to her had run its course, weaker-willed monarchs could come under lasting and undesirable influence from men who were able to dominate them. Alexander III, for all his physical strength and imposing appearance, was persistently influenced by Konstantin Pobedonostsev, his tutor as a young man and an archconservative. Alexander's cast of mind was naturally in tune with Pobedonostsev's conservatism, but the emperor did not possess the critical faculties necessary to analyse the impact of his policies upon a rapidly changing Russia. A contemporary noted that Alexander III 'did not manifest any outward brilliance, quick understanding or mastery... he did not learn things quickly'.[3] Nicholas II fell under the influence of both his wife, the strong-willed Alexandra, and the self-proclaimed holy man, Rasputin. The discovery that the imperial couple's only son, Alexei, suffered from the inherited disease of haemophilia threw the emperor and his wife into near-despair. Rasputin, a wily and manipulative man, was able to persuade the couple that he could exert a beneficial influence on the progress of Alexei's disease and he became able to exert influence over matters far removed from the illness of the heir to the throne. In the final years of the Romanov dynasty, Rasputin proved able to exercise influence over matters of policy and ministerial personnel, influence that was only brought to an end by his murder in December 1916 by members of Russia's noble elite.

Even though the imperial Russian monarchy was in many ways similar to the court of western European medieval monarchs, it was well aware of the need to establish its legitimacy and to sustain itself. The monarchy had its own dynamism, and successive rulers saw themselves as part of an historical tradition that stretched right back to the first Romanov rulers of Russian early in the seventeenth century. In 1913, the Romanov dynasty celebrated the tercentenary of gaining power in Russia and the event was used as a means of stressing the identification of Nicholas II and his predecessors with Russia as a whole. The Romanov tercentenary followed hard on the heels of the celebration of the centenary of the 1812 Russian victory over Napoleon and provided an exceptional opportunity for the monarchy to try to reassert the primacy of its position. Nicholas II and his empress travelled to the Volga cities, which had been the scene of the 1613 accession to power of the first Romanov, attempting to demonstrate that they were at one with their people. Government ministers were treated as incidental to the visit: the Prime Minister, Kokovtsov, had to organise his own transport to Nizhnii Novgorod, where the party embarked for the trip along the Volga. Large crowds turned out to see the royal couple, and they took this as evidence of the real bond that existed between Tsar and people. More perceptive observers, including the Tsar's cousin, Grand Duke Nicholas Mikhailovich, recognised the dangers inherent in mass popular demonstrations. 'They are just the same as they were in the seventeenth century, when they chose Michael as Tsar, just the same, this is bad', he commented to the emperor, all too aware that popular power could just as easily dislodge a dynasty as it had helped inaugurate Romanov rule 300 years previously.[4] Nicholas II was intent on making explicit the continuity between his own rule and that of his ancestors: the official portraits of the emperor and his wife that were prepared for the tercentenary celebrations show them both dressed in seventeenth-century costumes, making a direct connection between present and past. The monuments and ornaments that were produced for the 1913 celebrations also showed the continuity between the two eras: the

Fabergé egg produced for the imperial family included a miniature globe showing the extent of the empire's expansion over the three centuries of Romanov rule.[5]

The Monarch as Soldier

The images that monarchs chose as their representations had a fundamental consistency to them. The military was an essential part of the life of all Russian sovereigns, and each of them took clear steps to establish close links with Russia's armed forces. This had a practical political dimension, since support from the military was essential for the monarch to be able to rule. The Russian state depended heavily on its army to maintain internal order and a military presence in garrisons across the empire was a vital part of the state's strategy to prevent rebellion. The army had played a crucial part in bringing monarchs to power: troops were vital in allowing Catherine II to seize the throne, while the Decembrist revolt that followed the death of Alexander I in 1825 was largely a military affair. Troops loyal to the future Nicholas I were decisive in facing down rebellion from regiments lined up on St Petersburg's Senate Square on a freezing December day. Nicholas I never forgot the debt that he owed to the military – and nor did he forget the threat that could be posed to his regime by mutiny among Russia's armed forces.

Monarchs wanted to demonstrate their heroic roles as conquerors; this was easy for those Tsars who personally led Russia's armies to victory in war. Peter the Great was the model to which all his successors wanted to aspire as military leader: Petrine military triumph was one part of Peter's legacy that all later Romanovs could agree on, even if they held very different views about the visions of Russia's nationhood that the Petrine era represented. Catherine II and Alexander I both witnessed Russian military success during their reigns: Catherine's armies were victorious over the Turks in war between 1768 and 1774, and Catherine was responsible for expanding the Russian navy in the Black Sea. She took especial pride in Russian naval successes, claiming this as her 'personal achievement'.[6] Peter the Great's reputation as the father of the Russian navy was a part of his legacy that Catherine wanted very much to follow. At the very end of her reign, Catherine's troops were instrumental in the destruction of independent Poland and in securing the larger part of the Polish

lands for Russia. Alexander I's part in victory over Napoleon represented the high-water mark of Russian military power in Europe; a
century after Russian emergence as a European Great Power with
Peter I's vanquishing of the Swedes, Russian troops marched into
Paris, apparently cementing Russian pre-eminence on the European
continent.

Yet even though Russia's military prowess was most evident during
the reigns of Catherine and Alexander I, they were perhaps the two
of Peter the Great's successors who were least concerned to flaunt
their military credentials. It was rulers who were much less successful
in war who wanted to flaunt their devotion to Russia's armed forces
and to wrap themselves in the banner of the empire's heroic military
past. Even though Nicholas I was the most overtly military of Russia's
monarchs since Peter I, delighting in military ceremonial and paying
much attention to the detail of uniforms for the armed forces, his
actual record in war was much less impressive.[7] The discipline that
Nicholas sought to transfer from the parade ground to Russian society
as a whole proved to be insufficient in its original military context;
Russian defeat in the Crimean War when Nicholas's troops were
threatened on Russia's own soil by Britain and France exerted a fatal
strain on the emperor. He died in February 1855, exhausted by the
physical and psychological stresses that the destruction of his image
as 'the gendarme of Europe' exacted on him.[8] Nicholas II was also
a monarch whose devotion to Russia's army was not matched by
military success. Away from his family, Nicholas was at his happiest
when he was in the company of soldiers. He was commissioned into
the Preobrazhenskii guards regiment at the age of 19, and for the
rest of his life he demonstrated a deep devotion to the army and
navy. Nicholas was very conscious of his reliance upon his troops for
the maintenance of his authority, especially after the 1905 revolution,
and he did not stint on expenditure on the military budget. Two
public demonstrations of his commitment to his military heritage
stand out: in 1909 the jubilee of Peter the Great's triumph at Poltava
was marked with celebrations on the battlefield at which Nicholas
spoke of the unity of 'the tsar with the people' and where the apparent
enthusiasm of the crowds for the monarch prompted Prime Minister
Stolypin to remark that 'the revolution is over'.[9] The second event
was an intensely personal celebration: in 1912 Nicholas marked the
25th anniversary of his joining the Guards and, in an extraordinary
move, he marched in the parade as an ordinary officer, subordinate to

the regimental commander.[10] The emperor's devotion to his military responsibilities was best demonstrated in 1915 when, faced with a second summer of disastrous Russian reverses in the First World War, Nicholas himself took on the duties of Commander-in-Chief, even though assuming the post exposed the emperor to bearing the full brunt of responsibility for further defeats. Russia's military record was rather tarnished for much of the nineteenth century, but that did not prevent its rulers from harking back to earlier glories and from projecting an image that suggested they were each military conquerors on a par with Peter the Great.

The Monarch as Reformer

The second image that attracted Russia's rulers was that of reformer. Peter the Great had thrust reform onto Russian government and society in a way that was never to be matched again, and none of his successors could entirely ignore the significance of his reforms in enhancing Russia's international and domestic strength. Even though reform was a concept that rankled with some of Peter's successors, none of them could reject the Petrine inheritance completely. For some monarchs, the appeal of Peter's reforms was direct. Catherine II clearly saw herself as being in Peter's mould, and her erection of the equine statue of Peter on the Neva embankment in St Petersburg symbolised the attachment that she felt to him. The 'Bronze Horseman', as Pushkin entitled his marvellous poem centred on the statue, epitomised the dynamic and powerful state that Catherine wanted to build.

> I love you, Peter's great creation
> I love your harmonies austere

wrote Pushkin in 1833, the city of St Petersburg standing as a metaphor for the Russia that Peter had brought into being. Catherine displayed a significant interest in making changes to the Russian empire, corresponding with western European figures about the theoretical framework of rights and duties that was appropriate for Russia. She sought to codify Russia's laws, and her Great Instruction to the Legislative Commission that was to carry out the work implied that she wanted so see Russia follow the European path of enlightened absolutism. However, little came of the work of legal codification and Catherine's good intentions remained largely theoretical. Catherine's enlightened ideas were subordinated to the need to maintain control of her empire; reform was all very well as an aspiration, but it had to be tempered by the practical necessities that governing the Russian empire imposed on a monarch. The only Romanov who approached Peter the Great's record of reform in practice was Alexander II. But Alexander showed little desire to eulogise his ancestor; the bicentenary of Peter's birth in 1872 attracted only minor celebrations and Alexander himself played little part in them. The reforms of the 1860s never achieved the same impact as those 150 years earlier; by the middle of the nineteenth century the course of Russia's development was a source of bitter dispute and even the Tsar himself was cautious about proclaiming the virtues of change.

Peter I

Peter the Great stands as the Romanov to whom all his successors could look back with unstinting admiration. His accomplishments surrounded every later monarch in their daily lives. St Petersburg, the capital city from which they ruled the empire, was an entirely artificial creation, founded by Peter in 1703 to provide Russia with an outlet to the west and to exemplify the modern state that he was intent on building. The architecture of St Petersburg, with its Italianate lines and its absence of traditional Russian symbols, was a constant reminder of the path that Peter had chosen for Russia. The two central religious buildings of the capital – St Isaac's and the Kazan cathedrals – were both built in western styles, consciously echoing St Peter's in Rome. It was only in the 1880s that the centre of St Petersburg gained a major church that took its inspiration from traditional Russian forms, with the construction of a church on the spot where Alexander II had been assassinated. Peter's determination to push Russia onto the European stage was an ever-present part of life in the capital, where the skyline was dominated by the gleaming golden spire of the Admiralty building, symbolising Peter's maritime expansion into European waters. It is perhaps significant that Alexander III and Nicholas II, two of the most conservative occupants of the imperial throne, found St Petersburg a less congenial place to live than their country estates and limited their visits to the city. Peter the Great's engagement with Europe was predicated on military victory. His reign was dominated by war and campaigning and there was hardly a year during his more than 30 years on the throne as an adult when Russian troops stood idle. Peter's greatest triumph was to supplant Sweden as the dominant power in northern Europe and to transform the Baltic Sea from a Swedish lake into a Russian one. But Peter did not limit his adventurings to Russia's north-western frontiers. He also went to war with Turkey in 1711, a conflict which ended in Russian defeat and came close to being a major disaster. The treaty that ended the war required Russia to surrender significant territory on the Black Sea littoral to the Turks and for Russia's fleet in the Sea of Azov to be destroyed. Peter enjoyed more success when he went to war with Persia in 1722, acquiring new lands on the western shore of the Caspian Sea. The emperor was also keen to promote Russian expansion in the Far East and he provided funds for an expedition to explore the Kamchatka peninsula in the far north-east of Siberia. Russia's hugely expanded military role was the main determinant of policy during Peter's reign.

The expansion of Russia's army and navy had a dramatic effect on the government of the state: the colleges of War, the Admiralty and Foreign Affairs were recognised as the most significant parts of the administration and they ate up the greater part of the state's budget. By the time of Peter's death in 1725, Russia could put an army of 200,000 men into the field and Peter's military exploits made a substantial standing army a permanent feature of the Russian state. Peter the Great transformed Russia into a state that was dominated by its military commitment. The Tsar himself was most often depicted in military attire and, following the great victory at Poltava, Peter was represented as Mars, the Roman god of war, wearing Roman battle dress. The civil administration needed to be reformed to ensure that an expanded army and navy could be financed, manned and equipped. A modern military machine could only function if it was supported by the apparatus of a modern state. Peter imposed an entirely new system of government on Russia: a Senate was established in 1711, initially to govern Russia during Peter's absences from the capital, but it soon became the heart of Russian government and Peter ensured that the men appointed to it were tried and trusted associates. At the beginning of the eighteenth century, the functional parts of Russian government were haphazard and lacked any proper co-ordination. The Muscovite model of government was swept aside by Peter who, after attempting to add new institutions to the multitude of existing chancelleries (*prikazy*), abolished them all and established nine new colleges to coordinate the work of central government. A concomitant to effective civil administration was the need for efficient and reliable systems of collecting taxes to fund Russia's expansionist policies. Peter introduced a poll tax for the first time, giving the state a straight forward mechanism for assessing and collecting revenues.

The emperor himself was an imposing man. He was unusually tall, standing six feet seven inches, and physically towered over his contemporaries. Peter had modest tastes, eschewing the sophistication that was the fashion at western courts at the time, but he was well aware of the need to project an image of power and authority to his own people and to the outside world. Official portraits and images of the emperor almost all depict him in uniform or else draw on allusions from the classical world to show him as omnipotent. It was essential for Peter to be able to exercise absolute control over his subjects. The institution of serfdom made it easier to dominate the peasant population of Russia, but the nobility presented a greater challenge. Noble discontent could bring about the downfall of a monarch and Peter was determined that the nobility should be firmly tied to the state and rendered subservient to the institution of monarchy.[11] Peter wanted to institutionalise the nobility's service to the state and his expanded army provided an effective way of compelling young noblemen to become enmeshed in the apparatus of the state. A central innovation was the publication of a codified Table of Ranks in 1722 which allocated individuals to a particular social position and allowed them to advance upwards by royal patronage. The table was intended to offer an incentive to the nobility to give more effective service to the state, but it also ensured that the monarch had a decisive influence over the futures of noblemen and their families. Peter the Great's reign set Russia on a path that would endure until the end of the Romanov dynasty. His efforts ensured that Russia became a European power and that each of his successors had to maintain Russia's international status. The modernised state structure that he put in place provided Russia with the apparatus to sustain its international position. While he admired western European models and borrowed shamelessly from Europe, both in institutional terms and in using foreign experts to accelerate Russian development, Peter did not transform Russia into a western state. The fundamental social structures of Russia remained largely unchanged, with the symbiotic ties between monarch, nobility and serfs intact. In the words of the nineteenth-century thinker Peter Chaadaev, Russians picked up the 'cloak of civilisation thrown to them by Peter, but not civilisation itself'.[12] This view of Russian culture is harsh and extreme, but it contains an important kernel of truth: Peter had been able to transform Russia's external position, but the traditional features of Russia's society persisted long after his death.

The succession to Peter was confused. For five years, first his widow then his 12-year-old grandson reigned. His sudden death in 1730 brought to the throne the first of a formidable trio of women who were to rule Russia until the dying years of the eighteenth century. Empress Anna (1730–40) showed her mettle very quickly: within a month of having been placed on the throne by the privy council, she tore up the conditions she had agreed to as part of her accession (these included commitments never to remarry, and to consult the council on all important matters of policy) and asserted her autocratic power. But her interest in government did not last: in 1735 she delegated her powers to her ministers and for much of her reign she was dominated by Ernst-Johann Biron. Anna died after a decade on the throne and, after a short interlude during which the baby Ivan VI was installed as Tsar, she was succeeded by Elizabeth, the daughter of Peter the Great. The new empress sought to capitalise on her father's reputation but she too soon lost interest in the detail of government, perhaps as a result of illness. Elizabeth's death in 1761 brought her nephew to the throne as Peter III. He rapidly alienated both the military and the Church and was deposed after only six months in power by a Guards' coup that placed his wife on the throne as Catherine II.

Catherine II

Catherine proved to be one of the most significant rulers of the Russian empire, one of only two Romanovs who earned the epithet of Great. She had an unlikely background to become Empress of Russia: Catherine was born a minor German princess in 1744 and, at the age of 14, was invited to Russia as the potential bride for the 16-year-old Grand Duke Peter Fedorovich, himself the son of a German prince and Peter the Great's eldest daughter. Marriage followed the following year, but it proved to be an extremely unhappy match.

Catherine was thrown back onto her own resources and became adept at the political manoeuvring that was necessary to maintain her position at the court. Her husband's accession to the throne in 1761 was short-lived: six months later he was deposed and Catherine was installed as ruler of Russia. She had no intention of being the puppet of powerful nobles, and it was clear from the outset that Catherine would be an active and determined ruler. She drew heavily on the inheritance of Peter the Great to define her reign, symbolised in its first months when she was portrayed in the uniform of the Preobrazhenskii Guards. 'A man's dress is what suits her best' wrote the British ambassador,[13] and Catherine deliberately sought to demonstrate that she was the equal of her male predecessors. In 1763 she went on a physically demanding pilgrimage to pray at the shrine of St Dmitrii of Rostov, walking more than 75 miles, and then following this with a series of visits around her new domains. It was important for Catherine to establish herself as an independent monarch who, despite her foreign birth, was as devoted to Russia and its traditions as her predecessors. The empress had no truck with proposals to abolish or even moderate serfdom, despite her close engagement with Enlightenment thinkers, as she was well aware of the significance of serfdom in the empire's political and social structures. She displayed a disdain for the ordinary people over whom she ruled, writing that 'they will always be as ordinary as their nature; the flowering of the state, the passing centuries, the coming generations are all words that cannot concern them . . . the people never see more than the coming day; by their destitution they are deprived of the opportunity to extend their interests into the future'.[14] When peasant rebellion broke out in the early 1770s, Catherine dealt with it severely, fully aware that inchoate revolt could easily take hold in the popular imagination and become an unstoppable force that would sweep her armies aside. The Pugachev revolt of 1773–75 was the final instance of mass peasant rebellion in Romanov Russia; Pugachev himself was executed, although the empress ensured that he was beheaded, rather than subjected to more grisly forms of punishment.

The interests of the state took precedence over all else for Catherine. Following the Pugachev revolt, the empress took steps to improve the quality of provincial administration in an attempt to ensure that rebellion did not break out again in Russia's provinces. The provincial reform statute of 1775 was followed by a reform of municipal administration, and by a new charter for the nobility, defining their privileges. Catherine wanted to be remembered as an enlightened ruler who had continued Peter the Great's work of modernising Russia and who had used European models to improve the condition of the Russian empire.[15] Her policies accomplished some parts of these objectives, but they had a more profound impact on the way in which the empire was governed. Catherine's reign increased the level of centralised state control across Russia; she appreciated that, while Peter's reforms of central government had been effective, local government needed to be brought more firmly under the control of the St Petersburg government. She also understood the vital role that the nobility played in ensuring the survival of the state and was intent on preserving their position as the state's chief bulwark against rebellion. Catherine received the title 'Great' in 1767 from members of the Legislative Commission established to codify Russia's laws. Even though she protested that the appellation 'could only be determined by posterity', Catherine clearly wanted to be regarded as highly as Peter had been, and her reign demonstrated that the judgement made in the 1760s had merit.[16] Her greatness not consisted in making the wholesale and dramatic changes to Russia that had been the central feature of Peter's reign, but rather in consolidating the empire and ensuring that it remained a governable unit. Her more than 30 years on the throne were a period of tumultuous change across Europe, culminating in the French Revolution at the end of the 1780s. Catherine resisted the temptation to follow her intellect and liberalise Russia in line with the advice that she gained from abroad, but she also avoided the path of imposing an oppressive authoritarianism upon the empire.[17] Both options were open to the empress and each would have earned her plaudits from different quarters, but she trod a balanced path between them, almost the last of the Romanovs to do so. When Catherine died in 1796, she left a powerful and well-established Russia, a state that was continuing to expand its empire and which was fully recognised as a member of the European Great Power system.

The fate of Catherine's son, Paul I, was similar to that which had befallen her husband, Peter III. Paul's reign was brief, lasting only five years, and the militarism that he attempted to impose on the empire – and especially on the nobility – proved to be his undoing. Paul's authoritarianism was in very sharp contrast with his mother's careful balancing act and showed both the brilliance of her policies and the fragility of the Russian monarchy. Paul was unceremoniously murdered in his bedroom in the Mikhailovskii Castle in St Petersburg on a March night in 1801 by discontented nobles.[18] His successor, Alexander I, restored stability to Russia and his near-quarter century on the throne was characterised by the same careful equipoise that his grandmother had displayed. The succession of his brother Nicholas in 1825 brought to the throne a man who lacked subtlety and swung decisively towards imposing a rigid authoritarianism across the empire. His 30 years on the throne ended in the middle of the disastrous Crimean War and his son's accession in 1855 gave the promise of a very different tone to Russia's government.

Alexander II

Alexander II ruled Russia for more than 25 years and his reign demonstrated a very different style from that of other Romanovs. Alexander had received a traditional upbringing for males in the Russian royal family, with a heavy emphasis on military affairs. He came to the throne at the age of 36 and had been well schooled in the work of government, with appointments to a variety of official committees dealing with central topics in the affairs of the state. Alexander had also travelled widely, both across the Russian empire and in Europe. When he became emperor, there was little indication that Alexander II's convictions were likely to be radically different from those of his father. But, during the first decade of his reign, the Tsar enacted a series of reforms that touched almost every aspect of Russian life. The new Tsar had evidently been affected by the contrasts that he had seen between provincial Russia and the European states he had visited. His devotion to the military made Russia's defeat in the Crimean War all the more shocking and Alexander was forced to reflect on the reasons for the reversal in Russia's fortunes as a Great Power. In the space of 40 years, Russia had gone from being the most powerful of the European states to one that could not even achieve military victory on its own territory. The new emperor had to recognise that these 40 years coincided with the effective stalling of modernising policies at home. Russian international weakness appeared to be connected to the abandonment of the balance that had characterised Catherine's reign and it betrayed the Petrine legacy of Russian power. Alexander II needed little reminder of the centrality of Russia's international position in determining domestic policy and he acted swiftly to try to restore the state's prestige. The emancipation of the serfs in 1861 was central to Alexander's policies and he took the risk of offending the nobility by pressing ahead with freeing their enserfed peasants, so convinced was he that Russian backwardness had to be overcome. Modernisation followed in a variety of other areas: local government, the legal system, education, censorship and the army all underwent fundamental changes during the first part of Alexander's reign. The emperor believed that his policies would lead to Russian national renewal and would revitalise the link between monarch and people that had evidently become strained. The Tsar believed that the reforms of the 1860s showed the trust that he placed in his people by giving them greater autonomy in their lives, and Alexander expected that his efforts would be met with reciprocation from his grateful subjects. Reform, for Alexander II, was only a means to an end: the reforging of the historic bond between ruler and ruled that he believed had been an essential part in the success of the Russian state.

The emperor's hopes were cruelly disappointed as his subjects failed to demonstrate the appropriate level of gratitude for the reforms that he had graciously granted. In 1866 the first attempt was made to assassinate Alexander II, and for the remainder of his reign the emperor was never safe from the attention of terrorists. At the same time, the united front that had been presented by monarch and nobility for so long began to show evidence of fundamental structural flaws. Emancipating the serfs had been an essential step in moving Russia into the modern world, but Alexander II had failed to appreciate how it affected the central social bulwark of Romanov power – the nobility. Articulate and educated members of the nobility were quick to call, not for a return to serfdom, but for further reforms, changes that would strike at the heart of the Russian autocracy. Joined by a growing educated middle class, Russia's social elite began to turn its back on the monarchy, the traditional source of its authority. Alexander II was bemused by the reaction to his reforms. Relying on the eighteenth-century model of Russian government, he could not comprehend why he was being rebuffed by those very people he had intended to help. As one of his advisers wrote in 1870, 'The most powerful of all sovereigns of Russia, the most beloved and popular of Tsars, no longer believes in his power or in the benefit of the reforms he has accomplished.'[19] The Tsar felt lost and bewildered: the lessons of his predecessors no longer appeared to apply in mid-nineteenth-century Russia, and Alexander did not know where to turn for inspiration. The Russian monarchy suffered a crisis of confidence during the 1870s and Alexander appeared to recognise that the past no longer offered a reliable guide. He showed little enthusiasm for promoting the erection of a monument to Catherine II in St Petersburg and its dedication ceremony in 1873 was modest.

At the same time, the international situation was changing dramatically with the creation of a new united Germany on Russia's western borders. The old certainties of Great Power politics were fast disappearing. An opportunity for Alexander to revive his fortunes appeared to arise with war against Turkey in 1877. This offered the chance for the emperor to occupy the heroic role that Peter the Great had initiated, but there was also a more concrete aspect that Alexander believed could presage a resurgence in the position of the monarchy. Fighting against the Turkish infidel, Alexander II showed himself and Russia as coming to the aid of their Slav brethren in the Balkans. The Russo-Turkish war was an opportunity to appeal to the radical nationalism that had taken hold in parts of Russian opinion and to hark back to Russia's roots and Panslav past. The war proved to be successful in allowing Russia to dominate large areas of the Balkans, but the diplomatic settlement that followed showed that Russia was not able to capitalise on its victories at the negotiating table. The 1878 Congress of Berlin reduced Russia's gains, showing that Russian power was still far from its zenith at the beginning of the nineteenth century. Alexander II was unable to resolve the crisis of autocracy. He failed to comprehend the wider social and political context in which opposition to his regime was being voiced. By 1881 he was prepared to countenance the limited involvement of popular representatives in national government in the hope that this would retrieve the situation.[20] But it was not to be. On 1 March 1881, after giving preliminary approval to the formation of a limited consultative assembly and then inspecting his beloved troops, Alexander II was assassinated by a terrorist bomb in the streets of St Petersburg, barely a mile from the Winter Palace.

He was succeeded by his son, Alexander III, who took an entirely different approach in trying to restore monarchical authority and prestige. Whereas his murdered father had agonised over the reasons for popular rejection of his policies, Alexander III wasted no time on such reflections. For him the solution to the problems that beset Russia and its monarchy was clear: an aggressive reassertion of Russian

national identity. Built like an ox, Alexander III's physical appearance gave him the stature of the *bogatyr'*, the Russian hero of old
who single-handedly could defeat the most awkward opposition. The
emperor favoured wearing simple uniforms that echoed traditional
Russian dress and avoided the fancy and complex military apparel
that had been his father's favourite. During the Russo-Turkish war,
Alexander grew a beard for the first time and this too suggested a
reversion to an earlier heroic age before Peter the Great's condemna-
tion of beards as symbolising the backwardness that he wanted Russia
to escape from. While Alexander III rejected the Europeanisation of
Russia that had been an essential feature of Peter's reign, he could not
escape from the historical situation in which Russian found itself in
the 1880s. The emergence of a powerful Germany in central Europe
posed serious issues for Russia's foreign policy. It was impossible for
Russia to withdraw from Europe and return to the pre-Petrine age
when Russia stood on the margins of the continent, and Alexander
III therefore had to accept this part of his inheritance and engage in
European international politics. An alliance with republican France,
a state that embodied the antithesis of Alexander III's beliefs, was
signed in 1894.[21] Nor could Alexander turn his back on the processes
of economic change that had engulfed Europe during the nineteenth
century. The option of Russia remaining a peasant-based society was
no longer available by the 1880s – if indeed, it had ever been a realistic
possibility – and the international pressures that Russia faced made
industrialisation even more urgent. Alexander III presided over the
beginnings of Russia's first period of rapid industrial growth in the
1890s, persuaded by the wily Sergei Witte, Minister of Communications and then Finance Minister from 1892, that Russia had to adopt
this path if it was to retain its international position.

Alexander III's conception of the nature of Russia and its monarchy
was even more confused than that of his father. Rejecting the ideas
of political modernisation that he believed had brought about the
assassination of Alexander II, his son wanted Russia to return to an
earlier age. Alexander III embarked on a policy to Russify the empire,
by imposing the Russian language and the Orthodox religion on
non-Russian peoples. He believed that he was casting aside the alien
elements that had led Russia to crisis and that by reasserting traditional Russian statehood, he could again bring about that union of
monarch and people, which had become severely strained. Alexander
III immediately rejected his father's plans to introduce an element

of popular representation into the work of government and instead imposed a state of emergency across parts of the empire. His solution to the problems of governing the empire was a reassertion of the Muscovite tradition of unlimited autocracy. But the emperor's promotion of Russian national identity was limited and simplistic; he and his advisers failed to recognise that the work of Peter the Great could not be undone.[22] Russia was an integral part of the European political and economic system and it could not pick and choose which parts of a modernised state to adopt and which to reject. The genius of Peter the Great had been his recognition of the essential unity of his policies, comprehending that the nature of the monarchy was intimately bound up with Russia's economic and international fortunes. Alexander III, limited in intellect and advised by a disunited collection of ministers, believed that he could accept economic modernisation but reject the political and social consequences that were its inevitable concomitant. His early death in 1894 meant that he did not witness the final act of the Romanov dynasty, but its outlines were already in place by the time Alexander succumbed to kidney disease at the age of 48.

The final Romanov monarch was as devoted as his father to the Russian national idea. Nicholas II had no desire to embrace reform and attempted to reinforce the conservative policies of Alexander III. The monarchy proved unable to deal with the crises of revolution and war that assailed it in 1905 and after 1914, and its eventual collapse in 1917 came quickly. The Romanov monarchs were faced with very difficult challenges. They had to cope with ruling a state that had been thrust onto the world stage by Peter the Great, but which hardly possessed the political or economic resources to sustain this position. The solutions that these men and women chose, to try to maintain their inheritance, demonstrated their commitment to the task of ruling and did provide the Russian state with significant authority. Successive monarchs comprehended that their overwhelming priority was to sustain Russia's position and thus their own power and were prepared to use whatever means they believed was necessary to achieve this. The reluctance of Russia's monarchs to concede authority was a significant element in the persistence of their autocratic regime; the men and women who occupied the Russian throne during the eighteenth and nineteenth centuries both ensured the longevity of their regime, but also laid the foundations for its eventual downfall.

Chapter 3:   Service

The autocratic Russian monarchy devised a myriad of ways to impose its authority on its subjects. The power that the state could demonstrate, both through overt displays of force and through the imagery of authority that monarchs utilised, was a vital part in its efforts to maintain control over the population of the empire. The power of Russia's armies, on show not just in the international arena but also as a part of the regime's internal security apparatus, was a powerful deterrent to those who contemplated taking on the might of the Russian state. But, Russia's military power was far from being the only weapon in the state's armoury of control. There were sound practical reasons for this. The huge geographical expanse of the state – a constantly expanding empire – made it impossible for the Tsarist regime to deploy sufficient troops and police to ensure that it could maintain control simply by force or the implied threat that its army represented. Communication difficulties also made the actual exercise of control a difficult task. The problems of communicating across a huge empire in an age of primitive technology, combined with the severe climate that gripped much of Russia for large parts of the year, made a rapid response to problems a matter of hit and miss. Even though freezing and snowy winters made it very difficult for popular rebellion to occur in the countryside during those months, the threat of revolt during spring and summer was enough to be a continual worry to the state. The St Petersburg regime could never be sure that trouble might not break out hundreds of miles away from the capital and feared that, by the time central government learnt about it, a rebellion could have gathered many thousands of people to its cause and pose a real threat to the state. The solution that the state adopted to try to ensure that control could be exercised effectively in the empire's provinces was to harness the Russian nobility in such a way that the nobility's own interests would be served by their commitment to the state.

Nobility

The nobility's fundamental utility to the state came from their ownership of land and, before emancipation in 1861, their possession of serfs. While the state itself owned huge areas of land and the millions of peasants that farmed it, private landowning still played a larger role in the Russian rural economy. Serfs owned by private landlords made up almost 55 per cent of the total number of peasants in 1795, a proportion that had remained more or less constant throughout the eighteenth century.[1] Land and serfs provided their owners with a reasonably stable income and with the incentive to acquire more wealth by expanding their landholdings or by exploiting their existing land more effectively. Noble landholders were a stable part of rural society and the state believed that they could be used to provide a means of control over the peasant population. Peter the Great recognised that he needed to utilise the nobility, but that this was unlikely to be popular amongst the nobles themselves. He made state service compulsory for each male noble, beginning at the age of fifteen and ending only with disability or death. This process required the compilation of comprehensive records to ensure that eligible males did not evade the requirement for service and also to make sure that a sufficient number of nobles entered the military, rather than opting for the less demanding life of a bureaucrat. This Table of Ranks was a necessary part of the requirement for service, since it enabled the state to place each and every nobleman in order of precedence. The table was also a means of providing social mobility and of controlling entry to the noble estate. Nobility could only be gained by advancing to the eighth rank for civil appointment or the fourteenth for the military. There was no other means of attaining noble status: landownership did not automatically confer nobility, nor could it be bought. This transformed the Russian nobility into a single class that was bound together by common interests: they had to serve the state effectively if they were to be able to gain advancement up the Table of Ranks. This was not an entirely meritocratic process, however, since promotion was also dependent on a noble retaining the favour of the monarch and his advisers, so that the nobility also had to demonstrate continuing loyalty to the state if they were to prosper.

Compulsory service and the Table of Ranks placed significant burdens on the Russian nobility and service proved to be extremely unpopular. The predominance of military service was one important reason for this, since it meant the prospect of real danger for nobles and was likely to take them far away from their estates. But there were also advantages for the nobility: service to the state provided a regular salary and the government also established schools specifically to educate the children of the nobility to help prepare them for work for the state. These were important provisions, since the Russian nobility was far from being either universally wealthy or well educated. Most nobles owned only small numbers of serfs: evidence from 1777 showed that 32 per cent of noble landowners possessed fewer than 10 serfs and that a further 30 per cent had between 10 and 30. Only 16 per cent of noble landowners owned more than 100 serfs. This pattern continued into the nineteenth century, so that by 1858, 40 per cent of all landowners owned fewer than 20 serfs. Only a very small minority fitted the stereotypical picture of the Russian landowner possessing vast estates and with thousands of serfs under his control. Fewer than 1500 nobles owned more than 1000 serfs in 1858, although some of them did possess very extensive holdings. Count D. N. Sheremetev had more than 300,000 serfs in his ownership immediately before emancipation, and his family headed the list of wealthy nobles. Other families with stupendous wealth included the Vorontsovs, Stroganovs, Orlovs and Golitsyns. The regime recognised the value of making direct gifts to enhance the wealth and power of its favoured noble families and the continuing expansion of the empire meant that there were plentiful supplies of both land and serfs that the state could bestow upon its favourites. Between 1740 and 1801, monarchs gave away more than 1.3 million adult male peasants, together with their wives and children.[2] Nearly 400,000 of these went to only 111 recipients. Gifts could be made in recognition of especial service to the monarch: Empress Elizabeth gave serfs to each of the military officers who helped in her accession to the throne. But they could also be made on a whim or as a mark of favour to a lover: Catherine II gave Grigorii Potemkin more than 900,000 rubles on the occasion of his 40th birthday in 1779, partly in cash and partly in land. It was only the fortunate few, however, who were lucky enough to receive such immense gifts. Most of the Russian nobility scraped a meagre living from the land and needed to augment the income that they gained from farming with a salary from the state. The difficulties of farming in the Russian climate made agriculture a far from reliable way of earning a living, especially for nobles who had only modest holdings of land and serfs. Service was an unwelcome intrusion into their lives but was also an economic necessity for them.

On balance, the advantages that the nobility gained from service did outweigh the problems that it posed for them. After Peter the Great's death, the nobility tried to have some of the more burdensome aspects of service removed, but they did not want to close off the opportunities that it gave them for gaining preferment and income. In 1736, service was reduced from life to 25 years and one son in each noble family was exempted from service altogether. Nobles also became able to evade some of the more rigorous elements of service by registering their sons for service in infancy, thus allowing them to complete their 25 years while they were still young men. They also served less time in the lower ranks before gaining advancement, especially in the military, showing that merit was not the sole criterion for promotion. Compulsory service was abolished in 1763 by Peter III, but while some nobles took the opportunity to escape from the obligation altogether, some simply transferred from the military to less demanding posts in the civil bureaucracy. The vast majority of the nobility, however, continued to work for the state: they had become accustomed to the prestige and financial benefits that state service brought them. Peter the Great's insistence on compulsory service had brought benefits to the state that continued even when the requirements were relaxed.

One of Catherine II's pieces of codification was to issue a Charter to the Nobility in 1785. This document set out the privileges that the nobility enjoyed: they could only be deprived of their nobility, their property or their lives by trial by their peers. Corporal punishment for the nobility was abolished. They were exempt from personal taxation and from the obligation to have troops billeted on them. Nobles were granted the freedom to travel abroad and to enter into service in foreign states. They were given significant freedoms in dealing with their property; they could buy serf villages and could set up industrial enterprises on their estates, as well as being granted the right to buy property in towns and to set up enterprises there too. This charter represented an important step forward for the Russian nobility. It suggested that they had gained a degree of trust from the state and that the hard burden of service had not gone unrewarded. It clearly distinguished the Russian nobility from other elements of Russian society and gave them a set of privileges that no other section of society possessed. But the charter was not as impressive as it appears at first sight. While Catherine granted the nobility this wide range of rights, the charter contained no means by which the nobility could act to guarantee these rights. The state still held all the cards, and the privileges in the 1785 charter had no independent guarantor. The nobility could not use the legal system to uphold their rights and the autocrat had complete discretion in the actual implementation of the charter. When Paul I came to the throne, he again demanded compulsory service from the nobility and allowed the use of corporal punishment on them. The nobility had no means by which they could oppose Paul's abandonment of the charter other than to plot his overthrow.

The 1785 charter was also important as it established corporate institutions for the nobility. The nobles' formal collective identity had begin to take shape when assemblies were convened in 1766 to elect representatives to the Legislative Commission and the process was continued after the provincial reforms of 1775, when nobles had to select marshals of the nobility in each province and district of the empire to represent their interests. From 1785, nobles in each province were allowed to hold an assembly every 3 years and this assembly was given responsibilities to regulate the noble estate in its area. These local noble authorities would now maintain the official registers of the nobility for their area: this was an important devolution of power from central government, since it allowed the nobles themselves to apply the rules about who was qualified to become a member of the nobility. Noble assemblies were also given the right to make representations to the provincial governor, to the Senate or to the monarch about matters which concerned them. Lastly, the assemblies were to hold elections amongst their members to fill various posts in local administration, though all their nominations had to be approved by the provincial governor. The 1785 charter represented a natural progression in the process of the state lessening its direct control of the nobility, but it was far from delivering full rights to them, either as individuals or as a corporate body. There were sound pragmatic reasons for giving the nobles a greater say in the conduct of their own affairs. With the ending of compulsory service, a significant proportion of the nobility spent a much greater proportion of their time living on their country estates and it was important that the state should not completely lose their expertise and knowledge.

The state also needed to improve the quality of local administration: as the population of the empire grew and its physical boundaries expanded, it became more and more important for the St Petersburg government to be able to ensure that local control of its domains was effective. The best way to do this was to place significant responsibilities upon the nobility: the section of society that had the greatest personal stake in the stability and good government of their district. It was also important to try to disseminate the culture of the capital more widely. Russia in the eighteenth century was very much dominated by the twin cities – the two capitals – of St Petersburg and Moscow and the growth of the empire meant that it was vital to extend both the bureaucratic culture of the centre and the wider ethos of these developed cities out into Russia's provinces and districts. One of Catherine's motivations in setting up formal noble corporate bodies and giving them a degree of autonomy was to try to stimulate the overall development of provincial society. Providing a local focus for the nobility as well as giving them a limited role in the administration of their home regions was intended to strengthen their commitment to the countryside, rather than just seeing it as a place from which they needed to escape to the urban sophistication of St Petersburg or Moscow as often as possible. All the nobility in an area were able to participate in the work of the noble assembly and it provided an opportunity for the poorest nobles, with only a handful of serfs to their name, to mix with their more prosperous neighbours and for them to develop a sense of a common identity. Noble assemblies were given the power to own a building in the provincial or district town, and these did become a centre for noble social life, as Tolstoy describes in *Anna Karenina.*

The aims that Catherine entertained for the operation of the new noble corporate institutions were not wholly fulfilled. The state had viewed the granting of rights to the nobility as a means of strengthening the service bond that existed between nobility and state. The Pugachev rebellion had shown the brittleness of St Petersburg's hold on the Russian provinces and Catherine hoped that the nobility would grasp these new opportunities gratefully and commit themselves to playing a full part in the administrative life of the provinces. More was needed, however, to persuade the nobility that they should support the state in local administration. Most Russian provincial towns were a far cry from the great cities of the empire and many of the wealthier nobility who could afford to maintain a house in Moscow or St Petersburg spent as much of the year there as possible, usually returning to their country estates only during the summer. The nobles who did spend the entire year living in the countryside were usually the poorer gentry, and they had been more or less excluded from participating in the work of the new noble assemblies. The 1785 charter stipulated that a noble had to have achieved the rank of commissioned officer and to have an annual income of at least 100 rubles a year to be able to vote as a member of the assemblies or to be elected to a post by the assembly. Thus, many of the nobility who were actually available in the countryside year-round to take on the task of local administration were unable to play any real role in the work. Ambitious nobles viewed local government as a dead end, and most nobles who wanted to prosper and to advance their careers knew that they needed to obtain a military commission or else to find employment in a St Petersburg government department. The nobility's view of service was based on a very different premise from that of the Russian state: once compulsion had been removed from the equation, the nobility wanted to use service to the state as a means of maximising their own wealth and authority. They did not see service as a task that they were performing for the benefit of the state, even though that is how the St Petersburg government viewed the idea of noble service. The novelty of the new noble assemblies ensured that they were initially well attended, but interest soon tailed off among the nobility and it became difficult to find candidates for election to work in local government. The task of persuading the nobility to participate in the work of the noble assemblies was made no easier by the attitude that the established provincial bureaucracy took to the new institutions. Most provincial governors appeared to regard the noble assemblies as part of their own fiefdom and tried to impose their own preferences upon the assemblies. During Paul I's reign, the powers of the assemblies were reduced sharply. Provincial assemblies were abolished completely and, even after Alexander I's restoration of the assemblies' original structures and functions, they still failed to gain the interest of the nobility.

Serfdom and Emancipation

While service was an important role for the nobility, it was their relationship with their serfs that was the most crucial part of their function
from the point of view of the state. Serfdom had been institutionalised in Russia by the 1649 code of laws. This ended freedom of
movement for the enserfed peasantry, prohibiting them from leaving
their owners' estates and setting out the process for recovering serfs
who had abandoned their noble masters. The code deprived peasants
of their right to own personal property, instead considering all their
property as belonging to their masters. Peasants were deprived of individual legal rights and the 1649 code set the pattern for the Russian
rural world until emancipation two centuries later. Serfs of private
landowners were liable to provide their lords both with labour services
and with payments in cash or in kind. There were wide differences in
the precise type of service that peasants had to perform, as it was each
individual landowner who determined the mix of labour service and
in-kind payments. The level of dues that landowners required from
their serfs grew steadily during the eighteenth century, and peasants
had both to work more extensively on their lords' lands and to pay
them higher dues in cash or in kind. It has been estimated that by the
first half of the nineteenth century, landowners took at least one third
of both peasants' incomes and their total production.[3] The peasantry
also had to work in order to feed themselves and their families and
to earn sufficient income to be able to pay taxation.

The system of serfdom was intended to give the landowning elites
as large an income as possible from their land, by enabling them to
exploit the peasantry in a way that would not have been possible if the
peasants had been able to operate as part of an agricultural market
economy. But, it also fulfilled a vital function by working to deter
peasants from rebelling against landowners and the state. The powers
that landowners possessed over their serfs made the consequences
of disobedience potentially extremely severe, since the serf had no
access to the legal system to provide any protection against punishments that the landowner might impose. The restrictions on leaving
a landowner's land removed that option too for serfs, meaning that
they were largely doomed to live out their lives under the control of
their lords. This lack of mobility for the enserfed peasantry made it
easier for landowners to prevent their serfs becoming part of a landless, itinerant rural proletariat that could pose a threat to established

authority. Landowners' dependence on serfs for their own prosperity provided nobles with a powerful incentive to ensure that the system of serfdom delivered both economic benefits and also the social stability that the state wanted. The great peasant rebellions that took place during the seventeenth and eighteenth centuries appeared to the state to provide the justification for refusing to countenance any reduction in the burden of serfdom that the peasantry had to bear. Loosening the bonds that tied the peasantry to the land and to their noble masters would be a recipe for disaster and would only result in more frequent and more serious revolts.

The nobility thus provided explicit service to the state by becoming military officers or working in the bureaucracy, as well as operating as a part of the state's mechanisms of control over the peasant population. This was a situation that was sustainable well into the nineteenth century and it served the interests of both state and nobility. The state gained a reliable buttress in maintaining its own authority, while the nobility could be sure of receiving favours from the state in an effort to ensure that they remained committed to the maintenance of the autocratic regime. Power in this situation lay with the state, since the Romanov regime could take steps to deal with nobles who appeared to be dilatory in their duties. But, this position did not last. During the first half of the nineteenth century, the very concept of serfdom was being called into question. The moral case for emancipation was very powerful and Russia's continued espousal of serfdom placed it in an unenviable situation when compared with western European states. Growing levels of education among Russia's social elites exposed them to broader trends in European thinking, so that by the 1840s, Russian educated society looked upon serfdom as nothing less than a moral scandal. These considerations were given greater weight as arguments were advanced suggesting that a serf economy was less economically efficient than an economy based on free labour. In 1812, the Free Economic Society, a much-respected learned body, held a competition to debate the relative merits of hired and serf labour and its winner, a member of the staff of the Ministry of Finance, argued that free labour provided an improved economic outcome for agriculture.[4] There was also discussion of the structure of Russian rural society: the state was extending its bureaucratic competence and was coming to believe that it did not require the mediation of the landed nobility to act as a means of controlling the rural population. The state itself already controlled very large numbers of peasants and it seemed entirely feasible that privately owned serfs could be transformed into state peasants, as had occurred with the church peasants in the 1760s.

The final element in the discussions about the future of serfdom was the potential for peasant discontent. The spectre of the Pugachev revolt hung over Russia's rulers during the first half of the nineteenth century and they were deeply concerned that they would not be able to put down a further major uprising if the peasantry rose up in revolt against the institution of serfdom. Between 1816 and 1819 serfdom was abolished in the Baltic provinces of the empire, but the serfs in this region were not granted land when they were emancipated and further steps had to be taken to ensure that they were not left entirely landless. During Nicholas I's reign, the emperor summoned ten secret committees to discuss the 'peasant question' but almost nothing resulted from these detailed and prolonged debates. Nicholas I remained wary of the enormous step of emancipating the serfs and preferred not to interfere in a structure that was still performing reasonably well.

The death of Nicholas I and Russia's defeat in the Crimean War made a dramatic change to the situation. The ethos of government altered with the accession of a new Tsar and the death of Nicholas I allowed opinions that had only been discussed in private to be openly debated and to become part of the government's agenda. By far the most pressing issue that faced the new monarch and his government was serfdom. There was a recognition at the very top of Russian society that the situation had to change; Grand Duchess Elena Pavlovna had hosted a salon during the 1840s that had become a centre for the discussion of progressive ideas. Her patronage – she was Nicholas I's sister-in-law – made her regular social gatherings a safe environment in which the emerging generation of bureaucrats could debate their plans for the future without fear of retribution. Support also came from Nicholas I's younger son, Grand Duke Konstantin Nikolaeveich, who was an enthusiast for modernisation in many forms. He presided over the Imperial Geographical Society, one of the main official forums through which the empire was being explored and information was collected about the new lands and peoples that were ruled over from St Petersburg. While much of the discussion about the prospects for reform took place in the rarefied circles of the imperial bureaucracy and its associated institutions, there was also a wider perception across Russian educated society that Russia's humiliation in the Crimea and the end of Nicholas I's 'thirty-year tyranny of madness', as Konstantin Kavelin termed it, marked a turning point in Russia's development.[5]

The new emperor realised the necessity of making change, but he had to exercise considerable caution in bringing the process to fruition. Addressing the issue of serfdom meant engagement with one of the chief sources of Romanov power: it would require a reformulation of the relative position of serf and noble and could thus threaten one of the main ways in which the Tsarist state retained its hold on power. The prospect of tangling with this key social relationship also had implications for the position of the monarchy itself, since the state relied upon the nobility to maintain control of the mass of the rural population. Reform also had to be approached carefully, since the Russian state was in considerable financial difficulties in the aftermath of the Crimean War. Losing a war is always an expensive business and the Crimea proved to be almost ruinous for the Russian treasury: the state's deficit grew very significantly in the late 1850s and there was very little leeway to introduce any measures that would require additional government expenditure. By the middle of the nineteenth century, the Romanov state had become deeply conservative in its approach to making reform and the prospect of embarking on changes to the status of the tens of millions of serfs was one that gave the new Tsar serious pause for thought.

The process of emancipating the serfs was neither quick nor straightforward. Early in 1856, the emperor addressed the Moscow nobility, announcing that 'rumours have spread of my intention to abolish serfdom. . . . I have no intention of doing so immediately. But, of course, as you yourselves realise, the existing system of serf owning cannot remain unchanged. It is better to begin abolishing serfdom from above than to wait for it to begin to abolish itself from below.'[6] This was very far from being the clarion call for reform that it is often suggested to be, but the process of considering how serfdom might be abolished had appeared on the government's agenda and it would not now be easily dislodged. The normal bureaucratic processes of the Russian state began their ponderous progress in the wake of the emperor's speech. A detailed historical review of the previous two centuries of serfdom was prepared and, after it had been submitted to Alexander, he established a secret committee to prepare proposals on the peasant question. The committee immediately began to encounter the issues that lay at the heart of the abolition of serfdom. When the serfs had been freed in the Baltic provinces of the empire 40 years previously, their emancipation had been accomplished without granting any land to the freed peasantry. This model was seized upon by some of the members of the secret committee as providing a pattern that should be followed for the remainder of the empire. For the nobility, emancipating the serfs without land appeared to hold huge advantages. It would retain the nobles' fundamental wealth and would, at the same time, remove their liability to make basic provision for their serfs. This course of action would provide the landowning nobility with access to a labour force for their farms that could be employed on low wages, since there would be huge competition amongst the peasantry for work, and this would provide the landowners with cheap labour. This followed the pattern of the process which had taken place in the Baltic provinces, which had resulted in the serfowners retaining their land and power but which had done very little to improve the condition of the peasantry. At the same time, the nobility in the north-western provinces of Kovno, Grodno and Vilna were being persuaded by the local governor, General V. I. Nazimov, to request formal permission from the Tsar to begin discussing how they might approach the peasant question in their own region. Alexander II's response to them in November 1857 was to allow the nobility to establish committees to debate proposals for the 'systematic improvement of the serfs' way of life'. These committees came into being not just in the three north-western provinces, but right across European Russia in the first half of 1858. Their conclusions demonstrated that there was a multiplicity of views amongst the provincial nobility about the way in which emancipation could be carried out, although the thrust of the committees' reports was, unsurprisingly, towards minimising the impact of the measure on the nobility themselves. The nobility in general wanted to receive as much financial compensation for the loss of their serfs as possible and, in some cases, were keen to see the quantity of land which they would lose reduced to a minimum.

This disunity made it easier for the 'enlightened bureaucrats' at the centre in St Petersburg to determine the form which emancipation should take. This was helped by the stand taken by General Iakov Rostovtsev, a member of the secret committee – now renamed the Main Committee on Peasant Affairs – who had the ear of the Emperor. In the summer of 1858 Rostovtsev wrote to Alexander II to express his conviction that the serfs must be freed with land and that the state had to assist in the financial process by which this land would be transferred from noble landowners to their serfs. This proved to be a watershed in the process of peasant reform, and Alexander II instructed the Main Committee that these principles were to form the basis of legislation. The transformation of principle into practice proved to be exceptionally complex, and the Editing Commission which was established to prepare detailed statutes held more than 400 meetings over 18 months and produced 19 separate pieces of legislation to bring emancipation into law.

The legislation that was enacted in February 1861 declared that 'the serfdom of peasants settled on estate owners' landed properties, and of household serfs, is abolished forever' and with this freedom came the right for peasants to carry on their lives without having to seek their master's approval for their every action.[7] The process by which the freed peasants were to acquire land was, however, more gradual. For a transitional period of two years the peasantry had to continue providing either labour service or quitrent to their lords as before, but during this period charters were to be drawn up setting out the extent of the land which the peasants would gain and the precise nature of the obligations which they had owed to their lords. These details would form the basis for the calculation of the financial part of the emancipation settlement; the peasantry could buy the land which they were allotted and they had to make redemption payments for it over a period of 49 years, based not on the value of the land itself, but on the extent of the obligations which they had owed their lords. This did not, however, mean that the nobility would have to wait nearly half a century before they would receive compensation for the land which their former serfs would gain. The government realised that this would not be acceptable to serfowners and so the state was to advance most of the cost of the peasants' allotments to the nobility immediately, although in interest-bearing bonds, rather than in cash. Pressures on the state's finances meant that the government refused to subsidise the arrangements and the redemption arrangements had to be self-financing.[8]

Complicated formulae were set out to calculate the precise size of the allotments which the peasants would receive. But the landowner was allowed to reduce the size of these plots if, after the removal of the peasant allotments, he would be left with less than about half of his estate. While the emancipation did give individual peasants their legal freedom and the opportunity to own land, the government remained extremely cautious of releasing the tens of millions of serfs from all the bonds which restrained them. The existing structure of the peasant village commune was retained and substantially strengthened by subordinating the individual agricultural and financial autonomy of its peasant members to the communal will. The traditional method of strip farming remained intact, and with it communal control over the growing of crops. Moreover, the commune's tax-collecting powers were extended to include responsibility for redemption payments so that the redemption debt was calculated for an entire commune, rather than individually. The commune therefore needed to retain as many members as possible to ensure that the redemption debt which each peasant household had to pay was kept as low as possible. As well, there was no real incentive for an individual peasant to maximise his own income solely in order to pay off the redemption debt early, since each household's contribution was subsumed in the overall repayment made by a commune, although peasants who had paid off their debt could ask to leave the commune. The 1861 statutes covered only serfs of private landowners. It took a further five years for the government to proceed with the full emancipation of the state peasants, although the 1866 measures which enacted this took a somewhat different form. Instead of allowing the state peasants to move towards the outright ownership of the land they farmed, they were only to make a yearly rental payment for the use of the land. It took a further 20 years before a decision in 1886 allowed the state peasants to begin a 45-year redemption process similar to that of the private serfs.

The impact of the freeing of the private serfs was dramatic. It transformed the legal status of the landowners' serfs, and the half-century following the emancipation witnessed a resurgence in peasant farming as the market for both renting and buying land became much more active. But the most significant changes affected the landowning nobility. The terms of the emancipation settlement meant that in most of Russia, landowners could see up to two-thirds of their productive farmland allocated to their former serfs. In the steppe region, landowners could retain up to half of their productive land. There could be some relief for landowners, however, as the result of a provision inserted in the emancipation legislation late in 1860. This late amendment to the statutes permitted landowners to offer their peasants free of charge a small allotment of land that would be no more than one quarter of the maximum size set out in the legislation, as an alternative to the normal process of land allocation.

These pieces of land became known as 'beggar's holdings', anticip-
ating what fate held in store for those peasants who made this choice.
This provision was motivated by the desire of landowners to hold on
to as much of their farmland as possible and also by the belief that
peasants who opted for this would be so impoverished that they would
have to continue to work on the landowners' estates to be able to
survive. The process of emancipation represented a fundamental shift
in the balance of authority across the Russian countryside. This was
not because the peasants were gaining more land than they had previously worked: there were significant differences between regions, but
on average the peasantry emerged from emancipation with less land
to farm than they had been accustomed to working under serfdom.
The difference was that the actual ownership of land was being transferred from landowner to peasant and this unfroze the centuries-old
structures of landholding across Russia.

While the emancipation settlement had favoured the landowning
nobility at almost every turn by allowing them to retain as much land
as possible, in the years after 1861 the nobility did not show any great
inclination to maintain their dominant position. The nobility rapidly
divested themselves of their remaining land from the 1870s onwards.
By the early 1880s, the nobility had reduced their landholdings by
almost 20 per cent compared with 1862 and the process continued
apace during the following decades. A further 10 per cent reduction
took place in the 1880s and again in the 1890s, so that by the beginning of the twentieth century the nobility owned 40 per cent less land
than they had at the time of emancipation. Not all of the nobility
wanted to sell their land, but the proportion of land purchases by
nobles in the 40 years after emancipation also fell. During the 1870s,
noble land purchases accounted for 43 per cent of all land bought, but
by 1905 this had fallen to 26 per cent. It was the peasantry who were
taking the place of the nobility in buying land: only 18 per cent of land
purchases were made by peasants in the 1870s, but they accounted for
40 per cent of transactions by 1905. The average size of noble landholdings also declined. In 1861, only some 20 per cent of nobles were
landless, but by 1905 this had increased to more than 60 per cent of
the nobility. The proportion of nobles owning between 101 and 1000
desiatinas of land fell from 45 per cent to 13 per cent, with a smaller fall
in those owning up to 100 *desiatinas* from 33 per cent to 21 per cent.[9]
This was a startling development: nobility and landownership had
gone hand-in-hand, and land had provided the basis for noble power.

Yet now, the nobility were abandoning wholesale landownership and recognising that their futures lay away from farming and the rural world.

For those nobles who did remain committed to the countryside, their pattern of activity changed too. They had made a conscious decision to stay and make a living out of farming: some of them tried to become agricultural entrepreneurs by improving their estates and trying to add to them by buying or renting additional land. Those nobles who had chosen this path were in a more favourable position than the newly freed peasantry, since they had access to much greater financial resources that they could utilise for investment in their farming businesses. This process was assisted by the creation in 1885 of the Noble Land Bank. This was a belated attempt by Alexander III to counter the decline in noble power and landholding that was taking place by providing finance on favourable terms that would enable the nobility to continue to exercise a commanding presence in the countryside.[10] The bank lent money to the nobility, securing loans on their estates and charging low rates of interest. The nobility took rapid advantage of the bank's establishment, viewing its modest rates of interest as a useful means by which they could pay off existing debts and reduce their expenditure through taking out new loans with lower repayments. Noble mortgage debt grew more than three-fold between 1883 and 1914, reaching more than 1401m rubles by the outbreak of war in 1914, although this still only represented 20 per cent of the total value of the nobility's land. The nobility put these funds to a variety of uses. As well as spending on improving their estates, some nobles simply used the money to finance current consumption. Others borrowed against their land in order to be able to invest in new businesses away from the countryside. There was a clear process of transfer of noble capital from farming to business and industry, as the nobility calculated that they could make a larger return on their capital by investing it in new enterprises. It was emancipation that allowed them to take these steps. Without the burden of land and serfs, the landowning nobility were liberated from the shackles of being compelled to engage in agriculture – whether or not they had any interest or belief in the value of farming – and could make more rational economic decisions about their future.

This was an unintended consequence of the emancipation. The regime had framed the emancipation settlement with the aim of preserving as much as possible of the nobility's power and influence, but the statutes' authors did not understand the full import of the changes that they were making to Russian society. Emancipation was viewed primarily as a measure that would change the legal status of the peasantry by giving them their freedom and, at the same time, allow them to farm semi-independently. The limitations placed upon the amount of land that the freed peasantry could gain were intended to ensure that the peasants remained tied to the nobility, since their own landholdings would probably be insufficient to allow them to earn an adequate income and they would therefore need to continue to work for the landowning nobility to be able to survive. While this was a rational position to adopt while emancipation was being prepared, it failed to take into account the reaction of the landed nobility to the freeing of the serfs. The Russian state assumed that the nobility would continue to pursue an existence that was based on farming and the countryside, and that they would move to become employers of agricultural wage-labourers – their former serfs – thus ensuring that the fundamental patterns of Russian rural life remained unchanged. They did not bargain for the fact that the nobility viewed emancipation as an opportunity for them to make decisions about their future in a more rational fashion, unrestricted by the ownership of serfs. Some nobles found it difficult to make changes to their lives, resigning themselves to the gradual process of genteel decline that Chekhov captured in his plays. But very many nobility decided that they did not want to continue the life of country gentlemen and that they preferred living in Russia's growing towns and cities, earning a living in the expanding state bureaucracy, or else from Russia's growing business sector. The Russian nobility embraced the modernisation of Russia's economy and society with enthusiasm after 1861 and, indeed, their decisions were of considerable significance in advancing Russian modernisation.

Emancipation revealed a huge gulf between the state's perception of the nobility's role and the aims that the nobility themselves had for their own future. The Russian government showed little comprehension of the changing nature of society, and it believed that it could continue to rely on the nobility remaining committed to the traditional pattern of service. The bargain between state and nobility had rested upon the institution of serfdom: for the nobility service to the state was the price that they had paid for the state's support and maintenance of serfdom. It was clear that the state did not understand the nature of the compact that bound the nobility to the regime and that it believed that the nobility owed unconditional loyalty to the Romanov state. The nobility's desire to see the end of compulsory service and the various tactics that they had used to try to reduce the burden of service should have alerted the state to the innate dislike of the nobility for the system in which they found themselves. Once the legal constraints of serfdom had been lifted, the nobility found themselves in a strong position. They had been able to retain a significant proportion of their productive farmland and they had also been able to gain financially, as the state made payments to them for the land that had been allocated to their former serfs. Emancipation benefited the Russian nobility very considerably. They emerged from the 1860s with more substantial resources than they had ever enjoyed before: they had land unencumbered by serfs as well as gaining significant financial benefit from the payments they received for their land. But the aftermath of 1861 proved deeply damaging to the strength of the Russian state. Its success in sustaining the social order was severely damaged by the decision to emancipate the serfs. The nobility showed their disdain for their traditional lives and embraced modernisation with enthusiasm; in doing so they weakened the power of the state and, in the medium term, this served to undermine their own authority as Russia's social elite. The huge social authority of the Tsarist state began its decline in 1861.

PART II
RULING AN EMPIRE

Chapter 4:   Institutions

The expansion of the territory and population of the Russian empire at the beginning of the eighteenth century made it imperative for the institutions of government to be reshaped into a more coherent and effective structure. The domestic administration that Peter the Great inherited was haphazard and included more than 40 separate government offices, each with varying degrees of authority and jurisdiction. Peter the Great's process of modernising Russia included the tearing down of this disorganised central government and its replacement with a more cohesive set of institutions that could provide a more orderly means of administering Russia. Peter's reforms of government were not, however, simply a reorganisation of the institutions that were the intermediary between monarch and people; they also redefined the state's view of its role and its relationship to its subjects.

   The position of law was central to the organisation of Russian government. While western states were gradually absorbing the concept that law applied not just to the state's subjects, but also to the institutions of the state itself, Russia remained resolutely outside this tradition. Right up until the fall of the Tsarist regime, there was a reluctance to accept that Russia was ready for the rule of law. 'Institutions are of no importance, everything depends on individuals' said Konstantin Pobedonostsev in 1884, and this represented the essence of the Romanov state's conception of law.[1] The Russian state embraced the concept of law as enthusiastically as did any other and its fundamental laws declared that 'the Russian Empire is administered on the firm foundations of positive laws, institutions and regulations enacted by the Autocratic Authority'.[2] But, the mechanisms by which these laws were created and the ways in which they were applied demonstrated the difference that existed between the Russian understanding of the nature of law and the view that was taking hold in the West. The omnipotence of the Russian monarch did not allow for any restrictions to be placed on his power and the authority of the state was essentially personal in nature. The size and complexity of the Russian empire dictated that it could only be ruled through a complex set of institutions, but these institutions had to remain subordinate to the will of the monarch. The state also understood that its institutions of government could not operate haphazardly and that their authority, and that of the monarch, could only be exercised properly if it operated through regular channels. The monarch was the sole fount of Russian law before 1905 and, in effect, any minister who acted on the emperor's instruction had the power to issue decrees that had the full force of law. Law was 'any Royal Order signed by His Imperial Majesty or State Council opinion confirmed by him' and could thus take any number of forms.[3] There was no clear distinction in the Russian state between law and administrative order, thus allowing the state almost total latitude in its enactments. Laws did not have to be tested against any coherent body of principles before they could be enacted, and while they offered a guide for the operation of Russia's institutions, they did not exert any formal restraint on the authority of the monarch, the fount of all law. The state's subjects had no real redress against the state's laws, since both law and the responsibility for its application emanated from the same source: the monarch. Until the judicial reforms of 1864, the Russian state maintained a stranglehold over the operation of the legal system and there was no hint of any independent authority through the courts that would allow a Russian subject scope to challenge the authority of the state. Law remained subordinate to the interests of the state as a whole: the implications of this for the institutional structure and ethos of the Russian empire were dramatic.

The ethos that underlay Russia's institutions was expressed clearly by P. A. Valuev, the Minister of Internal Affairs between 1861 and 1868. He wrote that

The extreme friability of our [governmental] structure makes it necessary that we have an element of authority. [In Russia] the fascination, the spectre, of authority is all the power that the state has. Our new people view authority from the fashionable vantage point of so-called progress, and most of them see only arbitrariness in it. . . . They portray authority by their denunciations, as if it were a personal, special attribute of one or another person rather than a social force, entrusted for the attainment of social and state purposes.[4]

Russian institutional authority was contingent upon the personal power of the monarch and the structure that Peter the Great put in place in the early eighteenth century emphasised this. In 1711 he established the Senate, and this was followed between 1718 and 1720 by the dismantling of the Muscovite system of *prikazy* and its replacement by nine colleges. The Senate was initially to be a body of only nine trusted advisers whom Peter could rely on to govern the empire during his absences in the field with his armies. It had no formal definition of its power at its formation and, indeed, Peter deliberately left its area of competence very vague so that he could ensure that it acted as he wanted. For the first decade of its existence, the Senate functioned as a type of informal cabinet as well as acting as an appeal court for some significant cases. To replace the *prikazy*, nine colleges were established to deal with the central functions of the Petrine state: foreign affairs, war, the navy, revenue, justice, auditing, trade, mines and manufacture and the budget. Each college had ten members: a president appointed by the emperor, with a vice-president chosen by the Senate from three candidates proposed by the college, and the remaining eight members selected by the Senate from a list provided by the college.

These colleges formed the basis for Russian central government throughout the eighteenth century, but the position of the Senate became the subject of significant dispute. Soon after Catherine II's accession to the throne, Nikita Panin, one of the chief architects of the plot that had brought her to power, proposed to the new empress that she should establish a permanent imperial council. His memorandum to Catherine argued that

the principal, genuine and overall concern for the welfare of the state resided in the person of the sovereign. But the sovereign could not translate this concern into useful action except by sharing it out intelligently among a small number of persons specially selected for the purpose.[5]

Panin's proposal was for a council of six to eight members who would have to countersign every piece of legislation approved by the sovereign; he did not propose that the council should be able to issue legislation on its own, but it was clear that he intended the council to provide some check on the powers of the autocrat. The entrenching of the imperial council in the government of the empire would help to counterbalance the influence of favourites over the monarch and would make it much more difficult for a monarch to act in a capricious manner. Panin's imperial council would include a representative from each of the most significant areas of government, so that the importance of the colleges would be emphasised and government business relating to the central areas of the state's responsibility would be considered by the functional department that had responsibility for it. Catherine's reaction to Panin's proposal was initially favourable: she had only just acceded to the throne and was uncertain about the security of her own position as monarch. But her initial caution gave way to the realisation that the proposed imperial council would impinge on her own prerogatives as autocrat. One of her supporters wrote a memorandum arguing that

> [the plan] inclines towards an aristocratic form of government. The influential people, appointed by law to a council of state . . . can easily turn into co-rulers. The Russian sovereign must have unlimited power. An imperial council brings the subject too close to the sovereign and the subject may begin to harbour hopes of sharing power with the sovereign.[6]

Catherine's rejection of any encroachment on her powers was shown during the following year when proposals were discussed for the reform of the Senate. She wrote to one of her close advisers that

> The Senate has been established for the carrying out of laws prescribed to it. But it has often issued laws itself, granted ranks, honours, money and lands, in a word . . . almost everything. Having once exceeded its limits the Senate now still finds it difficult to adapt to the new order within which it should confine itself.[7]

Catherine issued an order reforming the Senate in December 1763, restricting its powers and confining it to a mixture of administrative and judicial functions. The Senate could now only issue decisions that were authorised by existing legislation; any new law could only be issued by the monarch. The Senate's legal powers were similarly circumscribed: the procurator-general, the link between sovereign and Senate, was given effective control of the Senate's judicial processes, so that its independence was very effectively constrained.

Ministerial Government

Peter the Great's colleges had deteriorated in importance during the second half of the eighteenth century and much power had been transferred to the procurator-general. Paul's accession to the throne in 1796 and his love for order and organisation prompted him to reinvigorate the system of colleges, resulting in a set of institutions that presaged the major reforms to be introduced by his son, Alexander I. Paul had intended to create a system of ministries, but these plans were interrupted by his murder in 1801. The following year his successor instituted a system of ministerial government that was to last until 1917. Alexander I and his closest advisers deliberately looked abroad for a model on which they could draw, since the collegiate system had proved to be unsatisfactory, The intention was to create a unified government that could govern Russia more effectively than the colleges had done, and France and Britain were taken as particular examples of how cabinet government could operate. The proponents of ministerial government argued that their ideas were fully in the Petrine tradition and that it would create a regulated and well-ordered state that would allow the authority of the emperor to permeate every part of its structure. The idea of ministries did not find favour with all of Russia's elite however, since some viewed them as running entirely counter to the tradition of Russian government. Opponents of ministerialism argued that its bureaucratic nature was alien to Russia and that it would pervert the nature of autocratic authority by allowing institutions to take precedence over the monarch's wishes. They believed that ministries would help to separate state from society and would drive a wedge between the emperor and his people.

Alexander I did express caution about the ministerial structure that he introduced and he was careful to ensure that it did not become a unified government that could establish itself as an autonomous source of authority outside his control. In September 1802, Alexander I created eight ministries to deal with the whole range of government functions: internal affairs, foreign affairs, war, navy, finance, justice, education and commerce. The ministers were each appointed by the emperor and reported directly to him; they did not come under the control of the Senate, despite the emperor's confirmation of the supervisory role that the Senate enjoyed over the executive arms of the state.[8] No minister acted as prime minister and none of the ministerial posts automatically conferred additional status on its occupant. Alexander I and his successors in effect operated as both head of state and head of government until the creation in 1905 of a true cabinet system of government. During the nineteenth century Russia had no proper cabinet; at times the Committee of Ministers fulfilled the role informally, but without a prime minister, it was very difficult for ministers to establish themselves as truly able to challenge the emperor.

This did not prevent vigorous and, at times, ferocious battles taking place in the bureaucracy between different ministers. Even though it was the war and navy ministries that ate up the lion's share of the state's budget, they did not exercise a decisive influence over the whole business of government. Their functions were too restricted and the ministers that headed them were often men of too limited a vision to give the military ministries an extensive influence over government policy. It was the Ministries of Internal Affairs, Finance and Justice that had the widest remit and it was they that formed the core of Russian government during the nineteenth century. Their inter-relationship both demonstrates the power that the ministerial structure could exercise, but also points to its potential weakness as an instrument in determining and implementing policy. The Ministry of Internal Affairs bestrode the Russian empire: the formal mandate of the minister was

> to look after the well-being of the people everywhere, the tranquillity, peace and public services of the entire Empire. He has under his direction all sectors of state industry, with the exception of mining, and also the construction and maintenance of all public buildings. Above that he is given the responsibility to endeavour by all means to avert shortages of food and all other necessities.[9]

This gave the ministry responsibility in three crucial areas of policy. First, it was responsible for policing the empire in its broadest form.

The ministry controlled both the regular police force that investigated crimes and apprehended common criminals, as well as – from 1880 – the political police, which became increasingly significant in the final decades of Romanov rule in trying to root out subversion. The second area of activity that the ministry covered was to act as the government's ministry of trade and industry. It was only in 1905 that a separate body was established to take over these functions from the Ministry of Internal Affairs, so that it dealt with a great range of social and economic issues for more than a century. These areas of its activity became more and more important as the Russian economy grew and they were one of the central battlegrounds in the Ministry's struggles for influence with the Ministry of Finance. Lastly, the Ministry of Internal Affairs was responsible for the detailed supervision of Russia's provincial administration through its control of the provincial governors. Since the governors played the central role in the administration of the provinces, with a remit that covered almost every aspect of life, this gave the Ministry of Internal Affairs huge powers over the lives of Russian subjects. There was a persistent tension between the policing and the social and economic functions of the ministry, since the need to maintain public order often conflicted with the state's desire to promote economic development. This was part of a wider ministerial conflict, as the Ministry of Finance developed from being simply an accounting body into an organisation that saw itself as being the chief guardian of Russia's economy. The increasing professionalisation of the finance ministry during the second half of the nineteenth century brought it into tension with the Ministry of Internal Affairs, as successive finance ministers tried to gain overall control of economic policy. The establishment of a separate ministry for trade and industry in 1905 showed their success in stripping the internal affairs department of its role in determining economic policy, but its supervision of provincial governors still gave it huge influence over the detailed implementation of economic and social policy.

The ethos of policing that permeated the Ministry of Internal Affairs emphasised the ability of the state to police the empire much as it wanted, without severe legal constraints on its powers. 'Administrative justice' was a fundamental part of the state's armoury, allowing it to deal with a variety of misdemeanours without recourse to the courts. The policing powers of the state allowed its bureaucrats to operate an entirely arbitrary system of law enforcement, confident in the knowledge that they could not be challenged in the courts. This

situation changed in the 1860s and tension between the Ministries of
Justice and Internal Affairs grew, especially after 1864 and the enactment of major reforms to the empire's judicial system.[10] The emancipation of the serfs gave the freed peasantry a legal standing for the first
time, making it more difficult for them to be treated arbitrarily, while
the legal reforms of 1864 began the development of what Wortman
has termed 'a Russian legal consciousness'.[11] The Ministry of Justice
increased very significantly in importance after 1864, and its staff
came from a background that challenged the police-orientated views
of the Ministry of Internal Affairs. The hallmark of legality that was
the preserve of the justice ministry brought it into increasing conflict
with the internal affairs department, and this was accentuated as the
problems of maintaining order in the empire intensified during the
second half of the nineteenth century. While these conflicts were a
normal part of ministerial government anywhere, in Russia they were
brought into sharp focus since there was no institutional coordination
of the government's policies and no institutional forum in which
disputes could be mediated.

Bureaucrats

This state of affairs greatly enhanced the importance of the individuals
who staffed the government machine across the Russian empire, both
at its highest levels in St Petersburg and in the myriad of government
outposts across the empire. Institutional structures were shaped by
the men who operated them, and the nature of Russian governmental
power allowed them considerable latitude in both the formulation
of policy and its day-to-day implementation. The numbers of bureaucrats increased significantly: more than 5500 officials staffed Peter the
Great's government machine at the end of his reign, and this had
grown to some 16,500 by the time Catherine II came to the throne less
than 40 years later. But this growth was insignificant compared with
the expansion in the bureaucracy that took place over the following
century. At the end of the Crimean War in 1856, Russian officialdom
numbered nearly 114,000 and this more than doubled to reach more
than 252,000 by 1913.[12] Even with this growth in the number of
officials, Russia still had only one quarter of the number of civil
servants per head of population that the British and French states
deemed necessary to run their government apparatus. While part of

this expansion in the bureaucracy can be accounted for by the growth of the empire – in terms of both territory and population – the complexity and intensity of government increased too, so that more and more officials were needed to administer the Russian state. The system of noble service to the state was intended to help fill the need for more officials, but when compulsory state service ended, many nobles simply took the opportunity to return to their estates and shied away from work as civil servants. The position was made all the more difficult as the tasks and nature of government became more complicated, all the time demanding better educated men to carry out the work of governing the empire. The eighteenth-century Russian bureaucracy had only a limited level of professionalism and it was essentially a hereditary caste. In the middle of the century, 90 per cent of the upper ranks of the bureaucracy were men whose fathers had served in the civil service, while for all officials in the fourteen ranks of Peter the Great's Table of Ranks, some 70 per cent were sons either of nobles or else of clerks in the bureaucracy. In the provinces, more than three-quarters of the clerks in the civil service came from a family whose members had worked in similar positions. The government of the empire was thus very much in the hands of a closed group of men, and newcomers found it very difficult to penetrate this world.

There were changes during the late eighteenth and early nineteenth centuries, as some nobles decided to make the civil service their primary focus, rather then concentrating on landowning. In 1755 more than 40 per cent of the most senior officials of the empire owned more than 500 serfs and nearly three-quarters of them had at least a single serf. But by the 1850s, the predominance of the landowning nobility in the bureaucracy had taken a substantial blow. Holders of large numbers of serfs made up only 20 per cent of the most senior officials, and some 40 per cent of this stratum of officialdom owned no serfs at all by this time. While this did represent a change in the nature of Russian officialdom, it lagged behind the general process of social change that was taking place in Russian society.

This development in the social characteristics of the civil service was accompanied by a growing professionalism among Russia's officials. Many eighteenth-century bureaucrats were retired soldiers, who found the civil service a rewarding and comfortable environment after the rigours of serving in the army or navy. Only a third of the senior officials of the empire in 1755 had any formal education, and this proportion fell dramatically when provincial officials are considered. Only 10 per cent of middle- and lower-ranking provincial bureaucrats had any formal education, so that when the civil service is considered overall, more than three-quarters of the men administering the empire had no formal education. This situation changed significantly by the 1850s. New universities were established in the first decades of the nineteenth century and in 1809 the government attempted to lay down minimum educational standards for promotion to the eighth rank of the civil service: this was the rank that conferred nobility and was thus of especial significance. This attempt to improve the quality of Russia's bureaucrats failed, since the number of students in Russian universities remained very small in the first half of the nineteenth century and the rules were formally abandoned in the 1830s. But, the educational background of Russia's civil servants was changing. By the 1850s, almost half of the men who served in the upper levels of the bureaucracy had received a university-level education. Officials lower down the bureaucratic structure fared less well, with only 14 per cent of lower–middle ranking officials and 4 per cent of the lowest set of civil servants having higher education.[13] These two groups, however, did show a considerably greater level of school-level education, so that almost all the civil servants at these levels had obtained at least a primary education. These raw statistics conceal even greater differences between Russia's bureaucrats: Nikolai Gogol's depiction of the banal and poverty-ridden existence of junior clerks in the St Petersburg ministries in his short story *The Overcoat* contrasts very sharply with the opulent lives that their wealthy and highly-educated superiors enjoyed. Provincial life could show up even greater disparities of status between the Petersburg-appointed provincial governors and their senior colleagues and the lowly officials who staffed the outposts of the empire in the depths of the Russian countryside.

The Russian civil service was gradually changing from being overwhelmingly based on kinship networks and patronage to a modern bureaucracy that valued professionalism and educational achievement rather than family links. This was a slow development and, even at the beginning of the twentieth century, the Tsarist civil service still had some of the characteristics of a traditional royal household. Recruitment to the top levels of the bureaucracy was never conducted on the basis of competitive examination, as was the case in Britain after the reforms of 1870, and much of the business of the bureaucracy was still based on patronage and corruption. This was true at all levels of the civil service, and was exacerbated by the poor wages that the most junior officials received. This encouraged them to take bribes and, alongside the absence of a clear framework of legality, this allowed the Russian government machine – especially in the provinces – to operate in an arbitrary fashion. Personal connections were also significant at the most elevated levels of the state in St Petersburg. The elite that governed imperial Russia during the last decades of its existence possessed a social homogeneity that set it apart from the remainder of the bureaucracy and enabled it to protect both its own privileges and the wider institution of Tsarism itself. Men rose gradually through the ranks before they arrived at the most senior positions inside the state's bureaucracy, a process that took decades and required both skill and good fortune. The men who dominated the bureaucracy in the empire's final decades had entered the state's service in the middle of the nineteenth century and were the products of a domestic and social environment that was very different from that which characterised Russia by the time they had reached positions of power.

During the reign of Nicholas II, more than half of the men appointed to the State Council, the body that best represents Russia's political elite, were landowners and more than two-thirds of this landowning group owned more than 1000 *desiatinas* of land. This ruling elite was bound together by other common interests. More than a third of the Council's membership had been educated at the empire's four elite schools – the Corps de Pages, the School of Guards, Sub-Ensigns and Cavalry Junkers, the Alexander Lycée and the School of Law. Service in the military provided an important link: a quarter of the State Council's members had reached high rank in Russia's armed forces, while a full third of the Council's members had been educated at military schools.[14] The evidence from Russia's most senior officials was that the process of professionalisation of the bureaucracy was proceeding only slowly. This is hardly surprising, given that men needed to have 20 or more years of service under their belt before they could hope to achieve promotion to the highest levels of Russian government. But change was taking place: there are examples of men such as A. V. Krivoshein, the grandson of a peasant, who nevertheless rose to become Minister of Agriculture in 1908. The glacial pace of change in the nature of the upper bureaucracy did have important advantages for the Russian state. It ensured that the government machine did not get rapidly overrun by men who were wholly out of sympathy with the ethos of the Romanov regime. The prolonged probationary period that most of them had to serve before they could achieve real power meant that the men who eventually rose to the top of the bureaucratic pile had been thoroughly imbued with the attitudes and practices that permeated the apparatus of the state. It was uncommon, although not unknown, for an outsider to break through the barriers to bureaucratic advancement and emerge in a position of power.

The best example of such a man is Sergei Witte, who was Minister of Finance from 1892 to 1903, and reappeared in 1905 as the saviour of the Russian state, negotiating peace with Japan and driving through the most significant set of constitutional reforms that the Romanov state had ever witnessed. Witte, however, had begun his career not in a St Petersburg ministry as a junior civil servant, but working for the Odessa Railway Company, and it was only after nearly 20 years of railway management that he was persuaded to take over as head of the Department of Railway Affairs in the Ministry of Finance. Witte's position as an outsider in the enclosed world of the Russian bureaucracy helps explain why he was able to make dramatic reforms in both the economic and political spheres, but also gives an insight into the mistrust that he engendered among some of the ruling elite, not least with Nicholas II himself. The emperor never forgave Witte for his part in pushing through constitutional change in 1905. After Witte's resignation in 1906 from government service and subsequent departure for a visit to western Europe, one of the Tsar's closest confidants, the Minister of the Imperial Court, Baron Fredericks, wrote to Witte suggesting that his 'return to Russia at the present time would be most undesirable'.[15] Witte was ostracised from the Russian establishment until his death in 1915.

Representative Government

During the second half of the nineteenth century there were a number of attempts to reform Russia's institutions of government. In particular, the question of popular representation and participation in the work of government was repeatedly debated. The controversy that was generated by this issue shows how significant it was to Russia's rulers. Any suggestion that an individual or group should have a formal role in the government of the state raised the hackles of the defenders of the autocratic *status quo* who viewed these plans as an attack on the prerogatives of the monarch. Opponents of such plans saw the issue in very clear terms: their sole concern was the preservation of autocracy and they were not prepared to concede that Russia's government – and thus the state's strength and prosperity – could be enhanced by any limit, however small, on the power of the sovereign.

In 1809, Michael Speransky advised Alexander I that the time was right to place some limits on monarchical power. Speransky was another example of an outsider who had penetrated the elite of the empire: he was the son of a village priest and had made his way up the bureaucratic ladder in the Ministry of Internal Affairs to emerge as Alexander I's chief adviser by 1807. Speransky's 1809 proposal was heavily influenced by western European theories of government, and he proposed a structure for Russia that would enshrine the separation of powers in the Russian state. The structure would be presided over by the emperor and State Council, but there would be a separate legislature – a State Duma – to be comprised of members selected by the Tsar from lists proposed by provincial dumas. Speransky was convinced that limitations had to be placed on the power of the monarch and that the rule of law had to take hold in Russia. He wanted to ensure that despotic government could never again emerge in Russia and to stamp out arbitrary administration. Speransky's proposals were clearly coloured by the experience of Paul I's reign and the need to resort to the deposition and murder of the emperor as a means of restraining his excesses. He wanted to entrench the position of the State Duma, which, even though it was not to be an elected body, would have the power of veto over legislation proposed by the emperor. Speransky was careful to hedge this power about very carefully, proposing that 'a law acknowledged by the majority of voices [in the Duma] to be inappropriate remains without effect'.[16] Alexander, however, was very conscious of his inheritance as an autocrat and was unwilling to sacrifice any of his authority. The emperor told one of his advisers that Speransky's proposal 'convinces me that he and his Ministries were indeed intriguing against the autocracy which I cannot and I do not have the right voluntarily to abandon to the disservice of my heirs'.[17] Despite the catastrophe of his father's reign, Alexander was not prepared to recognise that the state could be strengthened in the long term by making constitutional reform.

This was to be the reaction of his successors for almost a century. The issue of popular representation was not raised again during Alexander's reign and his successor, Nicholas I, was wholly committed to the principles and exercise of autocratic power. It was a full half-century before the subject again underwent serious discussion. For the first time in the history of Russia, the Great Reforms of the 1860s gave power to groups of elected representatives. The introduction of elected local rural councils – the *zemstvo* – in 1864, followed by municipal councils in 1870, marked a fundamental change in the nature of the Russian state and inspired both members of the governing elite and those outside this charmed circle to contemplate extending the principle to national government. In 1865 the Moscow assembly of the nobility urged Alexander II to meet with its representatives 'to deliberate on the general needs of the empire'.[18] The implication of their request was clear; they wanted to establish that they had a formal right to be consulted about the way in which Russia was to be governed. Alexander II made a robust response to their request, writing to them that

> The reforms which have been successfully completed during the ten years of my reign and those reforms even at present being completed by my orders sufficiently attest to my constant concern to improve and perfect in so far as possible . . . the various branches of the state structure. The right of initiative in the main aspects of this gradual improvement belongs exclusively to me, and is indissolubly bound to the autocratic power entrusted to me by God. The past, in the eyes of all my subjects, must be the guarantee of the future. To none of them is it allowed to give prior notice to my incessant care for the well-being of Russia, or to decide beforehand questions about the basic principle of her state institutions. No class has the right to speak in the name of other classes. No one is called to take upon himself before me petitions about the general welfare and needs of the state. Such departures from the order established by existing legislation can only hinder me in the execution of my aims, in no case facilitating the achievement of that end to which they might be directed. I am firmly convinced that in the future I will no longer be confronted with such hindrances on the part of the Russian gentry, whose centuries-long services to the throne and fatherland are always in my memory, and in whom my trust has always been and is now unshakeable.[19]

During 1865, the newly established St Petersburg *zemstvo* attempted to flex its muscles by actually offering advice to the emperor on how to govern the empire: Alexander II took a much more severe line: the *zemstvo* was suspended for a period and its members received a fierce rebuke from the Tsar for its impudence in attempting to encroach on his powers. The regime did not accept that the principle of popular representation could be extended from local government to the work of the national administration and it continued to resist calls for any form of national assembly. As the *zemstvo* became more entrenched in Russian provincial society, however, they became more confident of their position and began to assert their views more forcefully and regularly. Russian victory in war with Turkey in 1877–78 resulted in the creation of a constitutional and democratic Bulgaria and this prompted Russian liberals to question why Russia itself could not have representative institutions. Their opinions were intensified by the upsurge in terrorism that took place in the late 1870s. Most of the *zemstvo* reacted to the government's calls for assistance in combatting terrorism by passing resolutions that condemned the terrorists and vowed complete loyalty to the emperor, but a number went much further and again raised the issue of continuing the reforms of the 1860s and the need for fundamental constitutional reform. The Poltava provincial *zemstvo* emphasised that 'only by the joint efforts of the government and the entire *zemstvo* can we decisively overcome the propaganda undertaken by the enemies of government and of society'.[20] The most extreme example of *zemstvo* rebelliousness was from Chernigov, where liberal members made a comprehensive attack on the government's policies and refused to offer any support to the regime in its struggle with revolution. The local authorities responded to these attacks by prohibiting the public from attending the session at which the formal resolution was to be discussed, and when the emperor was informed of the views being expressed by the Chernigov members, he immediately ruled that *zemstvo* assemblies were to hold no further discussion of the terrorism issue. This did not prevent some *zemstvo* from pursuing the issue of constitutional change under other pretexts: a widespread cholera outbreak in 1879 provoked a number of *zemstvo* to call for the summoning of a national *zemstvo* congress, ostensibly to debate the best ways to tackle the cholera epidemic, but in reality a way of trying to unite opposition to the government and to press for some form of popular participation in the work of national government. The government refused the request for a national congress on this issue, as it had on every occasion when such a meeting had been mooted, stressing that it regarded the *zemstvo* as having an 'exclusively local character'.[21] But, even while the regime was refusing these requests, men close to the heart of Romanov power were contemplating just such a policy themselves.

Terrorists were becoming more audacious in their assaults on the regime. In April 1879, Alexander II was lucky to escape unhurt from an attempt to shoot him while he was out walking. This was followed by an attempt to blow up the imperial train and, in February 1880, by a dramatic bomb explosion in the Winter Palace itself in St Petersburg. The emperor was again fortunate to avoid death or injury, but this series of attacks on his life prompted the government to take action. A week after the palace bomb explosion, Alexander appointed General M. T. Loris-Melikov to head a Supreme Executive Commission devoted to the suppression of sedition and the restoration of order. Improving policing was a crucial part of Loris-Melikov's plans, but he also wanted to address the root causes of radical discontent. This required work in almost every area of government policy, but he initially rejected the idea of extending representation into national government, arguing that such reforms 'could be harmful [as] the people do not think of them and would not understand them, and the government is not yet ready to answer the criticisms that representation would express'.[22] But, as Loris-Melikov's experience of government deepened and he prepared more far-reaching plans for the reform of the Ministry of Internal Affairs, intending to turn it into the heart of the empire's government, he came to believe that the introduction of a limited form of representation could help to revitalise the autocracy. Loris-Melikov recognised that the existing method of legislating was inadequate since it was not based on any sound institutional framework. Introducing a limited degree of popular participation into the legislative process would help to provide an outlet for the increasingly vociferous calls by social groups to play a part in the political process. The proposals that Loris-Melikov put forward in January 1881 were deliberately presented as being firmly in the Russian tradition and owing nothing to European concepts of government. He used the model of the editing commissions that had prepared the emancipation legislation of 1861 and proposed a three-stage process for legislating. The first level would comprise commissions made up essentially of bureaucrats, but they could also include 'experts' appointed by the Tsar. It was the second stage that would include elected representatives: a General Commission would consider all legislative proposals. This commission would include members of the preparatory commissions, along with two representatives from each of the provinces with *zemstvo* and two representatives from each of the major cities of the empire. The final stage of the legislative process was to be the State Council, and Loris-Melikov proposed that its membership should be augmented by 10 to 15 representatives of the *zemstvo* and cities. After discussions with the Tsar and his senior advisers, popular representation was eliminated from this final stage of the legislative process, but the emperor was prepared to sanction the other parts of the reform and 4 March 1881 was set as the date for the formal enactment of Loris-Melikov's proposals. However, on 1 March Alexander II was assassinated and the idea of popular representation in government died with him.

Both the final two Romanov monarchs were wholly opposed to countenancing any form of popular participation in government, and the idea was swept from the regime's agenda for almost a quarter of a century after Alexander II's assassination. It took the revolution of 1905, and the threat that it posed to the very existence of the Russian state, to force the idea of popular representation back onto the government's agenda. In the middle of December 1904, faced with military disaster in the Far East and a cacophony of calls for domestic reform, the regime promised some concessions, such as easing press censorship and allowing greater freedom of religion, but Nicholas II, acting on the advice of the wily Sergei Witte, the former Minister of Finance, rejected granting members of local councils any form of participation in the work of central government. These concessions met with a frosty response from liberal groups and the aftermath of the events of 9 January 1905 – Bloody Sunday – demonstrated that the autocracy would have to do far more before it could reassert its authority. The concessions which the regime made during 1905 were wrested from it grudgingly. There was considerable debate inside the government about the best way of dealing with the revolution which threatened to engulf it. The policies of repression which had been the mainstay of the Russian state were called into question by Witte, who argued that instead of dealing with the symptoms of discontent, the government should address itself to the real causes of the strikes and rural uprisings.[23] Little by little the regime moved towards granting a constitution; in February the government announced that it would allow 'elected representatives of the people to take part in preliminary discussion of legislation', but when the details of the scheme were revealed in August its limitations were made clear. The State Duma, the national representative body, was only to be a consultative institution and elections were to be indirect with the franchise heavily skewed towards large landowners and the peasantry, excluding workers and most urban inhabitants. The huge renewed upsurge in discontent during the autumn forced the government to acknowledge that a consultative assembly was insufficient to satisfy its critics and Nicholas II accepted, albeit with severe reservations, that the Duma should be transformed into a legislative body. The October Manifesto which announced this change of heart also declared that the new Duma would be elected on a wider franchise than originally planned, and that the Russian people should be granted basic civil rights, including freedom of speech, conscience, assembly and association.

After October 1905 the Tsar increasingly resented that he had been compelled to concede a legislative parliament which limited his autocratic power. No longer could the emperor act precisely as he wanted, for now legislation had to be approved by the Duma before it could become law. The government moved to limit the effect of this concession as soon as it was clear that order was being successfully restored to the empire in the spring of 1906. New Fundamental Laws for the empire were issued in April 1906. The State Council was reformed to become the second chamber in the legislative process, to be comprised of both members appointed by the Tsar and representatives elected by corporate bodies in the empire.[24] This arrangement guaranteed that the State Council would be solidly conservative in outlook and able to block bills passed by the Duma, while the legislative process was completed by making the Tsar's approval the final condition for the enactment of a law.[25] The Fundamental Laws continued to describe the monarch as an 'autocrat', and he could issue emergency legislation when the Duma and State Council were in recess. Although such decrees had to be submitted to the legislature for approval within two months of it meeting again, the government deliberately used this power to allow field courts martial to operate between August 1906 and April 1907 while the Duma was not sitting and then let the legislation lapse rather than face its certain defeat by introducing it into the Duma.[26] More than 1000 death sentences were handed down by the field courts martial during their eight months of existence.

The budgetary powers of the legislature were severely circumscribed by the Fundamental Laws which exempted expenditure on the army, navy and imperial court from the Duma's jurisdiction. Although the franchise for the first elections to the Duma was limited and had been devised with the intention that a conservative peasantry would cast its votes for candidates who would support the Tsarist regime, this judgement proved to be very wide of the mark. The First Duma, which met in April 1906, was dominated by the Kadets – the Constitutional-Democratic Party – the embodiment of the liberal movement, and the Trudoviki, a largely peasant party more radical than the liberal Kadets.[27] Government and Duma found themselves wholly at loggerheads and after less than three months the Duma was dissolved and an interval of more than six months interposed before the Second Duma was to meet. These new elections produced a body little different from its predecessor and the situation of deadlock was repeated. After little more than three months the Duma was again dissolved, but this time the government took more radical action to ensure that the composition of the Duma would be more in line with its own thinking. On 3 June 1907, the day after the Second Duma had been dissolved, the government illegally altered the franchise by reducing peasant participation and increasing the representation given to landowners and urban property owners.[28] This had a profound effect on the results of the elections for the Third Duma, which resulted in the representation of the left being dramatically reduced so that the Kadets and Trudoviki together made up only 15 per cent of the deputies. The largest single group in the new Duma was the Octobrists, a centre party which took its name from the October Manifesto of 1905 which had set up the legislative Duma, and which the government hoped would be a reliable ally. Parties on the right also gained substantial support, taking one third of the seats.

While the Russian regime was concerned to ensure a pliant Duma, the government was also committed to making fundamental reforms. The constitutional changes of 1905 had also brought about for the first time the establishment of proper cabinet government, with the Council of Ministers transformed into a forum for the discussion of policy and its chairman taking the role of prime minister. Between 1906 and 1911 this post was occupied by Peter Stolypin, who enunciated a policy of 'pacification and renewal' for Russia. He believed that the two parts of this policy had to run parallel, for to relax the fight against terrorism would result in such havoc that reform could not be implemented, while to abandon reform would be to cease the attempt at removing the causes of the discontent which fed the revolutionary fervour. In 1906 and 1907 the government introduced a whole series of proposals into the Duma: a major agrarian reform; bills to extend civil rights; the reform of local government; changes to the education system; the reform of emergency powers and a bill to reform local justice. Stolypin intended fundamentally to alter Russia through his reform programme. He believed that 'renewal must begin at the bottom'[29] and declared that his reforms were predicated on the creation of 'a wealthy, well-to-do peasantry, for where there is prosperity there is also, of course, enlightenment and real freedom'.[30] This transformation of Russia would bring into being a class of independent peasant landowners, freed from the shackles of the peasant commune. In addition, Stolypin argued that the Russian state itself had to be transformed so that the ethos of arbitrary government was swept away and replaced with a commitment by the state to itself being governed by law. These twin areas of reform were designed to remove the underlying causes of discontent and to establish the Tsarist state as a strong and modern institution.

Reformers did not, however, have the political field to themselves in Russia after 1905. Nicholas II himself believed that the constitutional changes of 1905 had been wrung out of him and were an affront to his God-given autocracy. The success of the regime's repressive policies during 1906 encouraged the emperor and the conservative elite of Russia to believe that reform was no longer necessary and that the state could revert to its previous patterns of behaviour. There was also a considerable popular movement which supported the traditional position of the autocracy and which was able to mobilise considerable grass-roots support for the monarch. The new legislative processes proved to be cumbersome and, lacking a 'government party' in the Duma, the government found it very difficult to make progress with its legislative programme.[31] It is indicative that the only one of Stolypin's reforms to come into force – the agrarian reform – was enacted outside the normal Duma procedure. The rest of the government's reforms fell by the wayside during 1908 and 1909 as Stolypin realised that, if he was to remain in power and retain the confidence of the Tsar, he had to move to the right. The post-1905 Russian system of government had gone some way towards moderating the autocracy, but in the last resort it was the monarch who was able to dismiss ministers and to whose opinions, therefore, ministers had to defer. In 1911 Stolypin was assassinated in mysterious circumstances, and Russian government from then until the outbreak of war in 1914 reverted substantially to its pre-1905 character.

The institutions of government that Russia took with it into the First World War were unable to provide the degree of unity between state and people that the experience of intense and prolonged warfare demanded.[32] The Duma met only for short periods during the war. The government was very fearful of providing a forum in which opposition could be voiced and, after a single-day session in July 1914 to vote for war credits – the additional finance that the government needed to fight a war – the Duma did not meet again until the government permitted a three-day sitting in January 1915. Severe Russian military reverses in the spring and summer of 1915 meant that the regime had to accede to demands for the recall of the Duma, and the session in July 1915 witnessed vehement attacks on the government, with some going so far as to demand the arraignment of Sukhomlinov, the Minister of War, for treason.[33] Almost three-quarters of the Duma's deputies formed themselves into a group that demanded 'the formation of a unified government of individuals who have the confidence of the country and are in agreement with the legislative institutions about the need for the rapid implementation of a definite programme'.[34] This Progressive Bloc was viewed with utter disdain by Nicholas II: the experience of war made him all the more determined to hold on to his prerogatives. The Duma could only rant in impotent rage as Russia slipped closer towards catastrophe, reaching boiling point in November 1916 when Paul Miliukov, the leader of the Kadet party, delivered a speech in the Duma in which he asked: 'When the Duma declares again and again that the home front must be organised for a successful war and the government continues to insist that to organise the country means to organise a revolution – is this stupidity or treason?'[35]

The institutional structures of the empire that had proved effective in governing the Russian state during much of Romanov rule proved unequal to the task of coping with a full-scale war. Once Russia began to experience modernisation and to develop a more cohesive society, its institutional structure experienced growing stresses. Its highly centralised institutional structure did give the empire very great strength, allowing the monarch to impose his will across the state without fear of his policies being diluted or easily thwarted. But, this proved to be much less appropriate when a more complex society developed in Russia. The ministerial structure matched models of government elsewhere in Europe, but without a prime minister it was still entirely dependent on the emperor and allowed little opportunity for the government to reflect a more complex view of Russia. The deep conservatism of Russia's monarchs, and their dominance of its institutions, meant that their view of Russia's government met little institutional challenge until 1905. There was never a balance between the personal power of the monarch and the authority that the institutions of government could wield, and this proved to be a serious flaw once Russian society became more educated and independent. Russia's institutions were never able to escape from the dead hand of autocracy and to establish themselves as autonomous. They were never able to act as a means of mediating between the monarch and society, and while this was less of a problem during the eighteenth century, it was very difficult to isolate Russia from the trends that were taking place in western political thinking and institutional structures after 1800. Institutions were unable to modernise themselves without the agreement of the emperor and, even at the very end of the Tsarist state's existence, there was barely sufficient social pressure to bring about political change. Even the political changes of 1905 were rapidly compromised as the state hedged the new institutions about with restrictions. Russia's institutions were thus insulated from social pressure; in some ways this gave them great strength and power, but it was also a weakness that resulted in their ossification and meant that they became increasingly distant from the people of the Russian empire.

Chapter 5:   Provincial Authority

The dispersed Russian state, expanding rapidly across difficult terrain, could not rely on an administration in St Petersburg, situated in the far north-western corner of the empire, to govern the empire adequately. Distance and climate meant that the hold of the centre on Russia's provinces was inconsistent, especially in the period before railways began to spread their tentacles across the empire in the middle of the nineteenth century. It was therefore important for the state to devise methods of cementing its power across its domains, but the geography of the empire, together with the autocratic ethos of the Russian state, presented huge challenges to the St Petersburg regime. The physical nature of the empire made it more sensible for the central apparatus of government to devolve significant powers to the provinces, but this conflicted with the state's need to retain absolute control across the empire. The tensions between these two conflicting pressures persisted throughout the Romanov period.

Provincial Government

Peter the Great's reforming instincts extended into the provinces. He inherited a complex and confused structure of provincial administration, with no clear and consistent lines of responsibility. The main representative of pre-Petrine government in the provinces was the *voevoda*, but his duties varied from region to region, and Russian towns were in a particularly confused situation, with entirely haphazard

Figure 5.1 The Provinces of European Russia.
Source: Adapted from D. Longley, *The Longman Companion to Imperial Russia 1689–1917* (London, 2000), p. xiii.

administration. Border towns were often under the control of the Foreign Affairs department, with others being the responsibility of an assortment of regional and functional *prikazy*. This state of affairs was unsatisfactory in many ways; the disorganised state of local government made for inefficiency and meant that it was difficult to implement consistent policies across the Russian state. The absence of clear and consistent structures also made corruption much more common inside Russian local government and there was much evidence of local officials siphoning off funds into their own pockets and accepting bribes from the population whom they governed. Peter the Great took early steps to improve local administration: in 1698 he legislated to provide for the collection of taxes by officials other than the *voevody*, in an attempt to ensure that revenues did actually reach central government, and in the following year changes were made to municipal administration with the same aim. But these reforms only tinkered with the real problems of Russian local administration, so in 1708 Peter put in place a local government structure that, in its fundamentals, was to persist up to the collapse of Tsarism in 1917. He created eight provinces, each headed by a governor, giving these officials very substantial powers. They were to be responsible for the key task of tax collection as well as for ensuring that the army in their province was adequately manned and equipped.

Peter's governors were men of great power and influence, appointed because he could rely on their loyalty and probity.[1] But this viceregal model of local administration proved unsatisfactory for Peter once the military situation had stabilised somewhat in the following decade. In 1718 and 1719, Peter attempted to impose on Russia a model of provincial government based on the Swedish system. This reform reduced the authority of the provincial governor and attempted to impose a well-defined bureaucratic structure onto provincial administration. But the early eighteenth-century Russian state did not have the bureaucratic capacity to be able to implement a system of such complexity. This Swedish model of administration provided a forty-six-paragraph definition of the duties of the chief provincial administrator, and instituted a great range of official posts in the provinces to enable the administration to function. But provincial Russia during Peter the Great's reign was still an unsophisticated place, where the most basic tasks of maintaining order and collecting tax revenues placed great stresses on the local administrators. It was wholly unrealistic to expect that this environment could simply have an alien system of administration imposed upon it, especially since Russia had no real tradition of public administration to build on. Peter the Great's initial model of immensely powerful governors was more suited to both the tasks that local administration needed to perform and the tough conditions of Russian provincial life.

It was only in the reign of Catherine II that the Russian state began properly to construct a sound system of provincial administration. The limitations of the Petrine system very quickly became obvious to Catherine's advisers when they began work on the reform of local government in 1768. They discovered that the official maps of Russia's provinces were grossly inaccurate: 'the limits of many provinces were not indicated or incorrectly indicated, the limits of provinces and districts were not indicated at all', while two new provinces and some towns were not marked on the maps at all. Russia was only just reaching the stage where its bureaucratic capacity was sufficient to enable it to understand and organise its domains effectively. It took a considerable time before Catherine was ready to enact her plans for reform of local administration and it was only in 1775 that Russian local government was reformed. The European part of the empire was divided into provinces, each of 300,000 to 400,000 inhabitants, and these were then divided into districts (*uezdy*) of some 20,000 to 30,000 people. Initially, the reform created 25 provinces, but this doubled to reach 50 by 1796.

Each province was headed by a governor, and these men were to become the most significant figures in Russia's government outside St Petersburg. The provincial governor had the right to correspond directly with the sovereign and was given very wide-ranging duties. He was charged with 'the supervision of the proper functioning of all organs of local administration, the redressing of injustices and watching over the interests of the injured and oppressed'.[2] But his precise role was confused: there was no clear definition of the governor's exact status as he was variously described as the 'head' (*nachal'nik*), and the 'direct head' (*neposredstvenyy nachal'nik*) of the province as well as 'the representative of supreme government power' so that he had to fulfil a dual role as the highest government authority in the area and as the chief agent of the Ministry of Internal Affairs.[3] As the former, the governor had the right to inspect all government institutions in his province, irrespective of which ministry they came under, and to supervise the work of local self-government. As the latter, he was responsible for all the local branches of the Interior

Ministry, including the police force. The governor was chairman of the provincial administration board, four subsidiary boards dealing in the main with economic matters, and five other committees such as the local statistical committee and the military service board. It has been estimated that the nineteenth-century gubernatorial chancellery would deal with an average of 100,000 papers a year, with the governor himself seeing some 300–400 daily.[4] It is no wonder that a senior civil servant wrote that 'the Russian governor could be the busiest man in the world, if the quantity of work he performed was measured by the number of official papers which passed through his hands'.[5] In addition to these specific duties the governor was also charged with the preservation of the rights of the Orthodox Church, of the gentry and other estates and with the maintenance of public order. The Ministry of Internal Affairs was responsible for nominating candidates for gubernatorial posts to the Tsar, but despite the immense burden of work that the job entailed there were no fixed qualifications for it and it was evident that the volume of work threatened the governor's ability to perform his duties.[6] The governor's position was ambivalent: he was both the Tsar's viceroy in the province as well as being the representative of one particular ministry. The link with the monarch gave the governor a status that was unmatched in Russian government and imbued his position with the aura of autocracy that character-ised the monarch's own position. Although direct contact between governor and sovereign became increasingly uncommon, monarchs did take considerable interest in the reports that governors presented each year on the condition of their provinces, and the marginal notes made by the Tsar on governors' reports were discussed by the formal machinery of central government. While many gubernatorial reports were formulaic in nature, some governors took the oppor-tunity to make a clear statement about the economic and social needs of their provinces, in the hope that their pressure might result in improvements for their own province.[7] The Tsar could also take particular note of a governor's performance of his duties and single him out for attention. This was the case when Peter Stolypin was appointed as Minister of Internal Affairs in April 1906: he had been governor of Saratov during the revolutionary year of 1905 and his stalwart performance in putting down rebellion was quickly noted by Nicholas II, who was keen to see him take charge of the policing of the entire empire as Interior Minister. This 'viceregal' function provided the governor with powers that no other government servant enjoyed; he was able to exercise the absolute authority of the monarch on the smaller canvas of his province and could do so with little fear of challenge.

This authority was enhanced by the governor's connection to the Ministry of Internal Affairs, the chief powerhouse of government authority across the expanse of the empire. Governors were able to use the ministry's authority as the main engine of law and order to exert significant coercive authority in their province, but they were also able to sidestep some of the demands placed upon them by the ministry, asserting that they were responsible for the good of the province as a whole, rather than just being subordinate to the ministry. St Petersburg was never entirely confident about the extent to which provincial governors were over-reaching their authority: the Ministry of Internal Affairs ensured that it received police reports on the governors' activities and St Petersburg also scoured the local press for indications that things were not well in the provinces. An article that identified problems would frequently provoke a brisk request to the governor for a report on the issue discussed in the press. Governors were still able to keep a step ahead of St Petersburg, however, as a result of the sheer bulk of the tasks that they were supposed to carry out. Governors soon discovered that the level of supervision that St Petersburg could actually exercise over them was limited and that they had very great discretion in deciding which of the myriad of instructions they received from the capital required their attention. Governors disobeyed St Petersburg's instructions with considerable impunity: during the famine of 1891, the Viatka provincial governor prohibited the export of grain from his province, despite repeated instructions from the Ministry of Internal Affairs to allow it.[8] Even though the Ministry of Internal Affairs did have sanctions that it could use against recalcitrant governors, such as denying them decorations or awards, it proved very reluctant to use them. In part, this was due to the very high social status that many governors enjoyed: they were usually chosen from amongst the wealthiest members of the Russian nobility and financial and other sanctions would have little effect on this group of men. It was also true that, by the middle of the nineteenth century, the Russian gubernatorial cadre included men who had very extensive and penetrating knowledge of their own provinces. This was not true of all governors, however: in 1910, the governor of Riazan was sharply criticised both for incompetence and, along with his deputy, for corruption.[9] St Petersburg did have a grudging respect for the competence of the majority of governors and was reluctant to use its heavy hand too firmly, lest it stymie the work that the governors performed.

Catherine's reform divided each province into districts, but this proved to be less successful. The district had no figure who corresponded to the provincial governor. Although the average population of the nearly 500 districts at the end of the nineteenth century was approaching 200,000, the central official there was the local marshal of the nobility, a figure elected by his fellow nobles and without any formal links to the government. There was no organisation similar to the provincial administration board to coordinate local government in the district. This situation had arisen unintentionally; by an edict of 1766 the district marshal of the nobility was appointed only as the chairman of the local assembly of nobility, and he was elected by that meeting to represent noble interests, but the state progressively imposed more and more administrative tasks upon him, since it was unwilling to establish new institutions with an independent staff and preferred to use existing officials. The marshal of the nobility proved to be the most convenient of such officials, for he already played a prominent part in local life, he was unpaid and, since there was a shortage of qualified officials in the districts, he could be relied on to bring 'a sense of legality and general culture to the administration'.[10] By 1899, the code of laws listed, in addition to his duties concerned purely with the nobility, 11 bodies of which the marshal was chairman and a further 13 of which he was an ordinary member – and this was an incomplete description of the marshal's responsibilities.[11] Although much of the district administration was unified in the office of marshal of the nobility, this was a purely personal unity since the marshal had no administrative apparatus to coordinate the work of the various bodies with which he was connected and this, together with a shortage of nobles willing to take on the job, meant that the district administration became increasingly chaotic. The state had no formal means by which it could control the activities of the marshal of the nobility, and instead had to rely on the goodwill and efficiency of the hundreds of marshals. While some marshals did take their duties seriously and were prepared to act as unpaid civil servants, many marshals adopted a casual attitude to the government work that they were expected to perform and paid it only the most cursory attention. This made it very difficult for St Petersburg to exert proper control over the administration of the districts, and it helps to account for the concentration of power in the hands of the provincial governors.

The only official who was directly subordinated to the governor in the district was the police superintendent (*ispravnik*), an official who required no qualifications to be appointed, but whose responsibilities extended beyond the preservation of law and order to cover tax administration and conscription. Before the emancipation of the serfs in the 1860s, the process of exerting authority over the peasant population was easier, since it was clearly in the interests of the serf-owning nobility to keep a careful watch on their serfs. But after 1861, the government discovered that it was much more difficult to impose its authority in the countryside without this informal network and it sought other ways to ensure that its policies could be implemented in the depths of the Russian countryside. In 1889, the post of land captain (*zemskii nachal'nik*) was established as the main official responsible for the peasantry. The office of land captain was a substitute for the justice of the peace, and appointments were made by the provincial governor in consultation with the district marshal of the nobility. Each land captain had responsibility for a part of each district, with over 2400 covering the empire, and was responsible to the governor through the district conference of land captains, which was subordinated to the provincial board on peasant affairs. Both a property and an educational qualification existed for candidates for appointment as land captains, but the latter could be dispensed with if there was a shortage of suitable people, and this only served to accentuate the trend towards the appointment of local gentry, who were motivated by the salary offered rather than by the tradition of service.[12] Supervision of the land captains was carried out by the district marshal of the nobility and the governor, but this was ineffective since the governor's responsibilities meant that he was 'too busy to carry out actual inspections and so they remained on paper', whilst in the case of the marshal a land captain wrote that 'the marshal is a local noble and the land captains are local nobles, the marshal's electors. . . . The marshal is the defender of the land captains and not their controller.'[13] It was made even less likely that a land captain's decisions would be challenged by making the district conference of land captains the body which heard appeals against his judicial rulings, and it was noted that these conferences would never overrule an individual member's decision. The powers of the land captain included all the functions of the former justices of the peace, together with a number of new ones which allowed him to make decisions on complaints about peasant officials, to overturn resolutions passed by rural district meetings and to carry out police functions in areas where there were no other police officials,[14] this last being a particularly onerous task since there were only some 8500 village policemen under the control of the Ministry of Internal Affairs.

Most of the land captains' time was spent in supervising the work of peasant self-government. This existed on two levels; each village had its own meeting of the heads of peasant households, which elected one of their number to act as elder (*sel'skii starosta*), and this pattern was repeated in the rural district. The village elder dealt with the collection of taxes from his area, could try the most minor judicial cases – where the punishment did not exceed a fine of one ruble or detention for two days – and acted as a clerk for illiterate peasants. The rural district was a much more significant organisation; it had been set up in 1861 and was intended to contain not more than 2000 male peasants but by 1900 it exceeded this limit in many cases, although the territorial area remained constant with a diameter of about 25 miles. Rural district government was made up of the peasant meeting, which consisted of one representative for every ten households and the district elder, elected by the meeting. He was responsible for the maintenance of law and order and for implementing the decisions of the district meeting, which had responsibility for economic and social matters, in particular education and the dispensing of charity. It was difficult to get good candidates to stand for election as district elder, as Donald Mackenzie Wallace noted: 'The more laborious and well-to-do peasants, unless they wish to abuse their position directly or indirectly for their own advantage, try to escape election as office bearers, and leave the administration in the hands of the less respectable members.'[15] This resulted in widespread corruption amongst peasant officials so that it was not unknown for districts to have to pay their taxes twice over as the elder had lost the proceeds of the first collection through speculation. With the growth in size of the rural district had come a corresponding increase in the numbers entitled to attend the district meeting, making it an unwieldy body whose size hindered discussion and decision-making. The majority of the Russian population lived under the control of two officials, the land captain and the local policeman, both eventually responsible to the Ministry of Internal Affairs, with the peasants having no satisfactory method of redress against the officials' actions.

Nineteenth-century bureaucrats recognised that Catherine's reforms had only addressed some of the issues surrounding the local government of the empire. A rapidly growing population and an increasingly complex society demanded a much more sophisticated system of local government that would provide clear lines of responsibility that reached down deep into the Russian countryside. In the late 1850s, the Ministry of Internal Affairs began to consider how the provincial and district administrations could be reorganised, but it came to no final conclusions, since emancipation and the introduction of the *zemstvo* intervened in the process. A second major set of proposals for change came from an 1884 commission chaired by M. S. Kakhanov, Deputy Minister of Internal Affairs. Kakhanov recognised that local government was disconnected and in need of wholesale change: he recommended the unification of the different local institutions, giving the governor the power of supervision over all non-military government institutions and officials in the province. The writ of the provincial governor was to run through the districts too, with the district administration being subordinated to the governor, and district officials having only very limited autonomy. But Alexander III was disinclined to make any substantive changes to local government, instead wanting to concentrate on the strengthening of central power. Local government reform disappeared from the agenda until 1906, when the newly appointed Stolypin proposed reforming local government, drawing on his own experience as a provincial governor. He too envisaged the creation of a unified set of local institutions, dominated by the provincial governor, but his ministerial colleagues were very reluctant to see a single official given so much power and they acted to dilute his proposals.[16] The tensions over local government reform demonstrated the power of provincial officials: the governor was able to operate with few limits on his power but, at the same time, the extent of this authority meant that it was difficult for this power to be exercised effectively. Proposals to further entrench gubernatorial power caused concern since there was no guarantee that increasing the governor's authority would do anything to enable Russia's provinces to be governed any more effectively. At the same time, local government reform also provoked inter-ministerial rivalry and conflict in the capital. The governor's position as essentially a subordinate of the Ministry of Internal Affairs meant that attempts to increase his powers caused concern to other central government ministries who saw their own authority coming under threat. While there was general agreement from the middle of the nineteenth century onwards that Russia's local government was in severe need of reform; institutional conflicts made reform very difficult to achieve.[17]

The Zemstvo

While reform to the administrative structures of local government proved very difficult to accomplish in the nineteenth century, Alexander II was, nevertheless, able to introduce dramatic changes into the way in which Russia's provinces and districts were governed. He eschewed attempting to reform administrative structures, instead embarking on the much more radical step of introducing elected councils in the countryside and in Russian towns and cities.[18] This was a dramatic change, as far-reaching in its principle as the emancipation itself. The rationale of the state for making this change was very far from its embracing of the principles of democracy or of popular representation. The view of P. A. Valuev, the Minister of Internal Affairs, was that the introduction of elected local councils was a means of compensating the nobility for the loss of their power that had come with emancipation. The original intention was to create councils that were dominated by the nobility, without any desire to see them as properly representative of the population as a whole. But more radical reformers were able to extend the scope of the new zemstvo. The 1864 legislation that brought them into being set out two levels of zemstvo: in the province and in the district. Initially, zemstvo were established in 33 provinces and in the 359 districts that comprised them. The process of establishing the new institutions was gradual: more than 25 of the new provincial zemstvo were opened by 1866, but it then took nearly a further decade before the last zemstvo appeared in Ufa. No further zemstvo came into existence until the last years of the Tsarist regime; in 1911, they were established in six western provinces of the empire, and in 1912 three further provinces gained zemstvo. By the time the First World War broke out, zemstvo were operating in 44 provinces and 441 districts of the empire, with more than 60 per cent of the empire's population living in areas that possessed zemstvo.

Elections to the zemstvo were conducted through electoral curiae: members of the district zemstvo were to be elected directly by landowners, business owners and merchants. But, the peasantry also played a part in the process through a system of indirect elections. Peasant assemblies were to choose electors who then went on to meetings where they would elect members of the *zemstvo*. This process brought about significant representation for the peasantry in the new councils. The first elections to the district *zemstvo* resulted in the nobility taking 42 per cent of the seats, but the peasantry were close behind with 38 per cent of the members. This was still a gross underrepresentation of the peasantry, since they comprised some 80 per cent of the population, but it gave them a formal status in the Russian polity far in excess of anything they had ever enjoyed before. The members of the provincial *zemstvo* were elected by the district *zemstvo* assemblies and it was thus inevitable that noble representation in the provincial assemblies would be magnified. Almost three-quarters of the members of the first provincial *zemstvo* came from the nobility, and the peasantry only gained 11 per cent of the seats. The composition of the *zemstvo* changed in the following 20 years. There were significant increases in the numbers of merchants in some *zemstvo*, and there were sharp regional differences in the dynamics of noble and peasant representation. Overall, the proportion of seats taken by the nobility in the provincial *zemstvo* increased slightly to reach 83 per cent by 1883, but some provinces witnessed a decline in noble representation, a trend that was especially clear in north-eastern Russia.

The *zemstvo* assemblies met annually in the provincial and district towns and were chaired by the marshal of the nobility. These meetings rapidly became a focus for rural society, and were often accompanied by significant social activities. Everyday business was conducted by the *zemstvo* board, elected by the annual assembly, which was made up of a chairman and a minimum of two members, although the assembly could increase this to six members if it wanted. The *zemstvo* were given significant responsibilities. Their central duties were in the economic and social sphere, and they involved themselves in local economic affairs, education, health care and communications. They were given real autonomy by being able to levy taxation independently of central government, so that St Petersburg could not frustrate the ambitions of the new councils by simply starving them of funds. Indeed, central government found the *zemstvo* so useful that it contributed to their budgets, providing some 20 per cent of their total expenditure by 1914. The *zemstvo* themselves increased their own spending: the Tver provincial *zemstvo*'s budget doubled between 1868 and 1890 and then grew five-fold in the next 25 years. The state did try to place some limits on the way in which the *zemstvo* could operate in the first few years of their existence. In 1867, the chairmen of provincial *zemstvo* were given the power to deprive any *zemstvo* delegates of their right to vote, and they were also permitted to prohibit discussion of any issue considered to be 'outside the competence of the assemblies' and to exclude the public from meetings. At the same time, the government prohibited any form of contact between provincial *zemstvo*, fearful that a national *zemstvo* movement could emerge. These restrictions had only a limited effect, and the *zemstvo* quickly developed into the central providers of services in the Russian countryside.

Even critics of the new councils recognised that their work had some merit through their provision of basic medical and veterinary services, although the financial management of the *zemstvo* was the subject of significant attacks. One provincial governor attacked his *zemstvo* for seeing their independence from central government as the most significant element of their work and for then failing to take a proper interest in the real concerns of the province. He also condemned the *zemstvo* for what he perceived to be its policy of handing out jobs to the favourites of members, suggesting that 'the *zemstvo* appears to have been created for the personal benefit of its members and not for the population of the province'.[19] But others took a more positive view of the *zemstvo*, seeing them as a force for enhancing social cohesion. Boris Chicherin, a member of the liberal intelligentsia, described the *zemstvo* as 'the flower of the gentry', and was insistent that the presence of peasants was beneficial. He wrote that even though 'it was rare that one of them [the peasant deputies] would get up by himself to speak . . . their main significance was that they were witnesses to what went on in the meeting and could vote for those whom they trusted'.[20] This view was shared by Mackenzie Wallace who was present at the annual meeting of the Novgorod district *zemstvo* in 1870. He wrote that:

What surprised me most was that [the assembly] was composed partly of nobles and partly of peasants – the latter being decidedly in the majority – and that no trace of antagonism seemed to exist between the two classes. Landed proprietors and their ci-devant serfs, emancipated only ten years before, evidently met for the moment on a footing of equality. The discussions were carried on chiefly by the nobles, but on more than one occasion peasant

members rose to speak, and their remarks, always clear, practical
and to the point, were invariably listened to with respectful attention. Instead of that violent antagonism which might have been
expected . . . there was too much unambiguity – a fact indicating
plainly that the majority of the members did not take a very deep
interest in the matters presented to them.[21]

The *zemstvo* embedded themselves deeply into the fabric of Russian
local life during their half-century of existence. Their concern with
problems that affected the everyday life of ordinary Russians, such
as health, agriculture and the condition of roads, brought them
into contact with the population as a whole. *Zemstvo* that took their
responsibilities seriously needed to employ substantial numbers of
people: teachers, doctors and medical assistants, agronomists, veterinary specialists and civil engineers were some of the most significant
specialists who were attracted into the countryside to work. Teachers
were by far the largest professional group employed by the *zemstvo*:
by 1914 they employed more than 46,000 primary school teachers
across the empire, alongside 4300 agronomists, 2300 doctors and
some 9000 medical assistants.[22] This was the first occasion on which
significant numbers of professional people had been attracted to work
in Russia's villages and small towns and, although they represented
only a tiny proportion of the rural population, they enjoyed an influence that was wholly disproportionate to their number. This 'third
element' of rural government – the first two elements were the centrally appointed bureaucrats and the elected *zemstvo* members – were
able to influence both ordinary Russians and, more importantly, the
elected members of the *zemstvo*. The nature of the work of this 'third
element' did predispose them to take a view of rural society and its
needs that was far more sympathetic than that of the state's own
officials. Many of these teachers, agronomists and the like wanted to
work in the countryside because they believed that they could help
to ameliorate the conditions in which ordinary Russians lived. They
frequently stood in opposition to the autocratic state and believed
that the powers of Tsarism needed to be curbed. In 1900, the vice-
governor of Samara province warned of the emergence of the threat
that was being posed by 'rootless radical *zemstvo* professionals' who
had managed to convince the elected members to approve projects
that they themselves wanted to undertake. They were able to gain
such significant influence that the elected *zemstvo* deputies frequently

took only limited interest in the real work of the *zemstvo* and were happy to adopt proposals put to them by their employees.

Even liberal *zemstvo* members agreed about the apathy of most members: Dmitrii Shipov wrote that 'in essence the *zemstvo* board has no choice but to rely exclusively on the third element, since there is no participation by the assembly at all'.[23] This view of the influence of *zemstvo* employees was exaggerated: the real radicalism that was demonstrated by the *zemstvo*, especially around 1905, was the work of elected members from the nobility. Even though the state had tried hard to prevent the *zemstvo* from developing any form of national identity, it proved unable to contain national *zemstvo* agitation as tensions rose after 1900. National *zemstvo* congresses played an important part in the articulate agitation that eventually wrung the concession of the October Manifesto from Nicholas II, but these congresses were the work of liberally inclined *zemstvo* members, rather than their professional employees. *Zemstvo* staff were more important in the general development of professional associations across the empire, and the Union of Liberation, which came into existence in 1904, acted as an umbrella body for some of these bodies. While political parties were still prohibited, these professional groups could play a role, but once more usual forms of political activity had become possible, the significance of professional groups *per se* diminished.[24]

Well before the upheavals of 1905, the regime had tried to limit the reach of the *zemstvo*. Alexander III's attitudes allowed little place for representative institutions and he and his advisers sought to reduce the influence of the *zemstvo* and to ensure that their members were reliable men who would support the aims of the St Petersburg regime. In 1890, a new *zemstvo* statute was issued which made changes both to the electoral arrangements for the *zemstvo* and to their overall autonomy from the state. After 1890, the peasantry played a much less significant part in *zemstvo* affairs, losing their right to choose deputies independently. Instead, each peasant district would choose a candidate and the provincial governor would select which of these men would become *zemstvo* deputies. The 1890 statute also gave the governor the right to inspect the *zemstvo* executive board and all the institutions that the *zemstvo* controlled, while the governor could now suspend decisions of the *zemstvo* assembly. A decade later, the government legislated to limit the level of tax increases that the *zemstvo* could levy, restricting them to a 3 per cent rise each year. The taxation question was one which St Petersburg approached with great caution.

While restricting the spending power of the *zemstvo* appeared super-
ficially sensible as a means of restricting their influence, the range
of functions that the *zemstvo* dealt with made it much more difficult for the state to curb their financial powers. The St Petersburg
regime wanted to rein in the most articulate critics of the regime,
but it preferred to do this by utilising more traditional bureaucratic
methods of control.

The attempts at counter-reform of the *zemstvo* by Alexander III
brought the relationship between the state and institutions of self-
government into very sharp focus. In the quarter-century after their
foundation in 1864, the *zemstvo* became an essential part of Russian
government. Alexander III's regime could not propose their abolition, any more than it could contemplate the re-introduction of
serfdom. The process of reform that Alexander II had set in train
was irreversible, and the introduction of the *zemstvo* marked a significant weakening in the armour of Tsarism. Before 1864, the state
had reigned triumphant across every aspect of Russian government
and administration and was able, at least in theory, to exercise absolute authority over its servants across the empire. The introduction
of the *zemstvo* was a revolutionary departure for the Romanov regime
as it conceded both the principle that elected representatives could
play a part in the government of Russia and that these elected institutions could act autonomously of central government. Alexander II
did not recognise the enormity of the step that he was taking when he
established the *zemstvo*, seeing it merely as an incremental move that
helped to compensate the nobility for the loss of their formal power
over their serfs. But conceding that representative institutions could
play a part in the work of Russian government began the process
of undermining the solid ramparts of the autocratic regime. The
regime however believed that the work of local self-government could
be kept entirely separate from the activities of the state itself, with the
zemstvo being responsible for matters that were essentially economic
and social and that did not impinge on the political sphere, which was
the exclusive preserve of St Petersburg. This 'public theory' of self-
government held that the interests of central and local government
were discrete and that when it came to political matters, local self-
government had to acknowledge the primacy of the central state and
bow to the wishes of St Petersburg. This was an essentially naive view
of the functioning of government. Without any experience of working
with representative institutions at any level, and buoyed up by the

excitement of being able to make real reforms, Alexander II's advisers believed that this theory could be translated into practice and that distinctions between central and local areas of competence could hold firm. It very quickly became evident that this view of the relationship between St Petersburg and the *zemstvo* was unsustainable. The theoretical view that was adopted by Alexander III's ministers, especially D. A. Tolstoi and A. D. Pazukhin, saw the *zemstvo* as entirely subordinate to the interests of central government. From the 1880s onwards, the regime argued that the only interests in governing Russia were those of the state and that the function of self-government was to carry out those tasks that were devolved to it by central government. This 'state theory' lay behind the 1890 *zemstvo* statute, which declared that changes were being made to the *zemstvo* so that they 'in proper unity with other governmental institutions could carry out with greater success the important state business entrusted to them'.[25] But, this attempt to subdue the *zemstvo* by St Petersburg was doomed to failure. Once the genie of popular representation had been let out of the bottle, it could not be contained, other than by the complete abolition of the *zemstvo*.

By the time the First World War broke out, almost 500 separate *zemstvo* assemblies were operating across the empire. Thousands of Russians had been elected as *zemstvo* members and had gained a taste for participation in the work of self-government. Even though central government was extremely distrustful of accepting that autonomous institutions could play any part in the war effort, the *zemstvo* mobilised their resources to try to ensure Russian victory. Immediately war broke out in the summer of 1914, delegates from 35 provinces met in Moscow and resolved to establish an all-Russian union of *zemstvo*, and this was followed by the creation of a parallel union of towns. The government was insistent that the *zemstvo* union should restrict itself to dealing with military casualties, receiving wounded soldiers from the war ministry and then transporting them to rural hospitals. Central government continued to view the *zemstvo* as simply fulfilling one of the tasks of the state in a time of war, and did not want to allow them any autonomy in helping with the war effort. Circumstances intervened, however, to change fundamentally the role that the *zemstvo* played. It quickly became clear that the conflict would not be swiftly concluded, throwing into confusion the plans that the Russian military – along with every other combatant army – had made for the eventuality of European war. The extent and severity of the war meant that the plans that the military had made to deal with the evacuation of the wounded proved hopelessly inadequate and they rapidly had to turn to the *zemstvo* to take on a much greater share of the work. The *zemstvo* union organised railway trains to move wounded troops away from the battlefront and then equipped and staffed hospitals to treat them. They were quick to organise hospitals, so that within four months of the outbreak of war they were responsible for 1700 hospitals. By February 1915 the union of *zemstvo* had 45 trains under its control, transporting some 16,000 troops at any one time. This was only the beginning of the efforts that the *zemstvo* made: the military author-ities were overwhelmed by the sheer task of fighting the war and found themselves incapable of organising the efficient supplying of the troops. The union of *zemstvo* became heavily involved in schemes to increase the flow of munitions to the army at the front and to provide improved food supplies for the army by obtaining and deliv-ering meat for military rations. As well, the union involved itself in efforts to improve cleanliness and hygiene in the army. The unions of *zemstvo* and towns rapidly developed into one of the central supply organisations for the army: they took on the manufacture of goods, ranging across the whole spectrum of military equipment from shells to boots for the troops. By November 1915 the Moscow city council alone had manufactured 1.4 million caps and 2.1 million gasmasks for the army, as well as having organised the repair of 400,000 pairs of boots and 800,000 trench coats.[26] These direct contributions to the work of the military were matched by *zemstvo* contributions to work in the rear. Russian defeats in 1915 and the huge German advance onto Russian territory set in motion a vast flood of refugees fleeing eastwards as German troops occupied their home towns and villages. The state was bewildered by this great flow of people and was at a loss as to how to deal with refugees. It was evident that the provincial authorities lacked the resources and indeed the desire to cope with these hundreds of thousands of people on the move. It was only the *zemstvo* that possessed the experience of organising local services and could even hope to deal with the resettlement of the refugee popu-lation and they took on the task of inspecting and disinfecting the refugees, as well as dealing with problems of children who had lost their parents. By the middle of 1916, the *zemstvo* had established 300 orphanages to house some 50,000 children.[27]

Even though it was plain that the government itself was incapable of undertaking the tasks that the *zemstvo* were working on, there was significant resistance from the St Petersburg regime to the role that the *zemstvo* were playing in the war effort. Ministers denounced the *zemstvo* as merely being a front for the political ambitions of the Kadet party, the chief liberal opposition to Tsarism. Even during the greatest crisis that the Romanov state had ever endured, central government remained extremely reluctant to contemplate granting real power to elected institutions of self-government. This was not simply because the government distrusted the political ambitions of the *zemstvo*, but it reveals the fundamental contradiction between the autocratic ambitions of the Russian state and the principle of representative self-government. The state's preferred method of governing the provinces of the empire was to impose its power through officials who were directly responsible to St Petersburg and who could exercise authority with the same latitude as central government. For most of the Romanov period, the state did not recognise that there was any distinction between the spheres of competence of central and local government: local administration was precisely that – the administration on the local level of policies determined in St Petersburg. The ethos of the state was to exercise absolute control of its domains and this could only be done if there was consistency of approach at all levels of the state's apparatus. Even though provincial administrators did not always follow the directives of St Petersburg, the state could be sure that the basic style of government remained more or less the same across the empire. The autocratic monarchy was replicated in miniature many times over in Russia's provinces and districts, giving the state a reassurance that the population of the empire was being kept under close control and that its servants across the empire could, and would, take whatever measures were necessary to maintain order. The introduction of *zemstvo* and of elected municipal councils opened a chink in the armour of the state that could not be repaired. Conceding that the principle of representation had a validity in Russia ran wholly counter to the principle of autocracy and, for all the state's attempts to argue that these new institutions had only been brought into existence to perform the bidding of St Petersburg, it could not escape the fact that an autonomous source of authority had been brought into being.

Russian local government encapsulated the arguments that took place over the shape and form of the Romanov state as a whole. The introduction of local self-government offered the opportunity for the Romanov state to begin to renew itself and to modernise its political structures. The limited powers that the *zemstvo* and town councils possessed, along with their skewed social representation, gave the state the chance to rebuild its ties to the nobility, as Valuev had suggested when the idea of elected local government was being mooted. But, the regime was determined not to make compromises with the new elected councils; instead it treated them essentially as a part of the nascent opposition to Tsarism. The *zemstvo* themselves responded to this attitude from the state by increasingly seeing themselves as the custodians of Russia's social conscience, responsible for enhancing the lives of ordinary Russians. The roles of central and local government began to be polarised: the *zemstvo* providing schooling, healthcare, agricultural advice and the like while central government retreated to its core function of maintaining order and authority across the empire.

Chapter 6: Coercion, Police and Justice

The Petrine state was highly interventionist in its approach to government: Peter the Great was determined to transform Russia comprehensively, but his reforms met with overt resistance, and also encountered the inertia inevitable in trying to bring about change to a major state. Peter's approach was to coerce his subjects into complying with his policies: by temperament he was an impatient man who had no desire to wait to persuade people to his point of view. The ethos that Peter developed for his state was one where he set out the direction that he envisaged for Russia and then compelled the Russian people to follow him. The institutionalisation of compulsory service for the nobility was one element of this approach to ruling, but Peter's iron hand extended much further across society.

Peter the Great was intent on using all the resources at his disposal to impose order on Russian society. Maintaining public order was one of the most important tasks that provincial governors had to carry out and it was also one of the most challenging. Banditry was endemic in some parts of eighteenth-century Russia, with gangs made up of runaway serfs, army deserters and escaped prisoners who preyed on landowners, priests and ordinary peasants. Nobles themselves sometimes resorted to organising bands of brigands to rob their neighbours and thus enhance their own wealth and power. In the regions on Russia's western borders, there was a serious problem as escaped serfs attempted to flee into Poland to avoid being caught and returned to their masters. In the Russian heartland, where such peasants could not escape abroad, the authorities strove to track down people who were roaming freely and to return them to the serfowner or to the military. Early eighteenth-century rural Russia was in many ways a wild and lawless place, where the writ of central government hardly ran and where legality hardly applied. The state experienced considerable difficulties in imposing even the most basic level of control over its subjects and had only a rudimentary police force to use to provide order.

Policing

The formal coercive apparatus of the state remained quite limited: police numbers were small and it was difficult for them to exert authority in the Russian countryside. There was no national police force in Petrine Russia and formal police forces only existed in St Petersburg, Moscow and two dozen other towns. Their duties were limited and did not really extend into the maintenance of order: this was clearly a task that was beyond their ability and instead the police were restricted to matters such as fire prevention, controlling epidemics of disease and maintaining public decency.

It was the local authorities who held central responsibility for keeping control of the population. They were able to enforce laws and to impose penalties on lawbreakers. There was no real distinction between the administrative and judicial functions of the Russian state, and this helps to explain the persistent weakness of the formal policing function. The state held responsibility for legislating, enforcing the laws that it had enacted and then prosecuting and punishing lawbreakers. Without any separation between administrative and judicial functions, the state did not need to separate its policing functions from the rest of its administrative functions. Local authorities were given the power to supervise different sections of the population, although the nobility usually came under the jurisdiction of central government institutions. The most senior clergy were subject to the ecclesiastical authorities, but the civil authorities usually felt that they could deal with transgressions by ordinary local priests, especially if their offences were connected to disorderly peasant. Ordinary Russians could be dealt with by local administrative officials – there was no requirement for police involvement – and then subjected to a variety of punishments. The sanctions that could be imposed on lawbreakers were often very cruel. Imprisonment was relatively rare, since it was an expensive form of punishment and required significant bureaucratic capacity to administer. The main punishments imposed during the early part of the eighteenth century were much more brutal. Corporal punishment, mutilation and an assortment of other very harsh measures were the mainstay of Peter the Great's sanctions against lawbreakers, with beating and forced labour being the most common punishments meted out. The death penalty was used relatively sparingly. By the time Catherine II came to the throne in 1762, punishments were gradually becoming less barbaric, especially for the nobility. Fines and dishonour were increasingly imposed as penalties for the nobility, although the peasantry continued to be subject to corporal punishment.

Peter used the principles of his Military Statute of 1716 as the model for his approach to maintaining order among the civilian population. In his introduction to the statute, the Tsar wrote

> but when (with the Almighty's help) the army was brought to order, then what great progress was made with the Almighty's help against glorious and regular nations. Anyone can see that this occurred for no other reason than the establishment of good order, for all disorderly barbarian practices are worthy of ridicule and no good can come of them.[1]

Two years later, Peter argued that he could replicate the success of his attempts to impose order and discipline on the army more widely across Russian society. An edict on petitions of 1718 stated that

> His Majesty . . . has with the help of God brought it [the army] into such good order that it is known to all what the military nowadays is like when compared with the earlier forces and what fruits have been borne. Now that this has been accomplished, His Majesty . . . does not want the civil administration to be neglected but is taking pains to see that this, too, is brought into as good order as military affairs.[2]

Peter began by instituting a reform of the court system, using the Swedish model in this area as in so many others, and intending to give the judiciary independence in how they reached their verdicts and handed down sentences. The Tsar's efforts ended in failure. There was no culture of judicial independence in Petrine Russia and the attempt to impose a model that was foreign in both structure and ethos demonstrated the depth of administrative involvement in the legal processes of the Russian state. Local officials quickly undermined the new courts, refusing to give up their involvement in the maintenance of order and the dispensing of justice. Within ten years, the idea of independent courts had been quietly abandoned and the administrative and judicial functions of the state remained inextricably intertwined.

Catherine also turned her attention to the issue of policing, and her approach again demonstrated the different understanding of the nature of the police in Romanov Russia. The tradition of eighteenth-century cameralist thought viewed the police as being not primarily a coercive force, but instead an integral part of the state's efforts to mould and reshape society. This concept fitted well into the Russian situation of very fluid distinctions between the administrative and the judicial parts of the state, and it was reflected in Catherine's Police Statute of 1782. This dealt essentially with the policing of Russia's towns and it laid out in great detail the duties that the police had to carry out, defining them essentially as a means to regulate the urban environment: organising firefighting, inspecting buildings and overseeing street trading. They were given some limited authority to deal with minor offences such as public drunkenness and transgressions of regulations and were able to impose limited punishments on offenders. Catherine also made reforms to the policing of the rural world, putting in place a police commandant in each district to supervise the maintenance of order there, but the dominance of the serf-owning nobility in the countryside made rural policing a less significant issue for the state. It was only during the first half of the nineteenth century that proper attention was paid to the rural police, making the provincial governor responsible for policing, but even then there was no real supervision of regular provincial policing by central government. Although the governor was responsible to the Ministry of Internal Affairs for matters relating to public order, the ministry had no effective means of monitoring the way in which the provincial police operated. Indeed, the formal police force continued to be grossly undermanned with only a dozen or so policemen for each district. These men were assisted by peasant constables, elected by their fellows, usually under duress, and they were consequently unwilling to devote themselves wholeheartedly to the work of enforcing the law. In 1878, a new force of mounted rural police was introduced, but they numbered fewer then 6000 in total and rapidly gained a reputation for arbitrary and oppressive policing. The responsibilities of the nineteenth-century police continued to be diffuse and included the collection of a variety of statistical information, enforcing the regulations regarding military conscription and collecting taxes, along with the enforcement of the huge body of regulations and laws issued by the St Petersburg government. The government also gave the police the catch-all duty of being responsible for the 'morality, sobriety, loyalty and religious feeling' of the population of the district in their charge, something that was plainly beyond the capability of the handful of regular policemen in the area.[3]

Contemporaries were scathing about the abilities of the rural police. A Simbirsk provincial landowner wrote in 1872 that

> the present composition of the police gives little cause for comfort, although one does meet able and honourable individuals who are policemen. In most cases the police do not help matters but hinder them. It is clear that the effort that the police expend in using their fists and in unending cursing . . . is not only inappropriate, but undermines the work of the police . . . and harms it in the eyes of society.[4]

The police were condemned by a provincial governor as 'having lost the ability to distinguish the important from the insignificant in the mass of matters which, because of their enormous number, it is impossible to deal with in good time'.[5] The rural police were generally recognised to be corrupt, to be almost universally open to taking bribes and to have little regard for legality. In part, this was explained by the very low levels of qualifications that were demanded of a man who wanted to become a police officer: the district police officers had only to be literate, 'able to compose protocols and generally familiar with the work of the police service'.[6] They were poorly paid, earning less than the average salary for ordinary provincial officials, and the job did not attract men of high calibre. The situation was little better even in the capital. An 1881 inquiry into the St Petersburg police force revealed that many officers were only semi-literate and had only a very limited knowledge of the law, while the very low level of police pay made corruption a serious problem.[7]

The inadequacy of the regular police force meant that the regime could not rely on it to carry out the vital function of protecting the security of the state. This was an especial problem, for the Russian state stood apart from its subjects and was dependent on containing the ambitions of society if it was to retain its untrammelled power. The Decembrist revolt of 1825 was instrumental in alerting the Romanov state to the dangers that it faced from hitherto unsuspected quarters. Peasant rebellion had been the central threat that the eighteenth-century state faced and the regime had proved relatively successful in developing methods of maintaining social control in the countryside. Decembrism arose from an entirely different source – Russia's officer corps – and the realisation that Russia's social elites contained elements that wanted to see the downfall of the state jolted the new Tsar into action. In 1826 Nicholas I established a political police force, the Third Section of his personal chancellery, to monitor social and political matters across the empire. This was a significant development, since this new police force was not part of the regular ministerial structures of the state, but stood apart from the bulk of the government apparatus and was directly subordinated to the monarch himself. It exercised its powers through a uniformed gendarmerie that was initially 4000 strong and possessed very wide powers. By the early years of the twentieth century, the number of gendarmes had grown to more than 12,000, but only about 40 per cent of these men were actually involved in combatting sedition. The majority of the gendarmes were assigned to police the rapidly expanding railway network, and only some 2000 were involved in security work. The state encountered significant difficulties integrating the political police into the overall apparatus of the state: political crimes remained a relatively rare event in Russia before the 1860s and the Third Section gained very limited experience in preventing and investigating them. The sudden emergence of terrorism in Russia in the 1860s and its rapid development during the 1870s thrust the security police into prominence so that it underwent a series of reforms in the years after the first assassination attempt on Alexander II by Karakozov in 1866. In 1867, P. A. Shuvalov, appointed director of the Third Section in the wake of the failed assassination, attempted to extend the scope of surveillance of the Russian population by increasing the number of gendarme stations but this had little effect in preventing further terrorist attacks.

The Third Section failed to recognise the nature of the threat that the Tsarist state faced during the 1870s. The terrorist groups that were plotting to destroy the Romanov regime were highly disciplined and determined to bring about the downfall of the state. They proved successful in mounting a series of attempts on the life of Alexander II, including infiltrating the Winter Palace and planting a bomb that almost killed the emperor, and in 1881 were able to assassinate Alexander II on the streets of his own capital city. Alongside these dramatic attacks at the centrepiece of the state, terrorists were also able to launch numerous attacks on government officials, including the St Petersburg governor F. F. Trepov, and, humiliatingly for the political police, murdering the head of the Third Section itself, N. V. Mezentsev, in August 1878. The security police had been unable to establish sophisticated systems of surveillance and, more fundamentally, they had not understood the motivation or the determination of the groups that carried out these acts of terrorism. When Loris-Melikov took over as Minister of Internal Affairs in 1880, the reform of the security police was high on his list of priorities: when the new minister had visited Moscow shortly after his appointment he found 'strictly speaking, no one in charge of security policing'.[8] In August 1880 he abolished the Third Section, replacing it with a Department of State Police, responsible to the Minister of Internal Affairs. This move did place all the policing of the empire under a single authority, but the Department of Police quickly became one of the most labyrinthine institutions of the Russian state, with a hugely complex internal structure and frequent changes of senior personnel. Tellingly, the Police Department had 16 directors in the 36 years of its existence. These institutional changes to the system of political police had only a very limited impact on the effectiveness of the regime's attempts to curb opposition.

There was a major upsurge in terrorism during Nicholas II's reign, with more than 3600 government officials being killed or wounded during 1905 itself. In 1906, terrorists succeeded in exploding a bomb at the home of Stolypin, the new Minister of Internal Affairs, killing two people and seriously wounding two of Stolypin's own daughters. Stolypin himself was the victim of an assassin's bullet in 1911, when he was shot during a performance at the Kiev Opera House in the presence of Nicholas II. Violence became endemic in some parts of the empire in the last decade of the Tsarist regime, with the viceroy of the Caucasus, Count Vorontsov-Dashkov, reporting nearly 700 terrorist attacks in his region in 1907. Terrorism was most widespread during 1905 and 1906: in Poland, nearly 800 military and police officers were killed and in the Baltic region there were 1700 attacks and assassinations by terrorists during those two years. The political police were overwhelmed by this great onslaught, with one official writing that 'every day there are several assassinations, either by bomb or revolver or knife, or various other instruments, they strike and strike anyhow and at anybody . . . and no one is surprised that they have not yet killed all of us'.[9] This wave of terrorism differed from the attacks in the 1870s in that the terrorists' targets were indiscriminate: the first wave of terrorists had concentrated on attacking figures at the highest levels of the regime, but this new set of revolutionaries spread their fire to threaten any servant of the state. The political police proved incapable of stamping out terrorism, although it did decline after 1908. Some of the senior officers of the Police Department expressed what was almost admiration for the terrorists whom they pursued: the police colonel who interrogated Dmitrii Bogrov, Stolypin's assassin, described him as 'one of the most remarkable people I ever met. An astonishing man'.[10] Even though the Tsarist state devoted substantial resources to hunting down its opponents, employing several thousand informers alongside its regular police force, the might of the state was insufficient to prevent terrorism becoming a regular feature of Russian society. While the political police had the outward trappings of power, their weakness was revealed at times of crisis, when they proved consistently unable to stem the flood of violent opposition to the regime.

The Military

The Romanovs had to fall back on their armed forces to reinforce the internal security of the state. The army played a central role in the rise of Peter the Great's Russia to European prominence, and Peter put in place a systematic procedure for conscripting men to serve as soldiers. From 1705 onwards, one recruit had to be provided from every 20 households, but Peter made significant additional levies at times when he needed to strengthen his forces. This burden fell overwhelmingly on the serfs: the landowners selected which serfs were destined for the army, thus giving them a further level of control over the peasantry. However, the nobility did not escape, since the compulsory service that they had to perform was most often carried out in the army. Peter's army was immense: in 1711, it numbered some 170,000 men and this increased to 300,000 by 1725.[11] This placed a vast burden upon a state with a population of 15 million, in terms of both manpower and the resources needed to maintain such a huge army. The conditions of service were hard for the ordinary soldier. During the eighteenth century, conscription into the ranks was essentially for life; it was only in 1793 that service was set at 25 years. Ordinary troops never received leave, so when a young man was selected to be conscripted he was bidding farewell to his family and his home for ever.[12] Until 1800, a soldier's family might not even be notified of his death. Life in the army was tough, even when a soldier was not actually on campaign. Russian soldiers were poorly paid and then not always paid on time. Officers could also compel their men to work for them privately, often removing the soldiers to their own estates. Army rations were of poor quality and on campaign troops often had to fend for themselves, spending valuable time searching for provisions.

The army increased in size significantly during the Napoleonic Wars at the beginning of the nineteenth century, eating up more than 56 per cent of the state's total expenditure by 1808. The regime was concerned to reduce the burden that the military placed upon it, but it was also very reluctant to reduce the actual number of troops. Alexander I and his ministers were very conscious of Russia's position as the greatest European military power and that this had been built on its immense military forces. But, it was imperative to reduce the financial burden that the army represented, and Alexander began to establish military settlements that would engage troops in useful work, intending that the army should be utilised to work on the land, build roads and bridges and enable the soldiery to make a contribution to the local and national economy. Count A. A. Arakcheev was entrusted with the task of organising these military settlements and from 1816 onwards about one third of the Russian army's soldiers were settled on the land. These settlements intensified the burden on the ordinary Russian solider and they were intensely unpopular with the troops. They operated under very harsh codes of discipline and were often located in areas that proved highly unfavourable for agriculture, making the life of the settlers extremely tough. There were many instances of mutiny against the regime of the settlements, with an especially serious uprising taking place in the north-western provinces in 1831. The rebels killed some 200 people in their attempt to throw off the shackles of the military settlements, but the regime was able to re-establish its authority without too much difficulty and exacted ferocious punishments on the mutineers. Despite the military settlers' evident dislike for the system, the settlements continued to grow so that by 1850 they included 51,000 soldiers, along with more than 700,000 other residents. This 'state within a state' only came to an end at the end of the 1850s, as one of Alexander II's reforms.

The dismal performance of the army during the Crimean War prompted a major reform of its composition. In 1874 the Minister of War, D. A. Miliutin, pushed through the most far-reaching reform of the Tsarist army that was ever accomplished. First, every male Russian subject was made liable for military service, an inevitable consequence of the emancipation of the serfs, which had given legal rights to the entire peasant population. The 25-year term of service was abandoned and ordinary conscripted men were now to serve for 6 years in the active army, with a further 9 years in the reserves. The nobility still had the opportunity to serve for a lesser period, since the possession of educational qualifications could reduce the amount of time spent in the army: a man with a university education would serve only 6 months in the active army, with a further 14½ years in the reserves.[13] The Russian army continued to be overwhelmingly comprised of peasants: 85 per cent of the men who were called up came from the peasantry and fewer than 1 per cent from the nobility. The size of the army increased significantly in the wake of the 1874 reform, so that Russia could call up more than 750,000 troops when war broke out with Turkey in 1876 and by 1904 the army numbered more than a million men. Despite Miliutin's reform, the Russian army continued to preserve intact the class distinctions that had been a feature of the army before emancipation. The officer corps remained a noble preserve, drawing its men from Russia's elites.[14] Fewer than 30 per cent of the men who were eligible to serve in the Russian army actually entered military service, in contrast to France where more than 80 per cent did so, and post-1871 Germany where over half of eligible men became soldiers. The Russian army thus could not act as a 'school for the nation' in the way that other European armies did, integrating its population and producing a coherent and cohesive society. The opportunity reform offered, to use the military as a means of creating a new social framework for the Russian state in the wake of emancipation, was squandered.

The Romanovs used their army not only as a means of fighting battles with foreign powers, but also as an essential and integral part of the mechanisms of control that the state utilised. The weakness of the police, together with the state's absolute need to be able to deal rapidly with rebellion, meant that the military was an essential feature of life in every Russian province. The army was fully integrated into the structures of Tsarist government: the devotion of successive monarchs to the armed forces was evident, and generals played a significant part in the empire's government. By 1908, the army included 1424 full generals, of whom one third had begun their careers in the elite Guards regiments, and there was a significant crossover between the military and civilian spheres. More than 10 per cent of these generals occupied posts in the civilian administration, often as provincial governors or in the Department of Police, but they could also be found in less predicable areas of the government. General P. S. Vannovskii had spent his whole career in the army, rising to become Minister of War between 1881 and 1898, but was called out of retirement in 1901 to serve as Minister of Education for a year. The organisation of the army at a local level also ensured that it could easily be mobilised to support the civil authorities. During the eighteenth century, financial considerations meant that during peacetime the Russian army was billeted on the rural population for some eight months of the year. This saved the state the expense of constructing permanent barracks for its hundreds of thousands of troops, since during the summer most of the army was quartered under canvas and, while this had a deleterious effect on the quality of military training that troops received, it meant that the army was on hand in the provinces if it needed to be used to maintain order. It was only during the second half of the nineteenth century that an extensive network of barracks was constructed, concentrating the army in Russia's towns for most of the year.[15]

The state used the army extensively to deal with internal discontent. The Pugachev rebellion of the 1770s could only be put down by troops, but even then, victory over the rebels was not immediate. Even though the trained soldiers of the Romanov army were able to defeat Pugachev's disorganised rebels, the regime found it difficult to stamp out the revolt once and for all. The army was able to defeat Pugachev at Orenburg in March 1774 and to lift the six-month siege of the city, but even though General P. M. Golitsyn's army was able to kill more than a quarter of the rebel troops and to take almost half of them prisoner after the battle, Pugachev himself and his chief lieutenants were able to escape and to gather more followers around him. Only five months after the defeat at Orenburg, he appeared at the head of some 20,000 men before the city of Kazan and was able to overwhelm the defences of the city, putting it to the sword, with his supporters looting, raping and murdering the inhabitants. Even though government forces were able to chase Pugachev from Kazan and to again kill and capture many of his supporters, he himself escaped and it was a further two months before he was eventually defeated and captured. The army's difficulties in putting down this rebellion were partly a result of the size of the empire; Pugachev was able to criss-cross the eastern parts of European Russia and the size of the empire meant that the army could not be everywhere at once. The state learnt a hard lesson from this great peasant uprising and Arakcheev's policy of imposing military settlements can be seen as one, albeit belated, response to the events of the 1770s.

The internal security of the state could only be guaranteed by deterring the empire's population from rebellion. After the upheavals of the 1770s, there were no further serious popular revolts for more than a century. The state was able to project its authority across the empire in ways that ensured that the population remained quiescent during the first part of the nineteenth century. Nicholas I's ferocious regime ensured that the empire remained quiet for a generation, while Alexander II pre-empted the possibility of peasant rebellion by embarking on the Great Reforms, calculating that the emancipation of the serfs would ensure that the countryside would remain peaceful and that the peasant population would feel no motivation to rebel. Alexander's assumptions proved correct: challenges to the regime during the second half of the nineteenth century came from terrorism, rather than from peasant uprisings. But the absence of overt peasant disturbances did not mean that all was well in the Russian countryside and that the rural population had acquiesced in their acceptance of the autocratic regime.

The Russian countryside was transformed into a boiling pit of fury during the revolution of 1905. Peasants turned on landowners, burning down their manor houses, seizing their crops and livestock and plundering their estates. By the autumn of 1905, 478 of the 500 or so districts of European Russia had been affected by peasant disturbances, and there were only three provinces left entirely untouched by peasant rebellion. Thousands of landowners' estates were affected by rebellion, presenting the Romanov regime with its greatest threat since Pugachev. The sheer extent of revolt made it a difficult task for the state to restore order, all the more so since Russia was still in the process of extricating itself from an unsuccessful war with Japan, and many of its most effective troops were still in the Far East and unavailable for the work of suppressing revolution. During 1905 alone, there were more than 3000 separate instances of peasant rebellion where troops were sent in to restore order and, even though more than 120,000 troops were used to put down revolt, it proved extremely difficult for the army to restore order to the countryside. Peasant uprisings continued during 1906 and 1907, with a total of more than 5000 instances during those two years where military units were called upon to intervene. Fewer soldiers were used to deal with rebellion in 1906, with 29,000 troops being used, but the severity of their response was at least equal to that used in 1905 itself. The Baltic provinces suffered particularly from the use of military 'punishment battalions' that were sent to quell disorder in an environment where the authority of the state was close to collapse. The British consul reported from Riga in autumn 1906 that 'The Baltic provinces are paralysed. The revolutionists, or rather the bands of scoundrels which infest the forests, are keeping the whole country in such a state of terrorism that nobody seems to know what to expect next.'[16] Troops were ordered to use whatever force was needed to quell disorder, and between 1905 and 1908 some 3000 people were executed in the Baltic provinces and a further 1000 sentenced to deportation to Siberia.[17] The brutality used by the Tsarist authorities left a deep and lasting revulsion among the population of the Baltic provinces.

The power of the Tsarist state was intensified following the assassination of Alexander II. In August 1881, the state introduced emergency legislation that persisted until 1917. The 1881 statute allowed the government to declare areas of the Russian empire to be in a state of emergency and to impose one of two levels of exceptional measures. The lesser of these, 'reinforced protection', could be introduced when 'public order in an area is disturbed by criminal infractions against the existing state structure or against the security of individuals and their property or by the preparation of such acts'. The more severe level, 'extraordinary protection', was to be imposed when 'these infractions have put the local population into a disturbed state, making it necessary to take exceptional measures urgently to restore order'.[18] Reinforced protection laid the responsibility for maintaining public order on governors and governors-general and gave them substantial additional powers. Most significantly, they were able to issue regulations for the areas under their control 'to prevent breaches of public order and state security' and could punish infringements by detention for up to three months or by a fine not exceeding 500 rubles. Extraordinary protection provided all the elements of the lesser category, and gave additional authority to the local authorities. It was envisaged that if this level of emergency was declared then an official would be designated as commander of the region and he in turn could delegate his authority to others, particularly army officers. He could transfer criminal cases from the normal court system to courts-martial or else could deal with them through administrative means. Immediately the statute was enacted in the summer of 1881, reinforced protection was imposed on ten provinces, comprising a population of more than 27.5 million people.[19] From 1881 until 1888 the number of people living under reinforced protection remained between 27.5 and 28.2 million, dropping in 1889 to 22 million and in 1890 briefly to 17.8 million. For most of the 1890s, 20.6 million people were covered by this element of the legislation, but increased use was made of it from 1898 onwards so that by 1903, 30.6 million people lived under reinforced protection.[20] Roughly one quarter of the population of the Russian empire, therefore, was affected by this section of the legislation before 1905. The urban and rural uprisings which shook Russia during 1905 resulted in a huge extension of these emergency powers. Extraordinary protection was invoked for the first time in December 1905 and by February 1906 it affected five entire provinces, together with parts of a further ten, whilst eight provinces were wholly under reinforced protection, along with parts of 18 more. In addition to the powers which the 1881 statute offered, the government introduced martial law into 17 entire provinces and parts of 22 others.[21] By the spring of 1906 some form of state of emergency had been imposed across 70 per cent of the Russian empire.

The sanctions that could be imposed under this emergency legislation were far-reaching. Provincial governors could exile individuals from their own provinces, although exercise of the formal power of administrative exile was subject to confirmation by the government in St Petersburg. Requests for the exile of individuals had to be made to a committee comprised of representatives from the Ministries of Internal Affairs and Justice, and in the 13 years from 1881 until 1894 this committee approved more than 5000 requests for exile.[22] This type of exile not only removed individuals from one region but also compelled them to reside at other named locations, usually in Siberia or the less hospitable parts of European Russia.[23] The power to issue local regulations without any need for reference to St Petersburg was an especially powerful sanction. Street demonstrations were prohibited in Kiev in 1901, followed in 1904 by a prohibition on any meeting or gathering which breached the peace. This not only made participants in a meeting liable to punishment, but also imposed penalties on those in charge of the premises where such meetings were held.[24] Meetings in the Baltic cities of Riga and Iur'ev were only to be allowed to take place with prior permission from the police, and the police could instruct participants in any meeting to disperse if they felt it necessary. The regulation was repeated for the city of Riga in the summer of 1904, emphasising the penalties that would apply to those who opposed the actions of the police in the maintenance of public order.[25] The disturbances in the Baltic provinces during 1905 persuaded authorities there to issue a range of regulations to deal with disorder. The prohibition on street demonstrations in Riga was repeated in January 1906, and in an attempt to lessen the chance of demonstrations it was decreed that all gates leading onto the street must be kept locked each night from 5 pm until 6 am.[26] Individuals who actively opposed the government by obstructing railways or roads or by interfering with telephone lines were to be dealt with under martial law. As well, individuals and communities who withheld taxation were to be liable to fines and exile, with the added threat that their places would be taken by migrants from the interior provinces of the empire.[27]

The disruption caused to life inside the empire by disturbances was also the subject of regulations. Problems brought about in the supply of food in Riga, especially a strike by butchers, provoked a regulation prohibiting attempts to halt or interfere in trade,[28] while shopkeepers who closed their shops for political reasons were to face punishment. Particular attention was paid to the sale of alcohol and at times local authorities went to extraordinary lengths to control consumption. The inhabitants of Omsk and two other towns in the Steppe region had, from 1904, to produce a police certificate before they could buy alcoholic drink; civil servants had to show a certificate signed and stamped by their superior at work, and factory workers had to produce a document from their employer. Ordinary soldiers needed to obtain the permission of their commanding officer before they could buy alcoholic drink.[29] Considerable attention was paid to dealing with disturbances at work. The Baltic authorities made strenuous efforts in this direction; early in 1905 workers and agricultural labourers were warned that absence from work and refusal to obey police instructions to return to work would result in detention.[30] In 1906 work stoppages for political reasons were prohibited altogether and those inciting such strikes were to be punished under martial law: tramworkers were singled out as liable to a fine or detention, while newspaper editors who halted the production of an issue would also be dealt with under the 1881 statute. Riga tramworkers continued to be a focus of attention: in the summer of 1906 a regulation ordered them to return to work the following day or else face a fine. Those that remained away from work would be expelled from the region. The following year the Baltic Governor-General decreed that workers who had been dismissed from their jobs for agitating amongst their workmates were not to be re-employed in any industrial enterprise. The only exception to this was to be where the person could produce a police certificate of good behaviour.[31] The 1881 statute was immensely popular among provincial governors, since it allowed them to govern their provinces without any real interference from the capital and gave them the freedom to use the police and army much as they wanted. Contemporaries recognised the ferocious power that it conferred on governors: a Justice of the Peace wrote that: 'This statute [of 1881] is a terrifying weapon in the hands of the local administration, giving wide scope for settling personal scores, for revenge, for complete arbitrariness and lawlessness. The main defect of this legislation – its essential evil – is that the most valuable blessings of man, freedom and the inviolability of the individual, are entrusted to lowly police officials.' Even central government was very suspicious of the extent to which authority had slipped out of the hands of St Petersburg. Sergei Witte commented in 1906 that

> ... this has led to an exceptional situation: there has been created on the initiative of local authorities, without permission from central government, a whole series of small independent governor-generalships, acting wholly independently from one another, outside proper supervision by central government and utilizing, with the force of law, the widest powers towards the local population which stands almost outside the law...[32]

Even at a time when the very survival of the state itself was under threat, the regime was ambivalent about allowing its power to slip away into the hands of individuals over whom it had only limited control, but who could nevertheless use this authority to restore order. The 1881 statute was, however, a critically important part of the regime's armoury to protect its own security; it represented an assertion of the principle of autocracy even as opposition to the Tsarist state was attracting more adherents and developing ideologies that struck at the foundations of the Russian state.

Law

The 1881 emergency laws cocked a snook at the principle of legality. This sat firmly in the tradition of the empire's systems of dispensing justice. The formal legislation that set out the principles of the Russian legal system used much the same language as was used in western states during the eighteenth century. The 1649 code of laws declared that 'for people of all ranks, from the highest to the lowest, of the Muscovite state the law and justice will be equal for all in all cases', but in practice Russian justice was inequitable and almost wholly dependent on the whims of the state.[33] Any technical independence that the courts enjoyed was subverted by their practical subordination to the government. Law was a 'moral ideal' in Romanov Russia, and even though Catherine II made significant reforms to the legal system, they could not have any significant impact while the ethos of the state asserted the primacy of the autocrat over every part of society.[34] The personal power of the monarch and the institutional power of the organs of the state meant that legality was relegated to playing a minor role in the mechanisms of the Russian empire. The court system became notorious for its delay, inefficiency and corruption, while the majority of the population – the enserfed peasantry – were excluded from the normal processes of justice, since they possessed no legal standing as individuals. The situation only changed with the Great Reforms of Alexander II. In 1864 a system of civil and criminal courts based on western models was introduced, with clear lines of appeal and staffed by a judiciary whose independence was assured through good salaries, thus obviating the need to take bribes, and by their irremovability from office. No longer could judges be dismissed for delivering verdicts which displeased the government. Furthermore, jury trials were brought in for the first time in criminal cases, thus introducing another element which was outside the control of the government into the administration of justice. During the 1860s and 1870s an independent and articulate legal profession came into existence, encouraged by the new freedoms which lawyers had gained under the reform, and the courtroom became a focus for challenges to the authority and style of government of the autocracy. Lawyers came to be viewed by the regime as being in the same category as the *zemstvo* professionals – a source of autonomous opposition to the government – and the government made attempts to restrict their freedom. This proved more difficult than in the case of the local councils, however, since court proceedings could be openly reported in the press and speeches made by both defendants and their lawyers in the course of a trial could not be the basis for further prosecution.

These legal reforms had most effect on the populations of the large cities and especially on the judicial atmosphere in St Petersburg and Moscow, where the most significant and controversial trials took place. For the majority of the population, the peasantry, access to justice was rather different: those offences concerning solely peasants were dealt with by a village court, comprised of judges elected by and drawn from the peasantry themselves and operating under customary law. For minor disputes which didn't only concern peasants, a system of justices of the peace was established; these magistrates were elected by the district council and appeals against their decisions could be made to a higher authority. They proved to be of significant benefit in making justice more accessible to the population at large, since the JPs' courts worked quickly, cost nothing to those appearing in them and came to be perceived as delivering equitable judgements. Both in setting up courts to try serious offences and in the establishment of a system for providing justice at the lower levels, the regime found that its aims of improving the judicial system and providing the peasantry with proper courts backfired. Whilst these aims were largely satisfied, the 1864 legal reform also laid the basis for a substantial challenge to the foundations of autocracy itself: the autocrat's power to act unconstrained by any other source of authority. Independent courts meant that such an independent source of authority did now exist, that the regime could no longer act in an arbitrary manner and, perhaps most importantly, that there was a clear recognition amongst the population that this was now the case. What Wortman has called the 'development of a Russian legal consciousness' helped to weaken the Tsarist regime: instead of providing a buttress for the state, it gradually came to undermine the foundations of the autocracy.

The power of the Russian state was feared across Europe. The authority of Nicholas I, 'the gendarme of Europe', terrified people outside Russia while the regimes of his successors were held in hardly less awe. The sobriquet of 'Nicholas the Bloody' that the last Tsar gained reflected the brutal force with which his regime put down rebellion and dragged itself back from the brink of oblivion during 1905. Coercion lay at the heart of the state and was an inevitable consequence of the doctrine of autocracy; Russian monarchs denied the validity of any challenge to their authority and asserted that they held complete sway over every aspect of both state and society. Their power rested not on the consent of the people over whom they ruled, but on the ability of the monarch to dominate the empire by every means at their disposal. The Tsars rarely stinted in their efforts to exercise their authority and the Russian population appeared cowed by the power that the state demonstrated. The nature of the empire meant that the arbitrary power of the monarch was replicated count-less times by the police, the administrative authorities and the military so that the Tsar's subjects were drubbed into submission. But, this formidable power did not survive intact until 1917. The judicial reform of 1864 challenged the coercive power of the state head-on; the principles of legality that it rested on were anathema to the very concept of autocracy. Even though the state attempted to sidestep the new courts by making greater use of administrative justice and of courts-martial, it was not prepared to reverse the legal reforms of the 1860s. The year 1864 proved to be a turning point in the course of the Russian state's development: the twin introductions of the *zemstvo* and of an independent legal system were to pose a greater threat to the existence of the Romanov state than any opposition that came from the mass of its population.

Chapter 7:   National Challenges

Tsarist Russia was the largest state on the globe. At its greatest extent it stretched more than 4500 miles from the border with Germany in the west to the Pacific coast in the east, and from the Arctic Ocean in the north to the mountains and deserts of Central Asia in the south. The imperial state's expansion had come in a variety of ways. Military conquest brought Russia control of the Caucasus, although the imperial state continued to face persistent challenges from insurgency and its senior officials in the region lived under the permanent threat of assassination. Much of Central Asia was acquired by military means. The state gained some territory by treaty; in the 1790s the partitions of Poland snuffed out the independent Polish state, dividing it between Russia, Prussia and Austria-Hungary. Russia gained the largest part of the Polish lands, but the empire's Polish possessions caused St Petersburg persistent problems, as the Poles deeply resented the Russian presence and rebelled time and time again. But the largest part of the empire's domains was acquired by a gradual and seemingly inexorable process of exploration and discovery. The frozen forests of Siberia concealed a great treasure trove of natural resources, providing a powerful economic motivation for Russians to explore the difficult terrain. Initially, they sought animal furs, but later recognised the potential that Siberia's mineral resources offered, despite the problems posed by remoteness and climate. The process of Russian expansion eastwards was also assisted by the sparseness of the population of much of Siberia; there was no real opposition as Russians moved towards the Pacific.

Figure 7.1 Ethnic composition of the Russian empire, 1897

	Million	%
Russians	55.6	44.3
Ukrainians	22.3	17.8
Poles	7.9	6.3
Volga-Uralic peoples	5.9	4.7
Belarussians	5.8	4.7
Caucasian groups	5.7	4.6
Jews	5.0	4.0
Baltic groups	4.0	3.2
Kazakhs	3.8	3.1
Other European groups	3.2	2.5
Siberian peoples	0.7	0.6
Northern peoples	0.5	0.4
Others	5.2	4.1
Total	125.6	

Source: Abstracted from A. Kappeler, *The Russian Empire. A Multiethinic History* (London, 2001), pp. 397–9.

The Russian empire that developed during the eighteenth and nineteenth centuries was very different from other European-based imperial states. Russia took control of most of the Eurasian landmass by taking advantage of a power vacuum and of the weakness of its neighbours, who were unable to mount any real challenge to Russian ambition. While Russia did encounter opposition to its rule in some areas, for the most part it was able to acquire new territory without needing to use military force. The wars and suppression of indigenous opposition that were a feature of the growth of the British, French and Spanish empires featured much less prominently in the growth of the Russian empire, and this largely peaceful acquisition of territory was important in shaping Russian perceptions of their growing domains. The process of expansion led Russians to see their empire as being an integral part of the state, a perception that was accentuated by the contiguous nature of the imperial state. Russians never had to venture overseas to acquire their empire, instead drawing most territory and people into their ambit by moving across the landmass to the east and south of the Russian heartland. Although communications between the different parts of the Russian empire were just as difficult as in the maritime-based empires, this did not prevent Russians taking a very different view of the majority of the possessions that they acquired, viewing them as areas to be assimilated into the metropolitan state, rather than colonies to be subdued.

Asia

Russia's process of imperial growth was almost continuous throughout the eighteenth and nineteenth centuries. The Russians had begun to gain control of eastern Siberia in the mid-seventeenth century, signing the Treaty of Nerchinsk with China in 1689 in an attempt to regulate the border between the two states in the Pacific region. The very agreement of this treaty was highly significant as it demonstrated that the Chinese recognised the growing power of Russia in a region that had traditionally been in their sphere of influence. Russian exploration in the Pacific region continued apace, with the discovery of the Kamchatka peninsula by Europeans in 1697 and government-sponsored expeditions along the northern Pacific coast by Vitus Bering between 1725 and 1741. The Russian state recognised the importance of acquiring a greater knowledge of regions of which it had only a sketchy grasp and it continued to fund and support expeditions. These adventurings had varied aims: they were intended to consolidate Russian power at the peripheries of the empire by showing the flag and establishing outposts of the empire in remote and hostile regions.[1] There was also a conscious scientific purpose to expeditions, with their members seeking to identify the topography and resources of the areas that they investigated. The growing significance of Russia's possessions on the Pacific littoral had an important effect in stimulating the development of southern Siberia, since it represented the only practical route for communication with the Far East. Irkutsk became the centre of Russian Siberia by the end of the eighteenth century, with a population approaching 15,000 by 1800, and it also acquired the trappings of civilisation. The Academy of Sciences donated more than 1300 books to establish a public library in the city in 1782, and Irkutsk, standing at the southern end of Lake Baikal on the only practical route east, attracted settlers from European Russia and became the base for every expedition that ventured deeper into Russia's eastern lands. The importance of eastern Siberia for the Russian state increased during the nineteenth century, as other powers began to demonstrate a more consistent

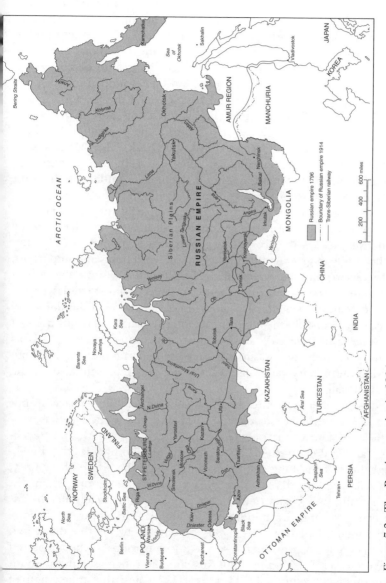

Figure 7.2 The Russian empire in 1914.

Source: Adapted from G. Hosking, *Russia: People & Empire 1552–1917* (London, 1997), pp. xiv–xv.

interest in the Pacific region. The appointment of General Nikolai Muraviev as governor-general of Siberia in 1847 marked a turning point in Russian attitudes to the area. Muraviev pursued an aggressive forward policy, exploring down the Amur River to its outlet into the Pacific itself. The establishment of a secure means of communicating with the Pacific coast rapidly encouraged the growth of new urban settlements on the coast: Vladivostok was only founded in 1860, but by 1900 it had become Siberia's largest city and the headquarters of the Russian Pacific fleet, succeeding in attracting more than 100,000 inhabitants in just half a century. By 1911, the populations of three other Siberian cities – Irkutsk, Tomsk and Omsk – also had exceeded 100,000 and 11 further Siberian cities had gained populations of more than 50,000. Siberia became a magnet for settlers of all kinds, and the St Petersburg government sought to encourage migration from European Russia eastwards.[2] This was partly intended to relieve pressure on the more densely populated areas of rural Russia, by promising settlers the prospect of generous allocations of land and the opportunity to grow wealthy if they moved east. It was also important, however, for the state to populate Siberia to demonstrate that Russia had indeed taken control of these vast lands. When Nicholas I sanctioned Muraviev's aggressive moves in eastern Siberia, he did so by declaring that 'where once the Russian flag has been unfurled, it must never be lowered',[3] and the clearest method of showing Russia's dominance of Siberia was to populate the region rapidly, rather than relying on military garrisons to act as the only representatives of the Russian state.

Russian expansion into Siberia was overwhelmingly peaceful, but Russia's experience in Central Asia and the Caucasus was very different. Many of the peoples of these regions were Muslim by religion and, although Russia had ruled the Muslim peoples that inhabited the region along the River Volga since the sixteenth century, Russia's southward moves provoked some intense opposition. St Petersburg only began to make a concerted effort to advance in this direction during the middle of the eighteenth century. New forts were established from the 1730s onwards between the Black and Caspian Seas to provide a base for Russian troops as they explored the Caucasus. During the 1770s Russian power increased in the south with military victory over Turkey in 1774, and the annexation of the Crimea in the early 1780s. It proved extremely difficult to take control of the mountainous Caucasus, however, as the Russians met with fierce resistance from the ethnically diverse population of the region. Guerilla war against the Russian invaders erupted in 1785 and proved to be an enduring feature of Russia's attempts to bring the region fully under its control. In 1829 Nicholas I ordered 'the final pacification of the mountain peoples or the extirpation of the rebels', believing that the success of his troops in war against Turkey could be replicated in the Caucasus.[4] The process of bringing armed opposition to an end lasted, however, for more than 25 years. Successive Russian commanders found it exceptionally difficult to mount successful military operations in the mountains against a determined opposition, and Russia's armies lost thousands of soldiers to the guerillas. It was only at the end of the 1850s that resistance was broken and that Shamil, the leader of the Caucasians, was captured. Russian authority was still unwelcome to many of the people of the region and when Alexander II visited Dagestan in the north Caucasus in 1871, he could only travel around the region under the protection of heavily armed guards. Russia had been expanding into the area east of the Caspian Sea since the first half of the eighteenth century, facing growing resistance from the Kazakh population as it did so. Kazakhs took part in the Pugachev revolt and they repeatedly attacked Russian settlers and garrisons, leading to a mass insurrection in the mid-1820s. Thinly stretched Russian troops found it very difficult to deal with these rebellions, even though the terrain was not as difficult as the mountains of the Caucasus. It took until 1846 before the Russians could put down the revolt by the Kazakh Middle Horde, but this was not the end of rebellion and fighting continued well into the 1850s.

Despite this, the St Petersburg regime was keen to expand further into Central Asia. Both economic considerations and international politics played a part in spurring Russia on to take control of Central Asia: defeat by Britain in the Crimea did not extinguish rivalry between the two powers, but instead stimulated Russia to challenge Britain's position in Asia. Russia was well aware that a move into Central Asia would be seen as provocative and Gorchakov, the Foreign Minister, made a spirited defence of Russia's actions in 1864 in a circular to the other powers. He wrote that:

The position of Russia in Central Asia is the same as the position of any civilised state which comes into contact with a semi-barbarous people, nomads without a fixed social organisation. In such cases the interests of frontier security and of trade relations always require that the more civilised state acquires a certain power over its neighbours, whose wild and turbulent customs make them extremely awkward. It begins by curbing raids and robberies and in order to limit these, the neighbouring peoples usually have to be subjected to some degree of control. When this result has been achieved, these peoples acquire more peaceful customs, but they in their turn are subject to attacks by yet more distant tribes. The state is obliged to defend them from these incursions and to punish those who carried them out. This creates the necessity of periodic and prolonged expeditions against a distant enemy, whose social structure makes him difficult to catch. If a state restricts itself to punishing the plunderers and then withdraws, the lesson will soon be forgotten and the retreat will be attributed to weakness; Asiatic peoples, for the most part, respect only visible and tangible strengths; the moral force of reason and of the advantages of education still has hardly any impact on them. Therefore the work has to be continually restarted. A number of fortified points are set up amongst a hostile people so as to put a rapid end to these endless disturbances; authority is set over them and this, little by little, makes them submit. After this second mission, however, other and yet more distant peoples soon begin to pose just the same dangers and require the same measures of restraint. Thus the state must decide on a definite course of action: either to refrain from this unending work and to condemn its frontiers to endless disturbances which will make well-being, security and education impossible there, or to move further and further forward into the depths of uncivilised countries, where with each step taken, the distances increased the difficulties and burdens for the state. This has been the fate of all states in such conditions. The United States in America, France in Africa, Holland in her colonies, England in eastern India – they have all been trapped on this path of forward movement, motivated less by ambition than by extreme necessity, and where the greatest difficulty is in being able to stop.[5]

Gorchakov's statement provided a classic legitimation of colonial expansion by imperial powers and his reasoning was repeated across Europe in the late nineteenth century, but his statement was aimed specifically at providing a justification for Russian advance in Central Asia. In 1864, a detachment of Russian troops moved southwards, capturing Tashkent in the following year. Russia established a new governor-generalship in Turkestan, defeating the Emir of Bukhara in 1868 and taking control of the region within a decade. Although the Russians did not face the same level of resistance that they had in the Caucasus and the Kazakh steppes, the Muslim population of the region did not become wholly reconciled to Russian dominance. Religious considerations meant that the population of the new Turkestan region was exempted from liability for military service. But the extreme shortage of manpower in the armed forces during the First World War prompted the St Petersburg regime to call up almost half a million men from the region for service in units behind the front lines in 1916. This move provoked immense and immediate opposition from the population of Turkestan: men simply refused to be conscripted, while violence erupted across the region in protest against the actions of the St Petersburg government. The rebels didn't just attack Russian troops in the region, but also vented their fury on government officials and on ordinary Russian settlers. The rebellion deteriorated into all-out war as the army distributed weapons to Russian colonists and punitive detachments were despatched across the region to put down revolt. Tens of thousands of people were killed and uprooted from their homes as the Tsarist state attempted to restore its authority in Central Asia.[6] Opposition to Russian rule was only just beneath the surface of society and was easily brought out into the open.

Europe

Russian expansion in Europe also brought significant difficulties for the Romanov state. The partitions of Poland at the end of the eighteenth century gave Russia a substantial segment of Polish territory, populated by several million Poles who adhered to Catholicism and had an abiding pride in the history and culture of their butchered nation. The Poles had a tradition of statehood that stretched back centuries, and Polish society was highly developed, with a substantial noble elite. The Poles deeply resented the snuffing out of their independence and, in the wake of Russian triumph over Napoleon and the confidence that it brought, Alexander I was prepared to go some way towards recognising their particular traditions. Alexander I's 1815 constitution for Poland gave the Russian monarch overwhelming authority, but it also allowed for the creation of a Polish parliament, to meet for a period of 30 days every two years. This Diet was to be elected, although the franchise was severely restricted, and the Polish population was granted a range of civil rights unknown in Russia itself, including freedom of the press and freedom of religion. Alexander himself addressed the opening session of the Polish parliament in 1818, going so far as to imply that the reforms he was introducing in Poland could be seen as a prototype for changes that might be implemented more widely across the empire. This proved to be no more than empty rhetoric, however, since Alexander I was never prepared to put liberal reform into practice in the Russian heartland.

Official attitudes to Poland changed dramatically in the autumn of 1830 when rebellion broke out in Warsaw. The growth of romantic nationalism across Europe had an intense impact on oppressed Poland, and Polish intellectuals argued for the restoration of the Polish state within its historic borders. At the same time, Nicholas I was taking steps to tighten the grip of Russia on its Polish domains by hunting down anyone who might be suspected of sympathy with the Decembrists who had attempted to deny him the throne in 1825 and arresting militant soldiers and students. Rebellions had broken out in France and Belgium in 1830, and the Poles believed that they could follow their example, throw off Russian rule and reclaim their independence. Rebellion raised its head in Warsaw in November 1830 and was initially successful. The Tsar's viceroy in Poland abandoned the city to the rebels, who promptly summoned a parliament and announced the end of Russian rule in January 1831. Nicholas I was enraged by the events in Poland. He despatched an army to suppress the revolt, but success was slow. The Poles still possessed their own army and were able to win early victories against the Russians: it was only in the late summer of 1831 that Russian troops retook Warsaw. Nicholas was determined to stamp very hard on the rebellious Poles, who had humiliated the Romanov state for almost a year in full sight of its European neighbours. Nicholas intended to impose the fundamental elements of Russian identity on Poland; autocratic government, the Orthodox religion and the essentials of Russian nationality. He abolished the Polish parliament and took steps to destroy the characteristics of Polish separateness. The Polish army was broken up, and Russian models were imposed on the legal and educational systems. The University of Warsaw was closed down and the

Orthodox Church was given a much greater role in Poland in an attempt to counter the influence of Catholicism. Nicholas also took steps to try to change the social structures of Poland and break the importance of the Polish nobility. Many Poles were stripped of their noble status, and Nicholas sought to promote the interests of the non-Polish peasantry against the indigenous Poles.

These measures persisted throughout Nicholas's reign, but when Alexander II ascended the throne he allowed some relaxation of the restrictions on Polish nationality. Even though these measures were limited in scope, they gave heart to Polish patriots who were already buoyed up by the successes of nationalism elsewhere in Europe. Poles demonstrated early in 1861 to mark the anniversary of their victory – albeit only very temporary – 30 years previously over Russian troops. Instead of following Nicholas I's example and responding with force, Alexander II appointed a new viceroy, the liberally inclined Grand Duke Konstantin Nikolaevich, and allowed him to make further concessions to the Poles. More latitude was to be allowed in the education system and the Russian grip on the administration of Poland was slightly relaxed. The Poles took these moves to be a sign of Russian weakness and unrest intensified, bursting into open rebellion in Warsaw in January 1863. Revolt spread very widely across Poland and also penetrated the north-western provinces of European Russia itself.[7] The rebellion came at a very sensitive time for Russia, following hard on the emancipation of the serfs and on defeat in the Crimea. Alexander II quickly recognised that the state's authority was at risk and executed a volte-face in policy. The St Petersburg government quickly became determined to break the Poles, ability to rebel once and for all. It took Russian troops the best part of a year to quell the rebellion and this was followed by very harsh retaliation to stamp out the traditional elements of Polish identity and autonomy. The St Petersburg regime wanted to break the influence of the Polish nobility: more than 600 Poles – mainly from the gentry – were executed and tens of thousands exiled to Siberia, while the Russian regime confiscated more than 3400 estates from Polish landowners both in Poland itself and in the north-western provinces of Russia.[8] The Catholic Church suffered severely: Polish bishops were all removed from their dioceses and many ordinary clergy were exiled or imprisoned.

The imperial state also moved to destroy every element of autonomy in the administration of Poland. This was epitomised by the replacement of the title of 'Kingdom of Poland' as the official Russian designation of the area with the geographically inspired title of 'Vistula region', and by the removal of any indication that Poland had a separate status within the empire. The office of viceroy was abolished and replaced with a governor-general, and the Russian system of provinces and districts was imposed across Poland, emphasising that Poland was now no different from any other part of the empire. At the same time, Poland was placed under martial law and the Warsaw governor-general was granted extensive powers to impose punishments and to regulate Polish society. The governor-general had to give permission before any form of public organisation or society could be established and severe censorship was put in place on every form of publication. The state also instituted a much more rigorous system of policing in Poland than in the rest of the empire, establishing a Land Guard to maintain order in the Polish countryside. Finally, a garrison of almost 250,000 soldiers was stationed in Poland to act as the final guarantee of peace.

The experience that the Poles endured after 1863 demonstrated clearly that the Russian state was prepared to respond to overt challenges to its authority with immense force. Armed uprisings were met with troops who showed little mercy in quelling rebellions. The state's instinctive response to open discontent from its subject peoples was to crush them and to impose on them the same ethos of government that the Romanovs applied to Russia itself. The imperial state faced a different type of challenge, however, in another part of its European domains. In 1808, Russia gained Finland from Sweden by conquest, providing St Petersburg with a greater degree of security since the Finnish border was only some 20 miles from the capital city. Alexander I's approach to his new territory was similar to the position he took in Poland. He established a governing council for Finland to take responsibility for legal and economic affairs, transforming it in 1816 into a Finnish Senate. Although the Senate's powers were closely circumscribed, it did take some steps towards establishing itself as a form of ministerial government. This stood Finland in good stead when Alexander II visited Helsinki in the first year of his reign and began to institute reform in this part of his domains, including the establishment of a Diet. In 1863 the emperor formally opened the first session of the Finnish Diet, declaring himself to be committed to 'the principle of constitutional monarchy inherent to the customs of the Finnish people'. He declared that we wanted to see an accord between the Finnish people and their sovereign and went on:

> This will be of great assistance to the well-being of the region, so close to my heart. . . . You, representatives of the Grand Duchy, must prove by your work, fidelity and composure in decisions, that in the hands of a wise people, ready to act as one with their Sovereign, with practical ideas for the development of their welfare, liberal institutions are not only not dangerous, but are a guarantee of order and prosperity.[9]

In 1869 the position of the Diet was formalised, establishing that it would be summoned every five years. The process of national awakening that was taking hold of much of Europe in the mid-nineteenth century had a dramatic impact on Finland. The establishment of the Finnish Literature Society in the early 1830s was a critical step in the development of Finnish culture, and in 1835 it published what was to become the nascent nation's emblematic epic, the Kalevala. The Finnish language moved from being spoken largely by the peasant population to become a fully-fledged literary language and a series of Finnish-language secondary schools were opened, so that by 1900 more than half of secondary school pupils were attending such schools. For much of the nineteenth century, Finland did not suffer the same depredations as large parts of the empire, and the Romanovs looked upon it with an unparalleled degree of benevolence. Finland continued to enjoy a very significant degree of autonomy: it possessed its own postal system and issued its own stamps, it had its own currency and coinage and had its own customs tariffs. Perhaps most strikingly, Finland possessed its own conscript army, established in 1878 against the advice of the Russian Minister of War, which was commanded by Finnish officers and used for local defence. The imperial army still maintained control of coastal defences, but the existence of a separate military force in Finland epitomised the level of autonomy that the Finns had been able to retain. As well, Russians had only limited rights in Finland: they had no vote in local Finnish elections, could not serve in the Finnish armed forces, and Russian teachers, doctors and sailors were restricted in their activities in Finland.

The position of Finland attracted the attention of the ideologues of Russian nationalism. In 1889, K. F. Ordin published a substantial account of the Russian acquisition of Finland, significantly entitled *The Conquest of Finland*, in which he argued that Finland had been granted no special privileges by Alexander I at the time of its absorption into the Russian state at the beginning of the nineteenth century. The implication of his argument was that Finland's autonomy was unjustified and that it should be curtailed to bring Finland into line with the overall ethos of the imperial state. The Finns challenged this interpretation of their history with great vigour, arguing that the relationship between Finland and Russia was one of equals and that, in effect, a treaty had been concluded between the two in 1808, confirming Finland's status as a constitutional monarchy and allowing the Russian monarch only to rule in Finland in accordance with a defined body of law. These opposing views struck to the core of the definition of the Russian state and the nature of its empire. At a time when St Petersburg was taking severe steps to limit Polish autonomy and was using its military might to subdue the peoples of the Caucasus and Central Asia, the position of Finland appeared increasingly anomalous.

The resurgence of conservatism that followed the assassination of Alexander II was manifested in a very different attitude to Finland and to Russia's empire as a whole by the Romanov state. In 1890 the separate Finnish postal system was abolished by St Petersburg, despite protests from Finland that the proper procedure had been ignored, as the Finnish institutions had not been consulted. But, the main assault on Finnish autonomy did not come until the end of the 1890s and the appointment of General N. I. Bobrikov as Governor-General of Finland. Bobrikov's military background was particularly appropriate as the St Petersburg government was planning to launch an attack on Finland's military autonomy. A new Conscription Act was prepared by the imperial Ministry of War, aimed at nullifying the 1878 legislation that had granted Finland its separate army. At the same time, St Petersburg was discussing how to ensure that Finland contributed a greater share of the empire's overall military expenditure. A. N. Kuropatkin, the imperial Minister of War, wrote that the military question was part of a more far-reaching objective,

the beginning of the true incorporation of Finland into the Empire, because it would bring the two peoples together, help Finns to learn the Russian language – which is nowadays entirely foreign to them – and above all cultivate in them the spirit of the unified

Russian army. The Empire's essential defence and security interests in the region of Finland require that this borderland – so close to the capital – be incorporated into the Empire more swiftly and completely than others.[10]

The imperial regime in St Petersburg refused to recognise not just that Finland should enjoy any autonomy, but also that the Finns could have any say in the determination of their own fate. Bobrikov's appointment as Governor-General of Finland in 1898 marked the beginning of a concerted attempt to destroy Finnish autonomy. The very manner of his appointment demonstrated the change in approach by St Petersburg; instead of conforming to the established method of issuing the decree through the Finnish authorities, the government promulgated it directly. When the Finns complained, the Minister of War shouted at them 'Get this straight, His Majesty the Emperor has by his will as Sovereign condescended to institute a new order.'[11]

St Petersburg intended that this 'new order' should mean the complete destruction of Finnish autonomy. Bobrikov's programme included the integration of the Finnish army into the imperial military forces and the levying of a proper share of the costs of the empire's armed forces on the Finns. He also wanted to ensure that the Governor-General took primacy over Finnish authorities, so that the Minister State Secretary for Finland – the chief Finnish official – was subordinated to him and could not act independently. Bobrikov was also intent on removing other practical manifestations of Finland's separate status by abolishing its separate currency and customs tariffs. He also wanted to allow Russians to play a full part in Finland by adopting Russian as the official language of the Finnish Senate and other parts of Finnish administration, as well as making its use compulsory in educational institutions. He turned his attention to education, intending to intensify the level of inspection of the Alexander University in Helsinki, seeing it as a hotbed of Finnish nationalism, and to institute proper checks on the textbooks that were used in Finnish schools to ensure that they presented a view of Finland's place in the empire that was acceptable to the imperial regime. Bobrikov also wanted to make sure that Russian views were adequately publicised throughout Finland and wanted to establish an official Russian-language newspaper. The new governor-general encountered immediate difficulties when he arrived in Helsinki to

take up his post. Although most of the members of the Finnish Senate
were fluent in Russian, they refused to use the language for official business, turning Bobrikov's chairmanship of the Senate into a
mockery. At the same time, his own staff was entirely made up of
Finns, so that the new governor-general had to deal with his own
confidential correspondence. This gave a flavour of the problems that
the imperial regime was to face as it attempted to impose its will on
the Finns. Bobrikov moved ahead to implement his programme, but
it provoked a significant campaign of largely passive resistance from
the Finns. When the new conscription law was introduced, fewer than
half of the men selected for the draft actually reported to the authorities, and those that did were subjected to cat-calling by crowds of
angry Finns. This in turn provoked violent reaction from the Russian
authorities, who used troops to disperse the demonstrators.

When Bobrikov attempted to bring about lasting change in the way
in which Finland was governed by redefining the roles of imperial
and Finnish authorities to give St Petersburg the deciding voice, half
a million Finns signed a petition against the 1899 February Manifesto that presaged the introduction of this change. Finns showed
their opposition to Russian rule by portraying Finland as the victim
of Russian repression. The poet Mandelstam wrote of Finland that
'in every house there hung, in a frame of mourning black, a picture
of a bareheaded girl named Suomi, above whose head there bristled
the angry two-headed eagle, while she fiercely clasped to her breast
a book with the label – Law'.[12] Bobrikov was shot dead in 1904 by
a lone assassin, and in 1905 Finland burst into outright opposition
as revolution took hold of much of the empire. The Finns, however,
had a very specific set of grievances and protested specifically against
the extinguishing of their autonomy that had been the hallmark of
Bobrikov's period in office. A general strike, attracting huge support
across Finland, took place at the end of October 1905 and alongside the regime's concessions outlined in the October Manifesto, the
St Petersburg regime caved in to Finnish demands and Nicholas II
issued a manifesto that withdrew all the legislation of the Bobrikov era.

The Finns took rapid advantage of the new situation, using it to
establish a modern parliamentary structure in Finland. In 1906 a
single-chamber legislature was brought into being, elected by all Finns
aged over 24 – both male and female – through a system of propor-
tional representation. But the imperial government had not finished
with its attempts to assert its authority over Finland. The Russian

state made one final attempt to impose its will on the Finns, by trying to assert unambiguously that St Petersburg had the deciding voice in whether legislation affecting Finland should be dealt with by the imperial government or by the Finns. This was part of the Romanov state's overall attempt to recover its authority in the wake of 1905 and when Stolypin, the prime minister, declared that Finland 'allegedly received a special state existence' at the time of its acquisition by Russia in 1808, it was clear that St Petersburg was preparing to make a further assault on Finnish autonomy.[13] The resurgence of conservatism after 1905 meant that the imperial government was able to push through its redefinition of legislative jurisdiction over Finland. But, the St Petersburg regime failed to take advantage of the new framework and it achieved little.[14] The course of the relationship between the imperial power and its Finnish domains is instructive in demonstrating both the power of the Russian state and the limitations of its authority in dealing with its imperial possessions. St Petersburg was able to use its mastery of the legislative process to ensure that it could gain control of the government of Finland and the imperial government had no qualms about imposing the Russian ethos of government on Finland. But faced with resolute and largely peaceful opposition from the Finns, the St Petersburg government was bewildered about how to respond. The violent uprisings of the Poles or the peoples of the Caucasus posed no dilemma for the imperial state: it responded to violence with its own brutal military force. But the Finns' passive resistance was unlikely to be broken by force and, by the second half of the nineteenth century, the Russian state was concerned about the international reaction that would be provoked by any significant use of force in Finland.

Attempts to Russify Finland ended in ultimate failure. But the St Petersburg regime had greater success in imposing uniformity on other parts of the empire. External manifestations of nationality increasingly found disapproval with the imperial government. Under Nicholas I, efforts were made to persuade the Greek Catholic population of Ukraine to convert to Orthodoxy and a Russian university was established in Kiev. In 1847, the prominent Ukrainian poet Taras Shevchenko was arrested for his membership of the Brotherhood of Sts Cyril and Methodius, a tiny organisation devoted to promoting Ukrainian nationalism, and was sentenced to 10 years hard labour. Use of the Ukrainian language in publications or public performances was completely prohibited in 1876, while at the same time the government resolved to offer financial support to a newspaper which was openly hostile to Ukrainian national ambitions.[15] The state rarely went so far as to totally forbid the public use of a language, recognising that such a policy was extremely difficult to enforce, but it did put great pressures on the non-Russian population of the empire to utilise Russian, rather than their native language, in every part of their contact with officialdom. In Poland, the Russian state sought to promote assimilation in the wake of the 1863 rebellion by insisting on the use of Russian in the courts and in local government. Russian became the language of local administration in the Baltic provinces in 1885, and Baltic legal reform in 1888 and 1889 brought with it the compulsory use of Russian in the higher courts. These reforms did not, however, affect the self-governing institutions controlled by the Baltic German landowners; they remained immune from this process of linguistic imperialism and continued to conduct their business in German. Alongside the use of Russian in administrative matters came a greater insistence on its place in education right across the empire. In Poland the native tongue could only be taught as a foreign language, so that Polish children had to use Russian when learning their own language at school. In 1863, the regime had prohibited the publication of all literature in Ukrainian aimed at the ordinary people,[16] while the 1876 Ukrainian language edict laid down that primary schools could not teach in Ukrainian – or Little Russian as the edict insultingly termed the Ukrainian language. It was also suggested that teachers who had been trained in Ukrainian provinces should be appointed to teaching posts in regions far from their homes and that schools in Ukraine should be staffed by teachers from the Russian heartland.[17] The imperial government regarded institutions of higher education in non-Russian areas with particular suspicion. It was all too aware of the role that universities had played in developing opposition to the state and did not wish to see this process accentuated in non-Russian areas by the addition of nationalist ideology to the already potent brew which was producing the nascent socialist movement in the 1880s and 1890s. This was one area in which the imperial government did act to restrict the privileges of the Baltic Germans: the German-speaking university in Tartu was compelled to provide instruction in Russian between 1889 and 1895 and in 1893 the city itself lost its German name of Dorpat and instead received the Russian name of Iur'ev.[18] In Finland, plans were made to institute new professorships in Russian law and Russian history at the Alexander

University in Helsinki and for these topics to be taught in Russian. Action had already been taken in the wake of the Polish rebellion to establish a new Russian-language university in Warsaw in 1869.

Religious affiliation was also a clear symbol of national identity through which the Tsarist regime sought to intensify the homogeneity of the empire. As well as providing encouragement to the Orthodox Church to proselytise amongst adherents to other religions, the government also took steps to make the Orthodox religion more attractive to others. In the Baltic provinces, land was provided for landless Orthodox peasants and financial support was made available to improve the quantity of Orthodox-controlled schools. During the 13 years of Alexander III's reign, it is estimated that 37,000 Lutherans in the Baltic region underwent conversion to Orthodoxy, although some returned to Lutheranism when religious toleration was increased after 1905. The Roman Catholic religion had suffered in the 1860s as the imperial government tried to break its ties with Polish nationalism. Catholic monasteries in Poland were closed down, the influence of Catholic priests was curbed and incentives were provided to encourage non-Catholics to buy land in Poland. As the Russian empire expanded into the Far East and Central Asia, intense activity took place to promote Orthodoxy. The All-Russian Orthodox Missionary Society was established in 1870 and by 1894 it was able to proclaim that nearly 60,000 'heathens and Muslims' had become Orthodox as a result of its work. A visit by the future Nicholas II to Siberia in 1891 provided the excuse for the forced mass baptism of members of the Buriat community.[19]

It was the Jewish population of the Russian empire that suffered the most direct discrimination as a result of their religion. The state imposed severe restrictions on Jews: they were permitted to live only in the Pale of Settlement in the western provinces of the empire, and only limited numbers of Jews could reside in Russia's towns and cities outside the Pale.[20] Jews had their choice of employment severely limited, as work in government service was almost entirely closed to them. Jewish access to education was restricted in 1887: in the Jewish Pale of Settlement, only 10 per cent of students in secondary and higher education could come from the Jewish population, a proportion that was reduced to 5 per cent in the rest of the empire, except in St Petersburg and Moscow, where only 3 per cent of students could be Jews. These quotas served to antagonise young Jews, who saw their ambition stifled by the Tsarist regime, and this discontent was further fuelled by frequent violent attacks on the Jewish community – pogroms – that were often officially sponsored and to which the Tsarist authorities usually turned a blind eye. It is unsurprising that revolutionary groups found it easy to recruit Jewish adherents and that Jews came to play a crucial part in the establishment of the Bolshevik regime that seized power in 1917.[21]

These visible expressions of nationality were not the only targets of the imperial government in attempting to extend the Russian nature of the state to all its component parts. The imperial army was seen as an effective method of promoting uniformity amongst the different peoples of the empire by inculcating Russianness into new conscripts. The Volga Germans lost their exemption from military service in 1874. The overall structure of the Russian army also contributed to this process: conscripts were dispersed among military units so that national groupings could not develop. The army aimed for no more than 25 per cent of any unit to come from non-Russian groups. As the work of the army was conducted in Russian, conscripts had to become proficient in the language and left the army with a firm command of it.

The Romanov state demonstrated considerable skill at acquiring and holding its empire together. The single unbroken expanse of the Russian empire gave it a very different character from the imperial regimes of other European powers. Despite the huge diversity of the lands and peoples that it gained, the Romanov regime was reluctant to view its new possessions as having any essential difference from metropolitan Russia itself. The Tsarist state was based on the imposition of a uniform ethos right across the state and there was therefore little room for allowing national or regional diversity. The concept of Official Nationality that Uvarov articulated during the 1830s showed that Russian nationalism was an essential component of the identity of the Tsarist state. Acquiring territories that were adjacent to the heartland of the Russian state did not allow the Romanov regime any real latitude in the approach that they took to their imperial domains. While the British and the French could use the physical separation of metropolis from colonies to allow their imperial domains significant variation in their level of autonomy and the style of government, the Russians were faced with a much more difficult situation. Driven by the need to maintain their authority unchallenged, the Romanovs could not risk allowing any of their possessions significant autonomy, lest calls for autonomy spread to the Russian heartland itself. This did not apply just to the methods and type of government that different parts of the empire acquired, but also to cultural matters. Permitting the development of national traditions in the empire would show that the Russian state was not the cohesive unit that was vital for its survival. The ill-fated Bobrikov articulated the imperial ethos with great clarity in 1898: 'Russia is one and indivisible. . . . Throughout the whole vast territory of Russia all who are subjects under the mighty sceptre of the Tsar must know themselves to be of one realm and share the love for a common fatherland.'[22] This statement demonstrated very plainly that the imperial government recognised no difference between the metropolis and its imperial possessions: as new territories were acquired they simply became part of Russia itself and their peoples were expected to embrace the elements of Russian identity with enthusiasm. The Russian state never established a separate government department to deal with the non-Russian peoples of the empire, and while some parts of the apparatus of government had more dealings with these groups, in particular the departments dealing with non-Orthodox religions, the Russian state was entirely averse to recognising that its territorial acquisitions required special treatment.

Cultural assimilation was to be the destiny of the peoples who were gathered into Russia's domains. The state was to integrate territory and population into its ambit with all the means at its disposal. The construction of railways during the nineteenth century was one tangible method of drawing together the empire, exemplified by the great project to construct the Trans-Siberian railway in the two decades after 1891. The project to lay thousands of miles of railway through deeply inhospitable terrain demonstrated the significance that the government placed upon giving a physical unity to the empire. 'Railway colonisation' was not unique to Russia, and the motivation for the construction of the railway was overwhelmingly political: during the 1880s the Finance Ministry consistently opposed spending money on the railway as it threatened the fiscal stability of the state.[23] The construction of the Trans-Siberian also provided a means by which Russian settlers could reach Siberia more easily and thus assisted the process of spreading Russian values into the east of the empire. This was particularly valuable since much of the Russian population of Siberia was made up of exiles and the government wanted to populate the region with a more stable and reliable group of people who could disseminate Russian values.[24]

Russia was not alone among the European imperial powers in trying to assert its own ethos and identity over its domains: the British and the French too wanted to ensure the dominance of the metropolitan power. The aggressive nationalism that the imperial state pursued for much of the nineteenth century both reflected the need of the Russian state to impose its own values on its subject peoples, while it was also a product of the development of nationalism that made some of the peoples of the Russian empire assert their own identity. The power of the state and its ability to constrain the national identity of many of its subject peoples did not, in most cases, destroy national sentiment. Instead, the intensification of Russian national identity merely sharpened existing nationalisms among the peoples of the empire, driving them into hibernation rather than extinguishing them. In the case of some peoples, such as the Poles, who had a highly developed national sense long before they were conquered by the Russians, the pressure exerted by the Russians served to accentuate their own existing identity. Russian attempts to impose an alien language and religion proved counter-productive and stimulated the Poles to develop a fierce and enduring loathing of their Russian masters. The impact of Russian imperialism came rapidly to the fore as soon as the authority of the state was weakened in 1917: the Finns, Poles and Ukrainians all jumped at the opportunity to achieve independence. Within six weeks of the Bolshevik revolution, Finland declared independence, while the Poles fought and won a war against the new Soviet state to regain their statehood. Ukraine was swallowed up by Bolshevik Russia in 1921, but the brief experience of independence from Russia whetted the Ukrainian appetite for autonomy.

The Russian imperial experience gave the Tsarist regime a reputation for unparalleled power and the other Great Powers lived in trepidation of further Russian expansion. The British feared for the security of their empire in India as the Russians swept south into Central Asia, while, in Europe, the Great Powers wanted to curb any further expansion by Russia into Slav Europe. Austria-Hungary was especially concerned by the appeal that Russian power held for the peoples of south-eastern Europe as the authority of the Ottoman Empire declined and the Orthodox population of the Balkans looked to Russia as the protector of Slav peoples everywhere. Russian imperial power persisted into the final years of the Tsarist state's existence and played a major part in determining the course of international relations in the late nineteenth and early twentieth centuries. The Anglo-Russian agreement of 1907 that dealt with imperial rivalry between Britain and Russia in Asia, and the Balkan crises that tore south-eastern Europe apart after 1900, both had their roots in the fear that Russia would use its imperial muscle to upset the balance of power and dominate both Asia and Europe. The Romanov state's expansion appeared to have no limits: the British believed that Russia had designs for making incursions into India, while the long-standing Russian ambition to acquire Constantinople and the Straits appeared to lie at the root of Russian interest in the Balkans. To the outside world, Russian imperial power was at its zenith after 1900 and gave little hint of the disaster that was to befall it.

Chapter 8:   Financing the Empire

The economics of the Russian state were significantly affected by both the Romanov regime's foreign and domestic policies. When Peter the Great set Russia on the course of expansion, he unwittingly put in place a model for the Tsarist state's finances from which it was never able to escape. The process of becoming and remaining a Great Power required Russia to commit huge financial and material resources to its military forces, and this was accentuated by the wider role that the army played in the Romanov state. The imperial ambitions of the Russian state further increased the demands that were placed upon the armed forces as troops were needed to subdue peoples from Poland to Central Asia and were required to garrison Russia's far-flung borders. The army's role in providing for the internal security of the state also placed further demands on the state to ensure that sufficient numbers of soldiers were available and that they were paid and equipped.

Expenditure

The structure of the Tsarist government meant that the state's spending took priority over the ability of the regime to raise revenue. The financial administration of the empire had little impact on policy making until the final decades of the Tsarist regime, and the function of the finance ministry and its predecessors was simply to raise revenue to meet the needs of the spending ministries. The weakness of the finance ministry was accentuated by the absence of any system of cabinet government until 1905: individual ministers were able to plead their case for additional spending directly with the monarch without any consideration of the overall impact that their requests would have on the finances of the empire. This gave the military and naval departments a particular advantage, given the close interest that successive Tsars had in Russia's armed forces. The identification of Russia's army with the prestige and identity of the Russian state itself meant that no monarch was likely to turn down a request from his generals for additional troops. The 'state's readiness to support its political dignity' was at stake when military expenditure was being discussed, as the Minister of War put it in 1879 when there were hints of a reduction in the army's budget.[1] Even though the military's protestations were not always well founded, their arguments did have a fundamental ring of truth to them. The Tsarist model of government was based upon military power, both at home and abroad, and any weakening of authority – whether real or perceived – could have a very damaging impact on the grip that the state had on power. The personal ties that monarchs had with the military also gave the generals a significant advantage in their position in the government: only the mid-eighteenth-century empresses did not experience a military education or serve as officers, so that every adult male emperor had a network of close contacts among the military. This gave the military a privileged access to the monarch that was not enjoyed by other areas of government, so that there was a continuing presumption that military spending would take precedence over everything else.

During the eighteenth century, Russia's army and navy consistently accounted for more than half of the state's annual budget, and at times this proportion increased to more than 60 per cent. Between 1700 and 1850 the overwhelming majority of this expenditure was devoted to paying, clothing and feeding soldiers. In the first part of the eighteenth century, almost 90 per cent of the cost of an infantry regiment was accounted for by these elements, with only a small proportion of the costs being accounted for by equipment. For cavalry regiments, the situation was different: almost 30 per cent of the costs of maintaining cavalry was taken up by expenditure on procuring and caring for the regiment's horses. Taking the army as a whole, by 1800 more than three-quarters of the army budget was spent on paying and feeding its soldiers. Weaponry accounted for only a small proportion of the cost of the army, reflecting the pre-industrial

technology and the basic muskets that were used.[2] A state's ability to
field an army in the early modern period was unrelated to its level
of industrial or technological development, but was instead simply
related to the state's ability to conscript men to serve and then its
continuing capacity to feed and clothe its soldiers. This was ideally
suited to the Tsarist state: the Russian rural economy made food
supply relatively easy to guarantee, while the authoritarian ethos of
the state made the conscription process reliable. While there was a
reduction in the proportion of the military budget that was expended
on troops themselves after 1860, it was only after 1891 that a significantly greater amount was spent on weaponry. This coincided with
Russia's first burst of industrial growth, as well as reflecting the increasingly rapid process of armament that gripped all the Great Powers
after 1890. It was only in 1913 and 1914 – on the very brink of the
First World War – that the proportion of the army's budget that was
devoted to weaponry and associated equipment exceeded 50 per cent
of the total.

The Russian navy's pattern of expenditure was different: the
construction of warships was an extremely expensive business, especially once modern ironclad vessels became the norm. Russia's limited
access to warm-water ports meant that the Tsarist navy was always
much less significant than its land-based armed forces. The only practical base for Russian ships was in the Baltic Sea, but access to and
from the open ocean required Russian vessels to pass through the
very narrow channel separating Denmark from Sweden. Russian naval
commanders were always concerned that passage could be denied
them if hostilities broke out in Europe and were very cautious about
expanding their fleet. The Black Sea was even more problematic for
Russia: the Straits that connected it to the Mediterranean were under
the control of the Ottoman Empire and there was always the possibility that a Russian Black Sea fleet could be cooped up and prevented
from gaining access to the open sea if hostilities broke out. Even
during the second half of the nineteenth century, the Russian naval
budget was less than one fifth of expenditure on the army. This position changed after 1900: in 1902 expenditure on the navy reached
100 million rubles for the first time, only falling back again in 1907
for three years and then increasing very sharply to reach 245 million
rubles in 1913. The huge cost of new capital ships drove the naval
budget up, so that its 1913 level reached more than 40 per cent of
expenditure on the army.[3]

The changes to the proportion of the military and naval budgets spent on weaponry that took place at the end of the nineteenth century had a significant impact on the state. While Russia's rural economy had been able to cope with growing crops and raising livestock to feed the troops and with producing textiles to make uniforms, the need for more sophisticated weaponry and equipment placed stresses upon the national economy. The undeveloped Russian industrial economy was not structured to produce the large quantities of armaments that a modern army needed, and the domestic iron and steel industry was anyway focussed on producing the materials needed for Russia's railway industry. The option of turning to foreign suppliers for Russia's armaments was also problematic. The Russian state had limited reserves of foreign currency and it was keen to conserve them. The economic policies pursued by Witte during the 1890s concentrated on encouraging foreign investment in Russia and on stimulating domestic industry, and the finance ministry was reluctant to expend precious resources on buying military equipment from abroad if it could be avoided. There were some types of military hardware that could only be procured from abroad: warships and other capital vessels were the prime example. Russia initially purchased ships from the construction yards on the River Tyne in north-east England, but then ensured that British shipbuilders established shipyards in Russia itself, thus reducing the foreign currency costs to the Russian exchequer.

Russia's persistent involvement in wars during the eighteenth and nineteenth centuries meant that there was little opportunity to reduce its military expenditure. The Napoleonic Wars proved to be an exceptional drain on the state's resources, and military spending rose to take up more than 60 per cent of the state's entire budget between 1810 and 1814. War with Persia and with Turkey in the late 1820s placed further stresses on the budget and, in late 1830, the Ministry of Finance indicated that any further conflict would cause significant problems. Expenditure was already likely to rise due to a series of poor harvests and the outbreak of cholera in some parts of the empire, and the Finance Ministry warned that any further war could not be financed from ordinary expenditure. Kankrin, the Minister of Finance, had already reported to Nicholas I that the government would face severe difficulties in finding the additional resources needed for conflict. Kankrin's view was not, however, shared by the government as a whole and the government's Finance Committee argued that difficulties could be overcome by printing money and by a number of measures that would enable the government to raise internal loans.[4] This approach to dealing with the financial pressures of war continued throughout the reign of Nicholas I. Discussions about managing the costs of the Crimean War in the mid-1850s resulted in the same measures being proposed. The Ministry of Finance issued more paper money as its first reaction to the increase in expenditure that was required by war, more than doubling the amount of paper money in circulation, but the Ministry did acknowledge that this solution was only sustainable if the war was short. It also recognised that this was a risky move to make, since the outcome of printing money would only become clear once the war was over: if the economy prospered, all would be well, but difficulties would arise if it weakened.[5]

During the 1860s, in the aftermath of the Crimean War and the very difficult financial situation associated with the process of emancipating the serfs, M. K. Reutern, the Minister of Finance, identified a pressing need to protect the value of the Russian currency and to stop resorting to the government relying on domestic loans to keep its finances afloat. He wanted the government to stop making purchases abroad and included the Ministry of War in his strictures, as well as insisting that the navy should stop making expensive foreign visits.[6] The government also made attempts to rein in military expenditure overall, but it never succeeded in achieving any substantial or lasting reductions. Throughout the nineteenth century, there were repeated efforts to restrain military expenditure and government committees regularly grappled with the problem of the cost of the Russian army and navy. A special committee met in 1818, followed by a review of military expenditure by A. A. Arakcheev in 1822, and a further attempt to rein in expenditure in 1835. This last review concluded that reductions in expenditure during the 1820s had produced a negative impact both on Russia's military forces and on the overall national economy, as a reduced demand for materials by the army had resulted in an overall reduction in the prices of domestically produced goods and this had affected both manufacturers and the treasury, since the government suffered a consequent loss of tax revenues. The dominant place that Russia's military strength played in the government's thinking is reflected in the results of the 1835 review: the committee could only suggest 'housekeeping measures' to limit military spending and then only if both economic and military conditions continued to be stable.[7] A further attempt was made to reduce overall government expenditure in 1861 but, in the aftermath of the debacle in the Crimea, no serious attempt was made to constrain military spending.[8] A committee chaired by A. A. Abaza looked again at military expenditure in the late 1870s, but in the aftermath of the Russo-Turkish war, it was again clearly impolitic to propose any major reductions in military spending. Abaza's committee had begun with the lofty ambition of moving beyond short-term solutions to the recurrent financial difficulties that faced the Russian government, and instead putting in place measures that would prevent ministries increasing their expenditure after their annual budget had been set. But by the middle of 1879, Abaza was compelled to admit that due to 'the alarming events of recent times', ministries had been unable to devote adequate attention to the work of his committee and that they had proved very tardy in providing the information he needed in order to proceed.[9] The Russian bureaucracy proved able to frustrate these plans; central authority was not yet well enough established to override the power of individual ministries, while successive emperors were heavily influenced by the needs of the military establishment and were unwilling to support the Ministry of Finance against the army and navy ministers.

The eighteenth-century Russian state devoted a substantial proportion of its expenditure to the court. In this it was little different from the other European powers, although the Russian court never approached the extravagance of Louis XIV's Versailles or the rigid formality of the Habsburgs in Vienna. Both Empresses Anna and Elizabeth were famed for their love of jewellery, but it was only during Catherine's reign that court expenditure grew significantly as a series of great palaces reached the final stages of their construction in and around St Petersburg. The Catherine Palace at Tsarskoe Selo was the most exuberant of these edifices, with its golden-domed chapel and richly decorated state-rooms. The court absorbed an amount equivalent to one fifth of ordinary expenditure on the army in the second half of Catherine's reign, as the number of courtiers increased and the Russian court became more sophisticated. Some 12 per cent of the state's budget under Catherine was devoted to the court and the empress's progresses around her domains required a substantial entourage: Catherine's 1787 visit to the Crimea needed 14 carriages, 124 sledges and 40 additional vehicles to accompany the imperial retinue. The court reached its zenith during the late eighteenth century, and Catherine's successors were more modest in their expenditure. The nineteenth-century court was more isolated from elite Russian society, with the final two Tsars and their families eschewing the splendour of the great eighteenth-century palaces and living in much more modest circumstances. Nicholas II spent most of his reign living at Tsarskoe Selo, not in the grand Catherine Palace, but instead in the modest Alexander Palace a few hundred metres away. His wife, Empress Alexandra, particularly disliked the ceremony of the court and the imperial couple attended only those functions that were an inescapable part of their duties. Their domestic life was simple and straightforward and they lived the lives of country nobles, enlivened with only rare bursts of extravagance, such as the Fabergé Easter eggs that became an annual feature.

The state's spending patterns underwent changes during the nineteenth century as the Tsarist regime's functions expanded. The Russian state had to play a substantial role in the process of stimulating Russia's economy, since Russia was very short of domestic sources of capital to finance investment. In particular, the state understood the critical role that railways could play in the general economic development of Russia and was prepared to make significant investments directly into constructing and running railways. The level of the state's expenditure on railways increased as Witte, with his background in the railway industry, rose to prominence in the Tsarist government. The Ministry of Communications took only 2.5 per cent of government spending in 1885, but the spurt of industrial growth that Russia experienced during the 1890s spurred on the government to devote significantly more of its budget to railway construction. By 1895, the Ministry's share of total government expenditure had risen to 11 per cent and it continued to accelerate to reach 20 per cent by 1908. An important reason for this dramatic increase in spending was the decision to proceed with the construction of the Trans-Siberian railway. The political imperative to draw the empire's lands closer together was intensified by the recognition of the growing importance of the Pacific region in international politics. The Russian state needed to be able to consolidate its position along the Pacific littoral, and a railway linking its possessions in the region with the European heartland of the empire was vital if Russia was to be able to supply its military and naval forces on the Pacific coast. The initial estimate for the construction of the railway was more then 350 million rubles, and this was at a time when the state's entire annual budget was only some 1400 million rubles. The building of the railway was to take more than two decades and its cost reached almost 500 million rubles in total by the time the project was completed.

Revenue

The development and management of a successful railway system during the second half of the nineteenth century was one indication of the growing bureaucratic competence of the Russian state's financial and economic apparatus. The most significant example of this was, however, the development of the state's involvement with the liquor industry. Russian consumption of alcohol was very high and it represented an important element in the Russian economy. During the eighteenth century, Catherine II's government established a system of tax farming to maximise the revenues that the state could obtain from the sale of alcohol. The regime's own administrative resources were not extensive enough to allow the state itself to take on the task of collecting revenue from the sale of vodka right across the empire and the use of a tax farm ensured that the state could guarantee this element of its revenues. In 1754, distilling had been established as a monopoly of the nobility and the introduction of tax farming in 1767 gave the government a fixed fee from each regional tax farm. Between 1767 and 1770 the Moscow and St Petersburg tax farms brought in more than 2 million rubles annually. While this system was useful in giving the regime a dependable source of income, it was also extremely profitable for the tax farmers themselves and the state became jealous of the amount of potential revenue that it was losing to them. In 1863, the government abolished the system of tax farming, confident that its own bureaucratic capability was now sufficient to collect the revenues from the vodka industry. This also represented the state's growing direct involvement in Russian industry and it was just one of the steps on the road towards the state's full control of the liquor trade. In the 1890s the government moved to establish a complete state monopoly on the vodka trade: the government became the sole legal purchaser for the products of Russia's distilleries. These gradual moves to enhance the state's role in the liquor industry involved it in extra expenditure: by 1912, it was costing some 200 million rubles annually to keep the industry going, but this was offset by the additional revenues that the state was able to achieve through its own control of the industry.

The Russian state was also involved in the salt industry. In common with other states, Russia recognised that this staple part of the diet could form a source of tax revenue for the state, and Peter the Great introduced a state monopoly on salt in 1705. This did not prove to be the same easy source of revenue as the liquor trade, since Russia's main salt deposits were located away from its main settlements and extracting salt and then transporting it to the Russian heartland proved to be expensive and difficult. The costs involved in the salt monopoly were high: in 1762 the state was spending one third of its gross revenues from the salt monopoly on the process of production and distribution, leaving it with only 2 million rubles as the net contribution to the budget from the salt business. The situation worsened significantly during the remainder of the eighteenth century, so that in 1791 the government for the first time made an actual loss on its salt operations.[10] The state tried to improve the position by increasing the retail price of salt and thus hoping to bring the business back into profit, but even this did not help and in 1818, the government gave up its monopoly on the sale of salt, eventually abolishing the salt tax altogether in 1880. The state's record of direct involvement in business was mixed: the Russian regime expended substantial amounts of its budget on the railway, liquor and salt industries, seeing a direct financial return only from its investment in the vodka trade. Rather than contributing to the treasury's coffers, the salt monopoly quickly proved to be a drain on the state's resources, while the railway industry had only an indirect impact on the state's finances, acting to improve the overall performance of the Russian economy and thus to increase the state's tax revenues, but making a substantial direct call on its finances.

The development of the state during the nineteenth century also had financial consequences. In common with other European states, Russia expanded its educational provision and central government spending on schools increased significantly. In 1881, total spending on education accounted for only 2.7 per cent of the state's budget, but by the time the First World War broke out in 1914, this had grown to reach more than 7 per cent. In 1895, the government's spending on primary schooling was only 2 million rubles, but this reached more than 82 million rubles 20 years later. The judicial reforms of the 1860s also required increased spending, as the system of courts grew more complex and the Ministry of Justice made repeated demands for increases in its budget to deal with the ever-growing number of cases that were coming before the courts. Lastly, the state had to make significant interest payments on its loans. Pressures on the state's budget were traditionally met by taking out loans and by printing money: by the end of the nineteenth century interest payments were costing the Russian state almost 100 million rubles a year. The Russian state's spending was not driven by any proper consideration of what the government could afford, but rather by the demands that the spending ministries placed upon the finance ministry. During the eighteenth century, the Russian government hardly had a proper budget-setting process, with 'an inadequate centralisation of financial administration, the lack of a central treasury, the secrecy of the budget, the unsatisfactory recording of business, the lack of accountability in agencies and the almost total absence of state fiscal control of expenditure'.[11] In these circumstances, it is all the more surprising that the Russian state was able to maintain financial solvency, but the regime proved consistently able to collect sufficient revenues to stave off financial crisis.

Peter the Great laid the basis for the financial stability of the Russian state by introducing a poll tax in 1721. The increased international role of Petrine Russia and the military resources that this demanded required a reliable source of income. The existing household tax was proving to be less successful since the peasant population was able to evade the full weight of the levy by artificially combining their families into a single household for the purposes of the tax collectors. The new poll tax was much more difficult to escape and it also proved relatively easy to collect. Initially, collection was the task of military detachments, which then used the revenue to maintain themselves, thus avoiding the need for a complex system of accounting. Once the pressures of the wars of the early eighteenth century had eased, the collection of the tax was transferred to the civil administration, and the government was able to give responsibility for collecting the tax to serfowners. Their power over the rural population eased the job of collecting taxes, although this part of their relationship with the serf population only served to increase the peasantry's resentment at their enserfment, since they saw their lords as also being agents of the state when it came to the lords having to extract the poll tax from them. The poll tax was, however, extremely successful during the eighteenth century. The tax base expanded significantly as the population grew with imperial expansion and with increased longevity among the population, while the ease of the tax's collection also meant that the state felt able to increase the level of the poll tax. By the end of the eighteenth century, the burden of the poll tax on privately owned serfs was a third higher than it had been when the tax had been introduced, and the total amount generated by the poll tax had risen to more than 10 million rubles annually, compared with just 4 million a year in the mid-1720s.[12] The poll tax slowly declined in importance during the nineteenth century, producing a steadily diminishing share of the state's revenues, and the emancipation of the serfs hastened the demise of the tax. Without serfowners in the countryside to collect the poll tax from their peasants, it became more difficult for the state to be able to guarantee the inflow of revenue and, after 1861, peasant tax arrears grew sharply. But the government was reluctant to abandon any source of revenue, especially at a time when the demands on the treasury were growing, and even at the end of the 1870s, the poll tax was still generating almost 60 million rubles annually. The position of the poll tax was considered by the government as part of a wider discussion of its taxation policies during the early 1880s. N. Kh. Bunge, Minister of Finance between 1882 and 1887, was keen to see a shift in the pattern of taxation, moving away from dependence on direct taxes and enhancing the importance of indirect levies. As part of this policy, the poll tax was gradually abolished between 1883 and 1886.

The greatest single source of indirect revenues came from the state's involvement in the liquor trade. The net revenue from the sale of vodka grew significantly during the eighteenth century: in 1765, the state gained 4 million rubles from this source but revenue more than doubled during the next 20 years to reach 9 million rubles in 1785, with a further acceleration in the growth of the tax yield during the next decade, so that the vodka trade contributed almost 18 million rubles to the state's income in 1795.[13] This represented a very substantial proportion of the government's overall revenues: in 1724 the liquor industry had contributed only 11 per cent of the state's overall income, but this rose to more than 40 per cent in the early 1780s before falling back to 24 per cent in 1805. During the nineteenth century, the revenue from the vodka industry contributed an average of 31 per cent of the state's total tax yields. The significance of this was not lost on the regime's financial bureaucrats. They understood both the exceptional importance of sustaining the revenue from the sale of alcohol, and also the potential that the business offered for providing the government with a dependable source of income at a time when the calls on expenditure were growing. This was part of the rationale for the state moving to take greater direct control of the vodka revenues by abolishing the system of tax farming in 1863. The cost of collecting liquor taxation was some 18 per cent of gross revenues during the 1850s, but by 1880, this had fallen dramatically so that only 3 per cent of the total revenue was eaten up by the cost of collection. The introduction of a full government monopoly on the production and sale of vodka significantly enhanced the revenues that the state received, but it also resulted in increased costs so that the level of net revenue remained static after 1894. When Russia entered the First World War in the summer of 1914, however, patriotic enthusiasm took precedence over financial prudence. The government initially declared a ban on the sale of alcohol during the process of mobilisation, and in October 1914, Nicholas II announced that he would abolish vodka sales permanently in Russia.[14] This created a very serious financial problem for the state, depriving it of the largest single source of its revenue: tax receipts in 1914 showed a decrease of more than 500 million rubles on the previous year, and the policy played a major part in the destabilisation of Russia's finances as the war progressed.

The Russian state was a major landowner and it received significant income from the peasants who lived on its land. While most privately owned serfs were liable both to carry out labour services for their owners and to make them financial payments, the state's peasants only had to make cash contributions to the government. This had been implemented by Peter the Great, keen to maximise government revenues for warfare, and the peasantry were viewed by the eighteenth-century state as a useful source of cash. Between 1765 and 1795 the state's yield from such payments rose from 2 million rubles to reach more than 12 million rubles at the end of Catherine's reign. However, the government became wary of further increasing the burden that these payments placed upon the peasantry. During the 1830s and 1840s, discussions took place about reforming the position of the state peasantry and the government rejected the option of significantly increasing these cash payments, arguing that this 'would disturb the tranquillity of the population and have dangerous consequences'.[15] Even when the state peasantry was emancipated in 1866, the regime took a conservative approach to the issue of the peasantry's cash payments. While the privately owned serfs moved immediately to a system of redemption payments for the land that they received upon emancipation, the state was wary of making any radical change that might threaten the security of its revenues from the state peasants. Instead, the government reformed the system of payments due from the former state peasants, only converting these into redemption payments in 1886, a full 20 years after emancipation. This move represented sound financial sense, since the yield from the redemption payments significantly exceeded the previous arrangements. Between 1887 and 1890, income from this source averaged 43 million rubles, a 30 per cent increase on the average of 32 million rubles that had been collected annually between 1880 and 1885.

The impact of Russia's budgetary policies on its population was considerable. Since the overwhelming majority of Russia's population were peasants, it was inevitable that they would bear the greatest burden of taxation. The impact of Peter the Great's introduction of the poll tax on the peasant has been widely debated. The emperor wanted to introduce a new and reliable source of revenue, but at the same time he was very conscious of the need not to antagonise the peasantry by making severe financial demands on them. Despite this, it has been argued, most notably by P. N. Miliukov in his writings before 1917, that the burden of taxation increased very substantially during Peter's reign and that, in particular, the poll tax generated 260 per cent more in revenue than the taxes that it replaced.[16] This argument is based on analysis of the total tax yield, rather than looking at the burden faced by each Russian household, and does not take into account the increase in population over the period and has thus been challenged by more recent commentators. It has been argued that the state's tax revenues increased partly because there were more taxpayers, but that this was also due to inflation and that the real tax burden on individuals remained more or less steady. It has even been suggested that the introduction of the poll tax represented a reduction in the level of taxation, after the government's need to increase taxes to pay for the Great Northern War.[17] As has been widely acknowledged, however, there is insufficient evidence to come to definitive judgements about the burdens of taxation in the early part of the eighteenth century. The Russian state did not have the bureaucratic capacity to maintain accurate records of its finances during this period and the budget-making process was still rudimentary. While complete evidence for the actual financial burdens faced by the peasantry during and immediately after Peter's reign is lacking, the perception produced by the introduction of the poll tax is much clearer. The population as a whole believed that the poll tax had resulted in significantly increased taxation. But this belief was related to the circumstances of the tax's introduction. The early 1720s were hard years for Russian farmers. Poor harvests and resulting high prices for grain helped to reduce the peasants' standard of living: many peasants were compelled to become purchasers of grain, rather than being able to sell their own produce. At the same time, the government moved to requisition grain, paying only very modest prices to the peasantry, to try to alleviate famine. The methods by which the new poll tax was collected also served to generate antagonism: the task of tax collection was initially handed over to the army, and the military sought to collect the new tax in cash. Even though the burden that the new tax represented may not have represented any substantial increase in the overall level of taxation demanded from the Russian peasants, their clear perception was that the poll tax did represent a considerable extra demand by the government.

The position of the peasantry in the second half of the nineteenth century was also complex. The government was very wary of making significant changes to the tax system until emancipation had bedded down. The system of redemption payments introduced a new financial burden for former serfs and the perception that gripped the Russian establishment after emancipation was that the peasantry were becoming more and more impoverished.[18] The government came to believe that it needed to try to alleviate the financial situation of the peasant if it was to prevent widespread rebellion. Alongside this, in the last part of the nineteenth century the state wanted to promote industrial growth in Russia. As Minister of Finance between 1881 and 1886, N. Kh. Bunge wanted to reduce the level of direct taxation on the peasantry, but the increases in indirect taxes in the 1880s and 1890s clearly had a significant impact on the rural population. The argument turns on the extent to which the reductions in direct taxation were balanced by increases in excise duties and other indirect levies. It has been suggested that in the first half of the 1880s, the overall tax burden on the peasantry was reduced: even though indirect taxation increased by some 10 per cent, this was more than compensated for by significant reductions in direct taxes. Urban residents paid more in taxation during this period, but the rural population saw its overall tax burden reduced by some 8 per cent.[19] This analysis is short-sighted, since it only considers the first part of the 1880s and fails to take into account the new impositions that were levied during the late 1880s and 1890s.

The increase in revenues that the government received from indirect taxation at the end of the nineteenth century suggests that the population was sufficiently prosperous to continue to consume taxed goods, even as the tax on them rose. The preponderance of rural dwellers in the Russian empire makes it improbable that it was townspeople who were the main purchasers of these goods and, in any case, significant numbers of the peasantry augmented their income from farming by wage labour in Russia's growing factories. It does appear as if the Russian peasant was, overall, sufficiently well off to be able to continue to consume manufactured goods, even as the government increased the taxation on them.

The Russian state's finances were put under significant stress by frequent wars and by the continual expansion of the empire's domains. This was especially true during the nineteenth century when warfare became more technologically demanding, and thus required greater resources, and as imperial growth accelerated into more hostile and difficult areas. The prolonged conflict with Napoleon, while bringing Russia huge prestige, also drained its coffers as the army marched westwards. This was followed by conflicts with Persia and with Turkey in the 1820s and, as the Russian state's financial apparatus became more sophisticated, bureaucrats began to warn of the dangers of continuing to let expenditure, especially on the military, continue to run unchecked. These interventions were initially rejected by the government, and even the state's Finance Committee saw no reason why Russia could not solve its problems by resorting to the traditional methods of printing money and taking out additional loans. It took several decades before the potential seriousness of Russia's financial position was fully appreciated by the government as a whole. The Crimean War proved to be ruinously expensive for Russia, requiring the levying of additional local taxation in the south to furnish the army with fuel, candles and straw, while Russia's eventual defeat meant that there was no opportunity to recoup any of its expenditure through reparations. The first reaction of the Ministry of Finance to the conflict was to print more paper money to cover the state's increased expenditure, and the amount of paper money in circulation more than doubled in the mid-1850s. The state found it difficult to retrieve the situation after the end of the war, as economic conditions deteriorated and Russia's overall financial position became more precarious. The war constrained Russia's ability to export goods, and this was exacerbated by a series of poor harvests in the 1850s that further reduced Russia's ability to export agricultural produce. The depredations of the war also meant that Russia needed to increase its flow of imports in the aftermath of the conflict to restore losses of equipment that it had suffered during the fighting, so that the empire's trade went into serious imbalance and foreign capital suffered a net outflow. The state's accustomed methods of dealing with budget difficulties were stretched to the limits by the end of the 1850s. Its debts to the banks had grown from 166 million rubles in 1845 to 441 million rubles 15 years later. At the same time, the amount of paper money in circulation had quadrupled to reach 93 million rubles in 1859, while Russian foreign debts totalled 365 million rubles by that year. It was clear that Russia had reached financial crisis point: the option of taking out further loans was hardly feasible, given the state's huge existing indebtedness both at home and abroad. Printing yet more paper money risked fuelling inflation and a consequent collapse in confidence in the ruble, both in Russia and among potential foreign investors.

Russia's financial difficulties were eased a little by the success of the 1863 abolition of the tax farm on the vodka industry and this helped to contribute additional revenues to the treasury. But, there was a fundamental – albeit slow – reassessment of the whole structure of Russia's tax system during the 1870s and 1880s. This followed the recognition by the Ministry of Finance that it was unlikely ever to be in a position to demand reductions in expenditure from the most greedy consumers of government revenue, the war and naval ministries. Even modest attempts to rein in the expenditure on the court brought no success: the Ministry of the Imperial Court firmly rejected a proposal to place the imperial theatres in private hands while the Minister of Finance's suggestion that the ministry's Committee on St Isaac's Cathedral could be abolished, since the building was now complete, met with disdain.[20] Instead, the Ministry of Finance began to shift towards increasing the proportion of revenues that it gained from indirect taxation, recognising both that these sources of revenue offered a greater potential to maximise tax yields and that the process of collection was also simpler. The success of the

1863 vodka tax reforms encouraged the state to be more adventurous in its imposition of indirect levies. During the 1880s the level of taxation on both tobacco and sugar was raised, resulting in a doubling of the revenue from tobacco between 1880 and 1895 and a more than ten-fold increase in the amount of taxation that the sale of sugar generated. By 1895, taxation on sugar produced more than 47 million rubles annually, almost 80 per cent of the amount that the poll tax had generated in the final years before its abolition. The Ministry of Finance, emboldened by these successes, imposed entirely new taxes on kerosene – used extensively for lighting Russians' homes before the introduction of electricity – and on matches. Between them, these two sources of revenue produced more than 27 million rubles a year by 1895. Finally, the government moved to make very substantial increases in import duties. This was prompted, not just by a desire to bring in more revenue, but by the calculation that an increase in the duties payable on imported manufactured goods would stimulate Russia's domestic industry to produce more goods for consumption at home. By the end of the 1880s, Russia's income from import duties had leapt by 40 million rubles annually, but the major tariff reform of 1891 accelerated the growth in revenues from this source so that in 1894 the government collected more than 183 million rubles from import duties. The Russian state became much more heavily dependent on indirect tax revenues than any other European power. By 1911, Russia took 84 per cent of total government revenue from indirect taxation, compared with 70 per cent in France and 59 per cent in Britain.[21] This proved to be an efficient way for the Russian state to collect its revenues; a rapidly expanding population made direct taxation a difficult option since it required a level and depth of bureaucratic competence that the state did not possess. The problems that had been demonstrated with the poll tax and with taxes on the state peasantry showed that it was much easier for the state to collect indirect taxes and that they were a more reliable source of revenue as they were levied on items that the Russian population consumed as essential or traditional elements of their lives.

Although at times the Russian state faced formidable difficulties in maintaining an even financial keel, in the long term it proved to be exceptionally successful at resourcing its activities. This was all the more remarkable, given the low level of economic development of most of its population and thus the limitations of the tax base. Russia's overwhelmingly rural economy did not produce the great wealth that the growing industrial economies of Britain, France and Germany were generating and that could then be tapped to produce tax revenues. At the same time, the demands that Russia's military commitments placed upon the state's budget far exceeded those faced by its fellow European Great Powers. Russia had to keep pace with its western neighbours in military terms, but on far weaker economic foundations. Russia's financial bureaucrats displayed very great skill at maximising their resources, even when they had little impact on determining levels of government expenditure, and they had a very clear awareness of the limitations of their own power, and of the opportunities that the nature of the Russian economy offered them. Successive Ministers of Finance knew the very nature of the Tsarist state meant that they could not constrain its spending on the army and navy, but they were also aware that both domestic and foreign financiers regarded the Russian state as immensely strong and therefore a good risk for lending money. The two went hand-in-hand: military power abroad and domestic oppression gave the Romanov state very great credibility when seeking finance on the international markets.

Even in the 1890s, when the tensions inside the Russian state were becoming more obvious, Russia was still able to draw itself even more tightly into the web of the European economy. In 1894 Russia and France signed a defensive alliance, but this had a far greater significance than being simply a political move by the Russian government. French acceptance of Russia as a formal ally and guarantor of its security against Germany had implications for the economic relationships that developed between the two countries. Witte's economic policies during the 1890s were aimed at creating the macroeconomic conditions necessary both to stimulate Russian domestic industry and to encourage foreign investment in Russia. Witte was well aware that, on its own, Russia did not have the financial resources to deliver the level of investment that was needed to industrialise. The government therefore had to create conditions that would attract foreign businesses and individuals to fund Russian industrial development. Alongside the reassurance that a formal alliance would give to potential investors, Witte also sought to provide reassurance about the stability of Russia's currency. Between 1897 and 1899 Witte completed a major monetary reform by moving Russia onto the gold standard.[22] The impact of this demonstration of both political and economic stability was to bring about a huge inflow of foreign funds – especially from France – into Russia's industries. By 1914, French investors held 14 per cent of the entire share capital of Russian listed companies and this represented a full third of the total of foreign investment in Russia.

Despite the unpromising financial and economic conditions that faced the Romanov rulers of Russia, they proved able to maintain Russia's economy and to sustain the national budget. Russia's financial and economic policy-makers were realistic about the limits of what they could achieve and the nature of the resources that the state could draw on to achieve their aims. They understood the overwhelming significance of Russia's military, even though it was a huge drain on the state's resources, and they also knew that they had to focus on maximising the state's revenues to meet the demands of the spending departments.

Conclusion: The Legacy of Tsarism

The Tsarist state was built on deep foundations. Its power was rooted in the state's fundamental ability to impose its will on its subjects by force, and this raw coercion was underpinned both by an intellectual legitimation of the Romanov autocracy and by a social compact between state and nobility. The institutional structures of the Russian state were built on these roots and provided a coherent means for the practical application of the autocracy's ethos and values. Although the state's coercive abilities were of vital importance to its ability to retain power, Tsarist Russia was not simply a police state. Marc Raeff argued that the eighteenth-century Russian state had much in common with the German states to its west, as they each sought to impose order on their societies. The 'well-ordered police state' that he described was founded on the concept of law that developed during the eighteenth century and the belief not simply that law could be used to control a society, but that it could also be a positive force in shaping all aspects of life. The European Enlightenment reflected these beliefs, and its adherents argued that the values of order and discipline that law represented could be extended across society as a whole. State and society could be organised on a rational basis, with the economy as much subject to these principles as any other area of life. The state itself should also be structured in a systematic way, with the formation of a professional bureaucracy that would implement law in a consistent manner. The police had a particular function in such a society; not only were they expected to maintain order, but they were also to act as agents of change, supervising all elements of society and generating social change.[1]

Raeff gives a more subtle view of Catherine II's Russia than Richard Pipes' portrayal of imperial Russia as the forerunner of the twentieth-century police states, prevented from going down this path only by the existence of private property and by the western values that had permeated Russia's social elites.[2] Russia's emperors and empresses were sustained in power by much more than simple coercion, whether this was the plain brutality associated with modern repressive regimes or the more nuanced concept of the police as the guardians of society. The absence of modern communications and the relatively low level of technological development in eighteenth- and nineteenth-century Russia meant that the levels of sustained terror that were to be utilised in the twentieth-century Soviet Union and other oppressive regimes were not an option for the Tsars. Simple force was not sufficient to maintain the Romanovs in power and the Tsarist state thus still needed to be able to persuade segments of its population of its legitimacy and to offer a justification for its remaining in power. The state received a series of reminders of the essential fragility of its position and of its proximity to disaster. The great popular revolt headed by Pugachev in the 1770s showed how important it was for the state to be able to prevent rebellion breaking out and the crucial significance of its dependence on the nobility to preserve social stability. The Decembrist revolt in the winter of 1825 showed that even members of its officer corps were prepared to stand up against the Tsarist state and take overt action to achieve change. The way in which significant numbers of the intellectual elite of Russian society became persuaded of the need to destroy the autocratic state posed a more direct threat to the public face of the autocracy. But the failure of their ideas to take hold more widely among Russians – even when revolutionaries succeeded in assassinating the Tsar in 1881 – demonstrated that the state still had substantial reserves of power. The revolution of 1905 was of such severity that the state could only preserve its position by making concessions to the rebels, but the regime's power was such that it was able to restore order in the aftermath of 1905 and reassert its authority, going so far as to claw back some of the concessions it made in October 1905. Force was, however, only one part of the Tsarist state's weaponry. The regime would have disappeared long before, if it had not been for its intellectual foundation, as articulated in the theory of Official Nationality. The position of the autocracy was further buttressed by the mutual dependence of state and nobility, providing the regime with a means of extending its control deep into Russia's countryside.

The Romanovs tailored the structure of the government of the empire to maximise their own authority. Institutions in both St Petersburg and the provinces gave the state the ability to deploy its power in ways that gave it extraordinary power over the empire's population. Lacking any legal check on its authority until 1864, the Tsarist state was able to ensure that the ethos of autocracy permeated every aspect of its administrative structures. The fluid boundaries between administration and justice, even after the legal reforms of the 1860s, ensured that the regime could act without any fear of formal challenges to its authority. The only method by which the people of the empire could demonstrate their discontent was through open rebellion, but the coercive forces of the empire were powerful enough to put down most instances of revolt. The Romanovs had no compunction about using brutal force to retain their position and the army and police were utilised to deal with opposition from any quarter, whether it be the peasantry seizing landowners' estates or the Poles rebelling against their Russian masters. The structure of the Tsarist empire and the Romanovs' insistence that their state was an integral whole, with a consistent set of institutions that hardly varied across their imperial domains, allowed the writ of St Petersburg to run right across the state. National groups were subordinated to the interests of Russia and the Russians, while the Orthodox Church played an important part in reinforcing the power of the Tsarist state and emphasising the Russianness of the empire as a whole. The imperial regime also proved adept at managing its modest financial resources to ensure that it was able to maintain its authority. While the Russian state expended very substantial resources on its army, this was a clear recognition of the important role the Tsarist state's military strength played both domestically and abroad.

The collapse of Tsarism in February 1917 was prompted in the short term by Russia's dismal performance in the First World War and its impact on Russian society as a whole. But, the crisis that gathered in Russia after the outbreak of war in the summer of 1914 fed on weaknesses in the structure of the Tsarist state that had been developing over the previous half-century. The gradual disintegration of the Romanovs' grip on power was brought to a head in 1917, but the overnight disappearance of the Russian monarchy did not mean that their impact on Russia had come to an end. The way in which the

Romanovs had ruled their empire had long-lasting implications for the nature of the Russian state and its society. The Tsarist regime set its face against any form of popular participation in national government until it was forced to concede the establishment of an elected Duma in 1905. Even then, Russia had no tradition of political activity on which it could draw to inform the activity of its new parliamentary institutions. The *zemstvo* had provided some outlet for Russia's nascent politicians, but the state had clamped down very severely on any attempt to give the *zemstvo* any national voice, while prohibitions on the formation of political parties remained in place until 1905. The new Duma had to find its feet without being able to draw upon any real political tradition. Unsurprisingly, the Duma found it difficult to make a significant impact on Russian society. The Duma had no formal connection with the empire's government, as ministers were not members of the Duma and the political parties represented in the Duma had no impact on the composition of the government. Much of the Duma's first years were spent in procedural wranglings as Russia's new politicians came to grips for the first time with real political activity. The Duma existed for less than a dozen years before the 1917 revolution brought it to an end, and in this brief period Russia was unable to develop any proper traditions of popular or democratic politics. The refusal of the Tsarist regime to contemplate any form of representative assembly until it was forced from a reluctant Nicholas II in 1905 had significant consequences for Russia's politics after the destruction of the monarchy. The Provisional Government that assumed power from the ruins of the monarchy initially sought to draw its legitimacy from the Duma, but this gave it only limited authority. Elections to the Fourth Duma had taken place more than five years previously and the Duma itself had met infrequently during the First World War, so that it was far removed from most of Russian society by the spring of 1917. The Provisional Government was very conscious that it had no mandate from the Russian people and was insistent that every real decision about Russia's future should be left until a Constituent Assembly had been elected. But, before these elections took place, the Bolsheviks seized power in Russia and the Constituent Assembly met only for a single day before it was unceremoniously disbanded by Russia's new rulers. The lack of any proper democratic tradition and the predominance of the autocratic ideal made it easy for the Bolsheviks to sweep aside the Provisional Government and to ignore the Constituent Assembly. Russia's new Bolshevik rulers had been brought up in an autocratic Russia and they had no experience of working in a democratic political environment. The Tsarist commitment to autocracy made it easier for another autocratic regime to replace them; the Bolsheviks were able to draw on many of the Tsars' traditions in consolidating their regime.

The Tsarist state's outward sign of authority was its army, its political police and its apparatus of coercion. The state was accustomed to responding to discontent with a show of force and the absence of a proper legal culture in Tsarist Russia meant that its actions could not be easily challenged. Both central and local government used violence as a means of maintaining their authority, whether it was by despatching troops to put down peasant uprisings or by using martial law to deal with discontent. The culture of state violence that developed during the eighteenth and nineteenth centuries proved impossible to eradicate in Russia. Lacking any powerful set of legal norms, and without any popular faith in the power of law, the regime that replaced Tsarism found it very easy to utilise the same methods when it came to power. The brutality that the Bolsheviks used to deal with opposition to their rule in the first years after 1917 was nothing new for Russia. Even after 1905 and the introduction of a new constitutional form of government, legality still held only very limited sway in Russia. The Tsarist regime itself sidestepped the new constitutional arrangements by making a unilateral change to the Duma electoral law in 1907, demonstrating very plainly that it still preferred to act according to its traditional values. The absence of any proper legal tradition and the state's continuing espousal of violence and coercion as a means of dealing with Russian society were intimately linked together. The Bolsheviks were simply continuing long-established political behaviour when they placed coercion at the heart of their regime and refused to institute an independent legal system. Russian society was used to being treated in this way and, while Stalin's vicious terror of the 1930s was far beyond anything that the Romanovs had ever attempted, the principles on which the state's use of violence was founded had changed little.

The Romanov state prided itself on its unchanging nature. Its monarchs looked back to the past for their inspiration and were intent on preserving Russia's political and social institutions as if frozen in the past. By its nature, Tsarism was deeply reluctant to institute reforms in Russia. It was a conservative regime that valued traditional structures and ways of behaviour and had an innate mistrust of the very concept of reform. The Romanovs believed that the enduring values that sustained their regime meant that change should be approached with great caution and that it was a last resort, to be contemplated only when the state was approaching crisis point. Successive monarchs shied away from the issue of reforming serfdom, even when it was plain that this method of economic and social organisation was no longer appropriate. In the same way, the state was reluctant to embark upon making even very limited political reforms: Loris-Melikov's plans for constitutional reform in 1880 came about only when Alexander II recognised that the level of animosity to the regime among sections of Russian society required a dramatic solution. The Tsar's assassination, however, persuaded his son Alexander III that Russia needed no further reform, since he believed that it was the reforms of the 1860s that had laid the ground for the emergence of revolutionary opposition to Tsarism. The state's failure to make timely reform meant that, when it was eventually forced into making change, reform came too late. Successive monarchs from Catherine II onwards had shelved plans for constitutional change presented to them by their advisers. Almost every monarch had drawn back from making major reforms. Only Alexander II stands out as prepared to take the risk of reform, but his conviction that change was necessary was very firmly conditioned by the circumstances in which he came to the throne. The death of Nicholas I in the middle of Russia's defeat in the Crimea presented Alexander with power at a time when Russia was experiencing a national humiliation. Alexander could not deny that reform was needed if Russia was to recover its position, and reform-minded bureaucrats were able to take full advantage of the position to drive through changes. But it was a full 40 years before the Russian state again contemplated reform, once more in the wake of defeat in war, intensified by widespread popular unrest in 1905. Nicholas II had no genuine commitment to reform, regretting his signature on the October Manifesto almost before the ink was dry, and failed to offer support to Stolypin when his prime minister proposed a further raft of social reforms in 1906. Tsarism's inability to reform itself meant that change only came about at times of crisis, usually long after the need for reform had first appeared. There was no significant alteration to Russia's rural world for nearly half a century after the emancipation of the serfs in 1861, even though the rural world was undergoing very rapid change. The state's reluctance to reform only served to intensify the pressures that it faced when it was eventually forced into making changes.

The regime's deep dislike for reform reflected the dominance of the interests of the autocrat in the Russian political system. The patriarchal attitudes that permeated Russia's elites identified the interests of the state with those of the monarch. The personal position of the autocrat thus directed the entire course of Russian government, with the interests of wider society having little impact on the way in which the state was governed. The absence of any real form of popular representation gave the Russian empire no forum in which the interests of state and society could be mediated, while the preponderance of the interests of the ruler made it very difficult for wider society to develop effectively. The Russian state viewed its population as its subjects, and was deeply reluctant to concede that they could have rights as citizens of the state. A civil society was very slow to develop in Russia: Russia's middle class was small in relation to the overall population of the empire and the regime had failed to provide the legal framework that would enable a cohesive society to emerge. The state was extremely suspicious of the formation of autonomous civil society: it remained difficult for Russians to form associations until 1905, with the state taking a very close interest in any group that could conceivably have any political slant to it. Censorship made it difficult to disseminate ideas across the empire and, even though restrictions was relaxed in 1865 and again in 1905, the state looked very unfavourably on material it considered to be subversive. It was difficult for Russians to engage in public discourse on social issues – and political activity was entirely prohibited until 1905 – so that Russians were unable to construct the dense network of professional and social networks that allow for the growth of a homogeneous civil society. Russia's middle classes were making some progress towards a modern social structure by the final decades of Tsarism, but this was painfully slow and the state remained deeply suspicious of attempts to construct anything that could represent an opposition to the regime. Russian society remained fragmented right up until 1917. This made it much easier for the Bolsheviks to take power, since the absence of a robust and cohesive society militated against the emergence of strong opposition to the new regime. The experience of war between 1914 and 1917 served to pull Russian society further apart as the regime became more and more isolated from society as a whole, and rejected attempts by powerful social groups to make a real contribution to the war effort. The formation of the Progressive Bloc in 1915 set Russian political society at loggerheads with Tsarism, with the government deeply suspicious of the motivations of the Duma politicians and they, in their turn, convinced of the incompetence of the state at a time of deep crisis. When the monarchy disappeared in February 1917, there was a sense of national relief, but no accord about what should replace it. The experience of war had atomised Russian society, making individual Russians focus more on their personal position than on the wider national interest. Russia's weak civil society made it easier for an extreme political party – the Bolsheviks – to seize power and retain it. Lenin and his party had focussed their attention on the urban working class and, after February 1917, on the army and navy, calculating that these groups held the key to a successful assault on the Provisional Government. Russian peasant society remained physically separate from the cities where the revolutions of 1917 were decided, while Russia's elites were arguing, apparently incapable of perceiving the broad needs of the country and more concerned with their own narrow sectional interests.

Tsarism proved to be exceptionally successful at protecting the position of the autocracy itself, imposing a centrally determined set of political and cultural values on the Russian empire. The Romanovs had constructed a state and society that were designed to maximise the power of the regime, but they had little concern for the broader issues of Russia's development. Russia remained essentially unmodernised until very late in the nineteenth century, when economic pressures compelled the regime to consider how a modern industrial economy could mesh with existing political and social structures. While elements of the Russian state recognised that a modern economy was incompatible with the politics of autocracy, Russia's rulers themselves refused to accept that they needed to make reforms if they were to survive. The Tsarist autocracy became increasingly dependent on its ability to coerce its population as it entered the twentieth century, losing sight of the need to sustain itself by creating a social and intellectual foundation for its rule. The success of the Tsarist state at maintaining itself in power came at the price of stifling Russia's progress towards modernisation. This weakened Russia's economy and retarded the country's social development, so that the crisis of the First World War hit Russia harder than other combatant states. The immense power that the Tsarist state had been able to deploy for much of the nineteenth century failed it during the

First World War; its army performed dismally against Germany while the regime was unable to mobilise the 'home front' effectively to support its military efforts. An unmodernised Russia proved impotent to fight a modern war. Tsarism's legacy was the disintegration of Russia's society once central authority eroded after the February Revolution, and the opportunity that this offered Lenin and the Bolsheviks.

Notes

Introduction: Building the Russian State

1. 'Dnevnik Nikolaia Romanova', *Krasnyi Arkhiv*, 20(1) (1927), p. 136.
2. T. Hasegawa, *The February Revolution. Petrograd 1917* (Seattle, 1981), p. 305.
3. V. V. Shul'gin, *Dni* (Belgrade, 1925), p. 300.
4. B. V. Anan'ich et al., *Krizis samoderzhaviia v Rossii 1895–1917* (Leningrad, 1984), p. 1.
5. R. Pipes, *Russia Under the Old Regime* (London, 1974), p. 138.
6. See C. Read, 'In Search of Liberal Tsarism: The Historiography of Autocratic Decline', *Historical Journal*, 45 (2002), pp. 195–210.

Chapter 1: The Ideology of Tsarism

1. A. Ascher, *The Revolution of 1905. Russia in Disarray* (Stanford, 1988), p. 162.
2. P. E. Kazanskii, *Vlast' vserossiiskogo imperatora* (Moscow, 1999 reprint), pp. 277–9.
3. S. S. Uvarov, *Desiatiletie ministerstva narodnogo prosveshchenia 1833–1843* (St Petersburg, 1864), pp. 2–3.
4. J. Cracraft, *The Church Reform of Peter the Great* (London, 1971), pp. 165–6.
5. D. Moon, *The Abolition of Serfdom in Russia, 1762–1907* (London, 2001), pp. 155–60.

6. R. Wortman, *Scenarios of Power. Myth and Ceremony in Russian Monarchy*, vol. I (Princeton, 1995), p. 384.
7. *Ibid.*, pp. 396–8.
8. J. Hartley, *Alexander I* (London, 1994), p. 124.
9. D. Field, *Rebels in the Name of the Tsar* (Boston, 1976), p. 1.
10. *Ibid.*, pp. 208–11.

Chapter 2: Monarchs

1. A. E. Presniakov, *Apogei samoderzhaviia: Nikolai I* (Leningrad, 1925), p. 46.
2. N. M. Druzhinin, *Gosudarstvennye krest'iane i reformy P D Kiseleva* (Moscow, 1946), vol. I, pp. 121–96.
3. S. S. Tatishchev, 'Imperator Aleksandr III. Ego zhizn' i tsarstvovanie.' Rossiiskii gosudarstvennyi istoricheskii arkhiv (RGIA), f. 878, op. 1, d. 4, l. 55.
4. R. Wortman, *Scenarios of Power, Myth and Ceremony in the Russian Monarchy* (Princeton, 2006), vol. 2, p. 476.
5. *Ibid.*, p. 455.
6. K. Rasmussen, 'Catherine II and the Image of Peter I', *Slavic Review*, 37 (1978), p. 65.
7. J. Keep, 'The Military Style of the Romanov Rulers', *War & Society*, 1 (1983), p. 78.
8. W. B. Lincoln, *Nicholas I: Emperor and Autocract of All the Russias* (London, 1978), p. 348.
9. A. Spiridovitch, *Les dernières années de la cour de Tsarskoe-Selo*, vol. 1 (Paris, 1928), p. 330.
10. Wortman, *Scenarios of Power*, p. 374.
11. E. V. Antsimov, *The Reforms of Peter the Great. Progress through Coercion in Russia* (Armonk, 1993), pp. 184–6.
12. P. Y. Chaadaev, *Philosophical Letters. Diary of a Madman* (M-B. Zeldin ed.) (Knoxville, 1969), p. 42.
13. J. T. Alexander, *Catherine the Great. Life and Legend* (New York, 1989), p. 65.
14. A. B. Kamenskii, 'Catherine II' in D. J. Raleigh (ed.), *The Emperors and Empresses of Russia. Rediscovering the Romanovs* (Armonk, 1996), p. 160.
15. N. V. Riasanovsky, *Russian Identities: A Historical Survey* (New York, 2005), p. 94.

16. S. M. Solov'ev, *Istoriia Rossii s drevneishchkikh vremen*, vol. 14 (Moscow, 1966), p. 74.
17. C. H. Whittaker, *Russian Monarchy. Eighteenth Century Rulers and Writers in Political Dialogue* (DeKalb, 2003), p. 150.
18. S. B. Okun', 'Bor'ba za vlast' posle dvortsovogo perevorota 1801 g.', *Voprosy istorii Rossii XIX – nachala XX veka* (Leningrad, 1983), pp. 6–7.
19. Wortman, *Scenarios of Power*, vol. 2, p. 92.
20. V. G. Chernukha, 'Aleksandr II i problema konstitutsionnykh preobrazovanii v Rossii', in *Dom Romanovykh v istorii Rossii* (St Petersburg, 1995), pp. 218–20.
21. A. Bokhanov and Iu. Kudrina (eds), *Imperator Aleksandr III i imperatritsa Mariia Fedorovna. Perepiska. 1884–1894 gody* (Moscow, 2001), p. 32.
22. H. W. Whelan, *Alexander III and the State Council. Bureaucracy and Counter-reform in Late Imperial Russia* (New Brunswick, 1982), p. 25.

Chapter 3: Service

1. D. Moon, *The Russian Peasantry 1860–1930* (London, 1999), p. 99.
2. J. Blum, *Lord and Peasant in Russia from the Ninth to the Nineteenth Century* (Princeton, 1961), p. 356.
3. S. L. Hoch, *Serfdom and Social Control in Russia: Petrovskoe, a Village in Tambov* (Chicago, 1986), pp. 23–4 and 118–19; Moon, *Peasantry*, p. 77.
4. T. Emmons, *The Russian Landed Gentry and the Peasant Emancipation of 1861* (Cambridge, 1968), p. 37.
5. 'Pis'mo K. D Kavelina k T. N. Granovskomu, 5-25 sentiabia 1848g', *Literaturnoe nasledstvo*, vol. LXVII (1959), p. 596.
6. G. Vernadsky, *A Source Book for Russian History from Early Times to 1917* (New Haven, 1972), vol. 3, p. 589.
7. *Polnoe Sobranie Zakonov Rossiiskoi Imperii*, (*PSZ*) 2nd series, vol. 36, pt. 1, no. 36657.
8. S. L. Hoch, 'The Banking Crisis, Peasant Reform, and Economic Development in Russia, 1857–1861', *American Historical Review*, 96 (1991), pp. 810–11.
9. S. Becker, *Nobility and Privilege in Late Imperial Russia* (De Kalb, 1985), pp. 38–9.
10. A. P. Korelin, *Dvorianstvo v poreformennoi Rossii 1861–1904 gg.* (Moscow, 1979), pp. 162–3.

Chapter 4: Institutions

1. A. A. Polovtsov, *Dnevnik A. A. Polovtsova* (Moscow, 1966), vol. I, p. 215.
2. N. K. Shil'der, *Imperator Aleksandr I: ego zhizn' i tsarstvovanie* (St Petersburg, 1898), vol. III, p. 4.
3. G. Yaney, *The Systematization of Russian Government: Social Evolution in the Domestic Administration of Imperial Russia 1711–1905* (Urbana, 1973), p. 263.
4. P. A. Valuev, *Dnevnik P. A. Valueva* (Moscow, 1961), vol. II, p. 324.
5. M. Raeff, *Plans for Political Reform in Imperial Russia, 1730–1905* (Prentice Hall, 1966), pp. 56–7.
6. I. De Madariaga, *Russia in the Age of Catherine the Great* (London, 1981), p. 43.
7. *Sborrnik imperatorskogo russkogo istoricheskogo obshchestva*, vol. 7 (St Petersburg, 1869), p. 345.
8. N. P. Eroshkin, *Krepostnicheskoe samoderzhavie i ego politicheskie instituty (Pervaia polvina XIX veka)* (Moscow, 1981), p. 107.
9. *Polnoe sobranie zakonov rossiikoi imperii* (St Petersburg, 1825), vol. 1, no. 20, 406.
10. N. N. Efremova, *Ministerstvo Iustitsii Rossiiskoi Imperii 1802–1917 gg.* (Leningrad, 1983), p. 88.
11. R. Wortman, *The Development of a Russian Legal Consciousness* (Chicago, 1976).
12. W. Pintner and D. K. Rowney, *Russian Officialdom. The Bureaucratization of Russian Society from the Seventeenth to the Twentieth Century* (London, 1980), p. 192; *Rossiia 1913 god. Statistiko-dokumental'nyi spravochnik* (St Petersburg, 1995), p. 265.
13. Pintner and Rowney, *Russian Officialdom*, p. 232.
14. D. Lieven, *Russia's Rulers under the Old Regime* (New Haven, 1989), p. 84.
15. S. Iu. Witte, *Vospominania. Memuary* (Moscow, 2002), vol. II, p. 483.
16. J. Hartley, *Alexander I* (London, 1994), p. 87.
17. Shil'der, *Imperator Aleksandr I*, vol. III, p. 38.
18. N. G. O. Pereira, *Tsar-Liberator: Alexander II of Russia 1818–1881* (Newtonville, 1983), p. 81.
19. T. Emmons, *The Russian Landed Gentry and the Peasant Emancipation in 1861* (Cambridge, 1968), pp. 410–11.
20. F. A. Petrov, 'Crowning the Edifice: The Zemstvo, Local Self-Government, and the Constitutional Movement, 1864–1881' in B. Eklof, J. Bushnell and L. Zakharova (eds), *Russia's Great Reforms, 1855–1881* (Bloomington, 1994), p. 203.

21. *Sbornik pravitel'stvennykh rasporiazhenii po delam, do zemskikh uchrezh-denii otnosiashchimsia (1870–1880)*, vol. 11 (St Petersburg, 1889), p. 79.
22. N. V. Golitsyn, 'Konstitutsiia grafa Loris-Melikova: Materialy dlia ee istorii', *Byloe*, nos. 4–5 (1918), p. 165.
23. RGIA, f. 1239, d. 1, l. 6.
24. A. S. Korros, *A Reluctant Parliament. Stolypin, Nationalism, and the Politics of the Russian Imperial State Council, 1906–1911* (Lanham, 2002), pp. 24–6.
25. M. Szeftel, *The Russian Constitution of April 23, 1906* (Brussels, 1976) analyses the structure in detail.
26. V. S. Diakin, *Samoderzhavie, burzhuaziia i dvorianstvo v 1907–1911 gg.* (Leningrad, 1978), pp. 26–7.
27. T. Emmons, *The Formation of Political Parties and the First National Elections in Russia* (Cambridge, MA, 1983), pp. 354–6.
28. S. E. Kryzhanovskii, *Vospominaniia* (Berlin, 1925). Chapter 4 is a description of the preparation of the new electoral law by its author, the assistant Minister of Internal Affairs.
29. RGIA, f. 1288, op. 1, d. 29, l. 3.
30. Speech by Stolypin to the Second Duma, 10 May 1907. *Gosudarstvennaia Duma. Stenograficheskie otchety*, II, vol. 2, col. 349.
31. V. A. Demin, *Gosudarstvennaia Duma Rossii (1906–1917): mekhanizm funktsionirovaniia* (Moscow, 1996), pp. 83–4.
32. E. Vishnevski, *Liberal'naia oppozitsiia v Rossii nakanune pervoi mirovoi voiny* (Moscow, 1994), pp. 165–6.
33. W. C. Fuller Jr, *The Foe Within: Fantasies of Treason and the End of Imperial Russia* (Ithaca, 2006) gives a full account of the fate of Sukhomlinov.
34. *Krasnyi Arkhiv*, vol. 50 (1932), p. 133.
35. *Gosudarstevannaia Duma. Stenograficheskie Otchety*, IV, vol. V, col. 48.

Chapter 5: Provincial Authority

1. A. Manko, *Bliustiteli verkhovnoi vlasti. Institut gubernatora v Rossii* (Moscow, 2004), p. 47.
2. *PSZ*, vol. XX, no. 14, 392.
3. A. I. Elistratov, *Gosudarstvennoe Pravo* (Moscow, 1912), chap. 30.
4. I. M. Strakhovskii, *Gubernskoe ustroistvo* (St Petersburg, 1913), p. 104.

5. I. Blinov, *Gubernatory* (St Petersburg, 1905), p. 262.
6. M. M. Shumilov, 'Gubernatorskie naznacheniia v Rossii 60-70-kh godov XIX veka' in A. A. Fursenko (ed.), *Rossiia v XIX-XX vv. Sbornik statei k 70-letiiu so dnia rozhdeniia Rafaila Sholomovicha Ganelina* (St Petersburg, 1998), pp. 207–8.
7. R. G. Robbins, *The Tsar's Viceroys. Russian Provincial Governors in the Last Years of the Empire* (Ithaca, 1987), p. 71.
8. R. G. Robbins, *Famine in Russia, 1891–1892. The Imperial Government Responds to a Crisis* (New York, 1975), pp. 55–7.
9. R. G. Robbins, 'The Limits of Professionalization: Russian Governors at the Beginning of the Twentieth Century' in H. Balzer, (ed.), *Russia's Missing Middle Class: The Professions in Russian History* (Armonk, 1996), pp. 259–60.
10. S. A. Korf, 'Predvoditel' dvorianstva kak organ soslovnogo i zemskogo samoupravleniia', *Zhurnal Ministerstva Iustitsii*, vol. 3 (1902), p. 93.
11. *Svod zakonov Rossiiskoi Imperii*, vol. 9 (St Petersburg, 1899), pp. 76–9.
12. A. Novikov, *Zapiski zemskogo nachal'nika* (St Petersburg, 1899), p. 52.
13. *Ibid.*, p. 38.
14. A. P. Korelin, *Dvorianstvo v poreformennoi Rossii, 1861–1904* (Moscow, 1979), pp. 197–8.
15. D. M. Wallace, *Russia on the Eve of War and Revolution* (New York, 1961), p. 351.
16. Osobyi Zhurnal Soveta Ministrov, 'Ob ustanovlenii glavnykh nachal ustroistva gubernskikh uchrezhdenii', RGIA, f. 1405, op. 543, d. 910, l. 65.
17. F. W. Wcislo, *Reforming Rural Russia. State, Local Society and National Politics, 1855–1914* (Princeton, 1990), p. 306.
18. V. A. Nardova, *Gorodskoe samoupravlenie v Rossii v 60-kh – nachale 90-kh godov XIX v.* (Leningrad, 1984), p. 11.
19. A. G. Kaznacheev, 'Mezhdu strokami odnogo formuliarnogo spiska', *Russkaia Starina*, vol. 32 (1881), p. 859.
20. B. N. Chicherin, *Vospominaniia. Zemstvo i Moskovskaia Duma* (Moscow, 1934), p. 22.
21. Wallace, *Russia on the Eve*, p. 30.
22. V. R. Leikina-Svirskaia, *Russkaia intelligentsia v 1900–1917 godakh* (Moscow, 1981), pp. 47–64.

23. T. Fallows, 'The zemstvo and the bureaucracy, 1890–1914' in T. Emmons and W. S. Vucinich (eds), *The Zemstvo in Russia: An Experiment in Local Self-Government* (Cambridge, 1982), p. 219.
24. H. Balzer, 'The problem of professions in Rusia' in E. W. Clowes, S. D. Kassow and J. L. West (eds), *Between Tsar and People: Educated Society and the Quest for Public Identity in Late Imperial Russia* (Princeton, 1991), p. 192.
25. *PSZ*, vol. 10, no. 6, 922.
26. P. Gatrell, *Russia's First World War: A Social and Economic History* (London, 2005), p. 42.
27. W. Gleason, 'The zemstvo union and World War I', in Emmons and Vucinich (eds), *Zemstvo in Russia*, p. 370.

Chapter 6: Coercion, Police and Justice

1. *PSZ*, vol. 5 (St Petersburg, 1830), no. 3006.
2. C. Peterson, *Peter the Great's Administrative and Judicial Reforms* (Stockholm, 1979), p. 324.
3. G. Yaney, *The Systematization of Russian Government: Social Evolution in the Domestic Administration of Imperial Russia* (Urbana, 1973), p. 335.
4. V. N. Nazarev, 'Sovremmenaia glush'', *Vestnik Evropy*, vol. 34 (1872), p. 167.
5. A. G. Kaznacheev, 'Mezhdu strokami odnoso formuliarnogo spiska', *Russkaia stariva*, vol. 32 (1881), p. 860.
6. N. K. Brzheskii, *Naturalnye povinnosti krest'ian i mirskie sbory* (St Petersburg, 1906), p. 174.
7. A. Leroy-Beaulieu, *The Empire of the Tsars and the Russians*, vol. II (London, 1894), p. 119.
8. 'Gr. Loris-Melikov i imperator Aleksandr II o polozhenii Rossii v sentiabre 1880 goda', *Byloe*, vol. 4 (1917), p. 54.
9. 'Pis'ma E. P. Mednikova' in B. P. Koz'min (ed.), *Zubatov i ego korrespondenty* (Moscow-Leningrad, 1928), p. 111.
10. A. P. Martynov, *Moia sluzhba v otdel'nom korpuse zhandarmov* (Stanford, 1972), p. xi.
11. J. L. H. Keep, *Soldiers of the Tsar. Army and Society in Russia 1462–1874* (Oxford, 1985), pp. 136–8.
12. Zh. Kormina, *Provody v armiiu v poreformennoi Rossii. Opyt etnograficheskogo analiza* (Moscow, 2005), pp. 102–4.

13. B. W. Menning, *Bayonets before Bullets. The Imperial Russian Army, 1861–1914* (Bloomington, 1992), pp. 21–3.

14. D. A. Rich, *The Tsar's Colonels: Professionalism, Strategy and Subversion in Late Imperial Russia* (Cambridge, MA, 1998), pp. 31–2.

15. E. K. Wirtschafter, *From Serf to Russian Soldier* (Princeton, 1990), p. 81.

16. A. Ascher, *The Revolution of 1905. Authority Restored* (Stanford, 1992), p. 242.

17. R. Sh. Ganelin, 'Ob istorischeskikh realiiakh stikhovoreniia Innokentiia Annenskogo "Starye estonki"', *Eesti Teaduste Akadeemia. Toimetised. Humanitaar- ja sotsiaalteadused*, vol. 42 (Tallinn, 1993), p. 104; and P. Ianson, *Karatel'nye ekspeditsii v Pribaltiiskom krae v 1905–1907 gg.* (Leningrad, 1926), p. 38.

18. *PSZ*, vol. I (St Petersburg, 1885), no. 550.

19. St Petersburg, Moscow, Kharkov, Poltava, Chernigov, Kiev, Volyhia, Podol', Kherson and Bessarabia.

20. RGIA, f. 1239, d. 1, l. 16b.

21. *Pravo*, no. 10, 12 March 1906, col. 910.

22. P. A. Zaionchkovskii, *Russkoe samoderzhavie v kontse XIX veka* (Moscow, 1970), p. 161.

23. See A. Wood, 'The Use and Abuse of Administrative Exile to Siberia', *Irish Slavonic Studies*, vol. 6 (1985), pp. 65–81.

24. 'Obiazatel'noe postanovlenie Kievskogo general-gubernatora', 9 April 1901 and 17 March 1904. RGIA, f. 1239, d. 1, ll. 215 and 216.

25. 'Obiazatel'noe postanovlenie dlya gorodov Rigi i Iur'eva', 7 December 1901. Eesti Ajaloo Arhiv (EAA), f. 296, n. 7, s. 2238, pp. 1 and 3.

26. 'Obiavlenie Lifliandskogo gubernatora', 7 January 1906. EAA, f. 296, n. 7, s. 2238, p. 18, and 'Obiazatel'noe postanovlenie dlya zhitelei goroda Rigi', 20 February 1906. *Ibid.*, p. 19.

27. 'Obiavlenie vremennogo Pribaltiiskogo general-gubernatora', 12 December 1905. *Ibid.*, p. 14.

28. 'Obiazatel'noe postanovlenie Lifliandskogo gubernatora', 16 December 1905. *Ibid.*, p. 15.

29. 'Obiazatel'noe postanovlenie dlya naseleniia Stepnogo kraia', 26 March 1904. RGIA, f. 1239, d. 1, l. 442.

30. EAA, f. 296, n. 7, s. 2238, p. 6. 12 March 1905.

31. 'Obiazatel'noe postanovlenie dlya g. Rigi', 12 January 1906. *Ibid.*, pp. 24, 23 and 33.

32. P. Kalinin, 'Po povodu usilennoi okhrany', *Pravo*, no. 48, 28 November 1904, cols. 3302–3.
33. R. Hellie (trans. and ed.), *The Muscovite Law Code (Ulozhenie) of 1649* (Irvine, 1988), p. 1.
34. Yaney, *Systematization of Russian Government*, p. 21.

Chapter 7: National Challenges

1. J. J. Stephan, *The Russian Far East. A History* (Stanford, 1994), pp. 35–6.
2. See P. A. Stolypin and A. V. Krivoshein, *Poezdka v Sibir' i Povol'zhe* (St Petersburg, 1911) for a clear statement of the government's aims.
3. W. B. Lincoln, *The Conquest of a Continent: Siberia and the Russians* (London, 1994), p. 192.
4. A. V. Fadeev, *Rossiia v Kavkaze v pervoi treti XIX v.* (Moscow, 1960), p. 340.
5. S. S. Tatishchev, *Imperator Aleksandr II. Ego zhizn' i tsarstvovanie* (St Petersburg, 1903), pp. 115–16.
6. See E. D. Sokol, *The Revolt of 1916 in Russian Central Asia* (Baltimore, 1954) and R. D. Crews, *For Prophet and Tsar: Islam and Empire in Russian and Central Asia* (Cambridge, MA, 2006), pp. 361–2.
7. T. Weeks, *Nation and State in Late Imperial Russia: Nationalism and Russification on the Western Frontier, 1863–1914* (DeKalb, 1996), p. 96.
8. A. A. Komzolova, *Politika samoderzhaviia v Severo-Zapadnom krae v epokhu Velikikh reform* (Moscow, 2005), p. 74.
9. P. Maikov, *Finliandiia, ee proshedshee i nastoiashchee* (St Petersburg, 1905), p. 525.
10. T. Polvinen, *Imperial Borderland. Bobrikov and the Attempted Russification of Finland 1898–1904* (London, 1984), p. 55.
11. *Ibid.*, p. 65.
12. O. E. Mandelstam, 'The noise of time' in C. Brown (trans.), *The Prose of Osip Mandelstam* (Princeton, 1965), p. 88.
13. Helsinki, Valtioinarkisto. KKK, 1909. I.3/25 (Fb 463), 'Po voprosu o prazdnovanii stoletnogo iubileia zavoevaniia Finliandii', 14 February 1909.

14. P. Luntinen, *F. A. Seyn 1862–1918: A Political Biography of a Tsarist Imperialist as Administrator of Finland* (Helsinki, 1985), pp. 195–7.

15. F. Savchenko, *The Suppression of the Ukrainian Activities in 1876* (Munich, 1970), pp. 381–3.

16. J. Remy, 'The Ukrainian Alphabet as a Political Question in the Russian Empire before 1876', *Ab Imperio*, vol. 2 (2005), p. 179.

17. D. Saunders, 'Russia's nationality policy: the case of Ukraine (1847–1941)', *Journal of Ukrainian Studies*, vol. 29 (2004), pp. 405–6.

18. H. W. Whelan, *Adapting to Modernity: Family, Caste and Capitalism among the Baltic German Nobility* (Köln, 1999), pp. 266–7.

19. P. A. Zaionchkovskii, *Krizis samoderzhaviia na rubezhe 1870–1880 godov* (Moscow, 1964), pp. 71–2.

20. J. D. Klier, *Imperial Russia's Jewish Questions, 1855–1881* (Cambridge, 1995), pp. 9–10.

21. E. Haberer, *Jews and Revolution in Nineteenth-Century Russia* (Cambridge, 1995), pp. 255–6.

22. 'Rech' finliandskogo general-gubernatora', *Novoe Vremia*, 2 October 1898, p. 2.

23. W. C. Fuller Jr, *Civil Military Conflict in Imperial Russia, 1881–1914* (Princeton, 1985), pp. 59–61.

24. L. P. Roshchenskaia and V. K. Beloborodov (eds), *Tobol'skii sever glazami politicheskikh ssyl'nykh XIX-nachalo XX veka* (Ekaterinburg, 1998) gives a useful insight into the experience of exiles.

Chapter 8: Financing the Empire

1. D. A. Miliutin to A. A. Abaza, 29 May 1879, RGIA, f. 1214, op. 1, d. 23, l. 1a.

2. W. M. Pintner, 'The Burden of Defense in Imperial Russia, 1725–1914', *Russian Review*, 43 (1984), pp. 238–9.

3. P. Gatrell, *Government, Industry and Rearmament in Russia, 1900–1914. The Last Argument of Tsarism* (Cambridge, 1994) p. 140.

4. 'Ob otyskanii denezhnykh ressursov na sluchai voiny', 1830–31, RGIA, f. 563, op. 2, d. 21, ll. 3–5 and 14.

5. 'O sredstvakh k pokrytiiu raskhodov po sluchaiu voyny', February 1856, RGIA, f. 563, op. 1, d. 6, ll. 2–6.

6. L. E. Shepelev (ed.), *Sud'by Rossii* (St Petersburg, 1999), pp. 114–59.

7. 'Komitet o sokrashchenii raskhodov po ministerstvam: voen-nomu, morskomu, inostrannykh del i vedomstvam: pochtovomu, putei soobshchenii i dukhovnomu. 1835', RGIA, f. 1172, op. 16, d. 1, ll. 54–7.

8. 'Komitet finansov. Po zapiske Ministra Finansov o finansovykh merakh: uvelichenie dokhodov; sokrashchenie raskhodov; svod rospisi. 1861', RGIA, f. 563, op. 2, d. 144, ll. 2–5. The War Ministry was able only to suggest savings of 881,000 rubles, out of a total annual budget of more than 90 million rubles.

9. 'Doklad Predsedatelia Osoboi Komissii A. A. Abaza s kratkim otchetom o deiatel'nosti Osoboi Komissii', 11 June 1879, RGIA, f. 1214, op. 1, d. 26, ll. 32–4.

10. J. P. LeDonne, 'Indirect taxes in Catherine's Russia. I: The salt code of 1781', *Jahrbücher für Geschichte Osteuropas*, 23 (1975), p. 188.

11. S. M. Troitskii, *Finansovaia politika russkogo absolutizma v XVIII veke* (Moscow, 1966), p. 221.

12. A. Kahan, *The Plow, the Hammer and the Knout* (Chicago, 1985), p. 133.

13. J. P. LeDonne, *Ruling Russia: Politics and Administration in the Age of Absolutism, 1762–1796* (Princeton, 1984), p. 257.

14. P. Herlihy, *The Alcoholic Empire: Vodka and Politics in Late Imperial Russia* (New York, 2002), pp. 64–5.

15. 'Osobyi komitet dia razsmotreniiu predstavlennogo Ego Velichestvu ot neizvestnogo obzora finansovoi chasti v Rossii, 1841', RGIA, f. 1175, op. 16, d. 118.

16. P. N. Miliukov, *Gosudarstvennoe khoziastvo Rossii v pervoi chetverti XVIII stoletiia i reforma Petra Velikogo* (St Petersburg, 1905), esp. pp. 471–91.

17. Kahan, *Plow*, p. 332.

18. See A. I. Engelgardt, *Letters from the Country, 1872–1887*, C. A. Frierson (trans.) (New York, 1993), for one of the main examples of this 'literature of social lament'.

19. See S. Plaggenborg, 'Tax policy and the question of peasant poverty in Tsarist Russia 1881–1905', *Cahiers du Monde Russe*, 36 (1995), pts 1–2, p. 58.

20. 'Zhurnal Komiteta Finansov, 4, 11, 18 & 25 noiabria 1861', RGIA, f. 563, op. 2, d. 115, ll. 13–16.

21. I. A. Mikhailov, *Gosudarstevennye dolgi i raskhody Rossii vo vremia voiny. Fakty i tsifry* (Petrograd, 1917), p. 132.

22. O. Crisp, *Studies in the Russian Economy before 1914* (London, 1976), pp. 98–9.

Conclusion: The Legacy of Tsarism

1. M. Raeff, *The Well-Ordered Police State. Social and Institutional Change through Law in the Germanies and Russia, 1600–1800* (New Haven, 1983).
2. R. Pipes, *Russia under the Old Regime* (London, 1974).

Bibliography

General Works

Dixon, S. *The Modernisation of Russia 1676–1825* (Cambridge, 1999).
Hartley, J. M. *A Social History of the Russian Empire 1650–1825* (London, 1999).
Hosking, G. *Russia. People and Empire 1552–1917* (London, 1997).
Lieven, D. *Empire. The Russian Empire and its Rivals* (London, 2000).
Longley, D. *The Longman Companion to Imperial Russia, 1689–1917* (London, 2000).
Raeff, M. *The Well-Ordered Police State. Social and Institutional Change through the Law in the Germanies and Russia, 1600–1800* (New Haven, 1983).
Rogger, H. *Russia in the Age of Modernisation and Revolution 1881–1917* (London, 1983).
Saunders, D. *Russia in the Age of Reaction and Reform 1801–1881* (London, 1992).
Waldron, P. *The End of Imperial Russia 1855–1917* (London, 1997).

Monarchs

Alexander, J. T. *Catherine the Great. Life and Legend* (New York, 1989).
Anisimov, E. V. *Empress Elizabeth. Her Reign and Her Russia* (Gulf Breeze, 1995).
Bushkovitch, P. *Peter the Great. The Struggle for Power, 1671–1725* (Cambridge, 2001).

198

Cherniavsky, M. *Tsar and People. Studies in Russian Myths* (New Haven, 1961).

Dixon, S. *Catherine the Great* (London, 2001).

Hartley, J. *Alexander I* (London, 1994).

Hughes, L. *Russia in the Age of Peter the Great* (New Haven, 1998).

Leonard, C. *Reform and Regicide: The Reign of Peter III of Russia* (Bloomington, 1992).

Lieven, D. *Nicholas II. Emperor of All the Russias* (London, 1993).

Lincoln, W. B. *Nicholas I: Emperor and Autocrat of All the Russias* (Bloomington, 1978).

Madariaga, I. de. *Russia in the Age of Catherine the Great* (London, 1981).

McGrew, R. E. *Paul I of Russia* (Oxford, 1992).

Pereira, N. G. O. *Tsar-Liberator. Alexander II of Russia 1818–1881* (Newtonville, 1983).

Ragsdale, H. *Paul I. A Reassessment of his Life and Reign* (Pittsburgh, 1979).

Raleigh, D. (ed.). *The Emperors and Empresses of Russia: Rediscovering the Romanovs* (Armonk, 1996).

Riasanovsky, N. V. *Nicholas I and Official Nationality in Russia* (Berkeley, 1959).

Riasanovsky, N. V. *The Image of Peter the Great in Russian History and Thought* (New York, 1985).

Whittaker, C. H. *Russian Monarchy: Eighteenth Century Rulers and Writers in Political Dialogue* (DeKalb, 2003).

Wortman, R. *Scenarios of Power: Myth and Ceremony in the Russian Monarchy*: 2 vols (Princeton, 1995 and 2000).

Central and Local Government

Ascher, A. *The Revolution of 1905*, 2 vols (Stanford, 1988 and 1992).

Bynes, R. *Pobedonostsev: His Life and Thought* (Bloomington, 1968).

Eklof, B., Bushnell, J. and Zakharova, L. (eds). *Russia's Great Reforms 1855–1881* (Bloomington, 1994).

Emmons, T. (ed.). *The Zemstvo in Russia: An Experiment in Local Government* (Cambridge, 1982).

Emmons, T. *The Formation of Political Parties and the First National Elections in Russia* (Cambridge, MA, 1983).

Field, D. *Rebels in the Name of the Tsar* (Boston, 1976).

Galai, S. *The Liberation Movement in Russia, 1900–1905* (Cambridge, 1973).

Haimson, L. 'The Problem of Social Stability in Urban Russia, 1905–1917', *Slavic Review*, 23 (1964), 619–42 and 24 (1965), 1–22.

Haimson, L. (ed.). *The Politics of Rural Russia* (Bloomington, 1979).

Hosking, G. *The Russian Constitutional Experiment. Government and Duma, 1907–1914* (Cambridge, 1973).

Korros, A. *A Reluctant Parliament. Stolypin, Nationalism, and the Politics of the Russian Imperial State Council, 1906–1911* (Lanham, 2002).

LeDonne, J. *Ruling Russia. Politics and Administration in the Age of Absolutism, 1762–1796* (Princeton, 1991).

LeDonne, J. *Absolutism and the Ruling Class. The Formation of the Russian Political Order, 1700–1825* (New York, 1991).

Lieven, D. *Russia's Rulers under the Old Regime* (New Haven, 1989).

Lincoln, W. B. *Nikolai Miliutin. An Enlightened Russian Bureaucrat* (Newtonville, 1977).

Lincoln, W. B. *In the Vanguard of Reform. Russia's Enlightened Bureaucrats 1825–1861* (DeKalb, 1982).

Manning, R. T. *The Crisis of the Old Order in Russia. Gentry and Government* (Princeton, 1982).

Orlovsky, D. *The Limits of Reform. The Ministry of Internal Affairs in Imperial Russia, 1802–1881* (Cambridge, MA, 1981).

Pearson, T. S. *Russian Officialdom in Crisis. Autocracy and Local Self-Government, 1861–1900* (Cambridge, 1989).

Pintner, W. and Rowney, D. K. *Russian Officialdom. The Bureaucratization of Russian Society from the Seventeenth to the Twentieth Century* (London, 1980).

Raeff, M. *Plans for Political Reform in Imperial Russia* (Englewood Cliffs, 1966).

Ransel, D. *The Politics of Catherinian Russia* (New Haven, 1975).

Robbins, R. G. *The Tsar's Viceroys. Russian Provincial Governors in the Last Years of the Empire* (Ithaca, 1987).

Starr, S. F. *Decentralization and Self-Government in Russia, 1830–1870* (Princeton, 1972).

Szeftel, M. *The Russian Constitution of 1906. Political Institutions of the Duma Monarchy* (Brussels, 1976).

Verner, A. *The Crisis of Russian Autocracy. Nicholas II and the 1905 Revolution* (Princeton, 1990).

Wcislo, F. *Reforming Rural Russia. State, Local Society and National Politics, 1855–1914* (Princeton, 1990).

Whelan, H. *Alexander III and the State Council. Bureaucracy and Counter-reform in Late Imperial Russia* (New Brunswick, 1982).

Yaney, G. *The Systematization of Russian Government. Social Evolution in the Domestic Administration of Imperial Russia* (Urbana, 1973).

Zaionchkovskii, P. A. *The Russian Autocracy under Alexander III* (Gulf Breeze, 1976).

Zaionchkovskii, P. A. *The Russian Autocracy in Crisis, 1878–1882* (Gulf Breeze, 1981).

Society and Service

Balzer, H. (ed.). *Russia's Missing Middle Class. The Professions in Russian History* (Armonk, NY, 1996).

Bartlett, R. (ed.). *Land Community and Peasant Commune in Russia. Communal Forms in Imperial and Early Soviet Society* (London, 1990).

Becker, S. *Nobility and Privilege in Late Imperial Russia* (DeKalb, 1985).

Clowes, E., Kassow, S. D. and West, J. L. *Between Tsar and People. Educated Society and the Quest for Public Identity in Late Imperial Russia* (Princeton, 1991).

Crisp, O. and Edmondson, L. (eds). *Civil Rights in Imperial Russia* (Oxford, 1989).

Edelman, R. *Gentry Politics on the Eve of the Russian Revolution* (New Brunswick, 1986).

Emmons, T. *The Russian Landed Gentry and the Peasant Emancipation of 1861* (Cambridge, 1968).

Field, D. *The End of Serfdom. Nobility and Bureaucracy in Russia, 1855–1861* (Cambridge, 1976).

Frölich, K. *The Emergence of Russian Constitutionalism 1900–1904* (The Hague, 1981).

Hamburg, G. M. *Politics of the Russian Nobility 1881–1905* (New Brunswick, 1984).

Hoch, S. L. *Serfdom and Social Control in Russia, Petrovskoe, a Village in Tambov* (Chicago, 1986).

Kingston-Mann, E. and Mixter, T. (eds). *Peasant Economy, Culture and Politics of European Russia 1800–1921* (Princeton, 1990).

Macey, D. *Government and Peasant in Russia 1861–1906. The Pre-history of the Stolypin Reforms* (DeKalb, 1987).

Moon, D. *The Russian Peasantry, 1600–1930* (London, 1999).

Moon, D. *The Abolition of Serfdom in Russia* (London, 2001).

Pallot, J. *Land Reform in Russia 1906–1917* (Oxford, 1999).

Robinson, G. T. *Rural Russia under the Old Regime* (Berkeley, 1932).

Worobec, C. D. *Peasant Russia. Family and Community in the Post-Emancipation Period* (Princeton, 1991).

Yaney, G. *The Urge to Mobilize. Agrarian Reform in Russia, 1861–1930* (Urbana, 1982).

Zaionchkovskii, P. A. *The Abolition of Serfdom in Russia* (Gulf Breeze, 1978).

Coercion and Justice

Balmuth, D. *Censorship in Russia, 1865–1905* (Washington, DC, 1979).

Bushnell, J. *Mutiny amid Repression. Russian Soldiers in the Revolution of 1905–08* (Bloomington, 1985).

Curtiss, J. S. *The Russian Army under Nicholas I* (Durham, NC, 1965).

Daly, J. *Autocracy under Siege. Security Police and Opposition in Russia, 1866–1905* (DeKalb, 1998).

Daly, J. *The Watchful State. Security Police and Opposition in Russia, 1906–1917* (DeKalb, 2004).

Fuller, W. C. Jr. *Civil-Military Conflict in Imperial Russia, 1881–1914* (Princeton, 1985).

Fuller, W. C. Jr. *Strategy and Power in Russia 1600–1914* (New York, 1992).

Geyer, D. *Russian Imperialism. The Interaction of Domestic and Foreign Policy, 1860–1914* (Leamington Spa, 1987).

Judge, E. H. *Plehve. Repression and Reform in Imperial Russia 1902–1904* (Syracuse, 1983).

Kagan, F. W. *The Military Reforms of Nicholas I. The Origins of the Modern Russian Army* (New York, 1999).

Keep, J. *Soldiers of the Tsar. Army and Society in Russia 1462–1874* (Oxford, 1985).

Lauchlan, I. *Russian Hide And Seek. The Tsarist Secret Police in St Petersburg, 1906–1914* (Helsinki, 2002).

LeDonne, J. *The Russian Empire and the World, 1700–1917* (New York, 1997).

Luntinen, P. *The Imperial Russian Army and Navy in Finland 1808–1914* (Helsinki, 1997).

Menning, B. W. *Bayonets before Bullets. The Imperial Russian Army, 1861–1917* (Bloomington, 1992).

Miller, F. *Dmitrii Miliutin and the Reform Era in Russia* (Charlotte, 1968).

Monas, S. *The Third Section. Police and Society under Nicholas I* (Cambridge, MA, 1961).

Rich, D. A. *The Tsar's Colonels. Professionalism, Strategy and Subversion in Late Imperial Russia* (Cambridge, MA, 1998).

Sanborn, J. *Drafting the Russian Nation. Military Conscription, Total War and Mass Politics 1905–1925* (DeKalb, 2003).

Squire, P. S. *The Third Department. The Establishment and Practice of the Political Police in the Russia of Nicholas I* (Cambridge, 1968).

Wildman, A. K. *The End of the Russian Imperial Army. The Old Army and the Soldiers's Revolt (March–April 1917)* (Princeton, 1980).

Wirtschafter, E. K. *From Serf to Russian Soldier* (Princeton, 1990).

National Challenges

Becker, S. *Russia's Protectorates in Central Asia. Bukhara and Khiva, 1865–1914* (Cambridge, MA, 1968).

Blobaum, R. E. *Revolucja. Russian Poland, 1904–1907* (Ithaca, 1995).

Brower, D. R. *Turkestan and the Fate of the Russian Empire* (London, 2003).

Brower, D. R. and Lazzerini, E. (eds). *Russia's Orient. Imperial Borderlands and Peoples 1700–1917* (Bloomington, 1997).

Carriere d'Encause, H. *Islam and the Russian Empire. Reform and Revolution in Central Asia* (Berkeley, 1988).

Chmielewski, E. *The Polish Question in the Russian State Duma* (Knoxville, 1970).

Crews, R. *For Prophet and Tsar. Islam and Empire in Russia and Central Asia* (Cambridge, MA, 2006).

Forsyth, J. *A History of the Peoples of Siberia. Russia's North Asian Colony* (Cambridge, 1992).

Gatrell, P. *A Whole Empire Walking. Refugees in Russia during World War I* (Bloomington, 1999).

Geraci, R. *Window on the West. National and Imperial Identities in Late Tsarist Russia* (Ithaca, 2001).

Geraci, R. and Khodarkovsky, M. (eds). *Of Religion and Empire. Missions, Conversion and Tolerance in Tsarist Russia* (Ithaca, 2001).

Hamm, M. *Kiev. A Portrait, 1800–1917* (Princeton, 1993).

Kappeler, A. *The Russian Empire. A Multiethnic History* (New York, 2001).

Khodarkovsky, M. *Russia's Steppe Frontier. The Making of a Colonial Empire, 1500–1800* (Bloomington, 2002).

Kirby, D. (ed.). *Finland and Russia 1808–1920. From Autonomy to Independence* (London, 1975).

Kirby, D. *A Concise History of Finland* (London, 2006).

Klier, J. *Imperial Russia's Jewish Question, 1855–1881* (Cambridge, 1995).

Layton, S. *Russian Literature and Empire: Conquest of the Caucasus from Pushkin to Tolstoy* (Cambridge, 1994).

Lohr, E. *Nationalizing the Russian Empire: The Campaign against Enemy Aliens during World War I* (Cambridge, MA, 2003).

Löwe, H.-D. *The Tsars and the Jews: Reform, Reaction and Anti-Semitism in Imperial Russia 1772–1917* (Chur, 1993).

O'Rourke, S. *Warriors and Peasants: The Don Cossacks in Late Imperial Russia* (London, 2000).

Paine, S. C. M. *Imperial Rivals: China, Russia and their Disputed Frontier* (Armonk, 1996).

Polvinen, T. *Imperial Borderland: Bobrikov and the Attempted Russification of Finland, 1898–1904* (London, 1995).

Schimmelpennick van der Oye, D. H. *Toward the Rising Sun: Russian Ideologies of Empire and the Path to War with Japan* (DeKalb, 2001).

Stephan, J. J. *The Russian Far East: A History* (Stanford, 1994).

Subtelny, O. *Ukraine: A History* (Toronto, 1988).

Suny, R. G. *The Making of the Georgian Nation* (Bloomington, 1994).

Thaden, E. C. *Conservative Nationalism in Nineteenth-Century Russia* (Seattle, 1964).

Thaden, E. C. (ed.). *Russification in the Baltic Provinces and Finland, 1855–1914* (Princeton, 1981).

Thaden, E. C. *Russia's Western Borderlands, 1710–1870* (Princeton, 1984).

Vucinich, W. S. *Russia and Asia: Essays on the Influence of Russia on the Asian Peoples* (Stanford, 1971).

Weeks, T. R. *Nation and State in Late Imperial Russia: Nationalism and Russification on the Western Frontier, 1863–1914* (DeKalb, 1996).

Whelan, H. W. *Adapting to Modernity: Family, Caste and Capitalism among the Baltic German Nobility* (Köln, 1999).

Finance

Crisp, O. *Studies in the Russian Economy before 1914* (London, 1976).

Gatrell, P. *The Tsarist Economy 1850–1917* (London, 1986).

Gatrell, P. *Government, Industry and Rearmament in Russia, 1900–1914: The Last Argument of Tsarism* (Cambridge, 1994).

Gerschenkron, A. *Economic Backwardness in Historical Perspective* (Cambridge, MA, 1962).

Kahan, A. *The Plow, the Hammer and the Knout* (Chicago, 1985).

LeDonne, J. 'Indirect taxes in Catherine's Russia. I. The salt code of 1781', *Jahrbücher für Geschichte Osteuropas*, 23 (1975), 169–90.

LeDonne, J. 'Indirect taxes in Catherine's Russia. II. The liquor monopoly', *Jahrbücher für Geschichte Osteuropas*, 24 (1976), 173–207.

Index